Old World
MYTHOLOGY

Old World
MYTHOLOGY

Myths and Legends of Europe, Africa, and Asia

CHIEF CONSULTANT
Dr. Alice Mills

GLOBAL BOOK PUBLISHING

Managing director	Chryl Campbell
Publishing director	Sarah Anderson
Project manager	Dannielle Doggett
Art directors	Stan Lamond
	Kylie Mulquin
New title development manager	David Kidd
Chief consultant	Dr. Alice Mills
Commissioning editors	Jody Lee
	Margaret Malone
Editor	Julie Stanton
Picture research	Jody Lee
	Margaret Malone
Cover design	Kylie Mulquin
Designers	Wendy Farley
	Alex Frampton
Cartographer	John Frith
Typesetting	Dee Rogers
Index	Glenda Browne
	Jon Jermey
Production	Ian Coles
Foreign rights	Belinda Vance
Publishing assistant	Jessica Luca

First published in 2003 by
Global Book Publishing
Level 8, 15 Orion Road, Lane Cove,
NSW 2066, Australia
Ph: (612) 9425 5800   Fax: (612) 9425 5804
Email: rightsmanager@globalpub.com.au

ISBN 9781740480161

This publication and arrangement
© Global Book Publishing Pty Ltd 2007
Photographs from the Global Book Publishing Photo Library (except where credited otherwise on page 183)
Text © Global Book Publishing Pty Ltd 2007
Maps © Global Book Publishing Pty Ltd 2007
First printed in English in 2009

Printed in China by SNP Leefung Printers Limited
Film separation Pica Digital Pte Ltd, Singapore

Photographers
Global Book Publishing would be pleased to hear from photographers interested in supplying photographs.

Captions for preliminary pages and section openers
Page 1: Wooden initiation mask from Kwele, Congo
Page 2: Five-headed Shiva, Indian painting *c.* 1730
Page 5: Detail from *Unicorn* by Annibale Carracci (1560–1609)
Page 7: Pseudo sarcophagus of Osiris, first–second century CE
Pages 8–9: Glazed brick relief of lion, Ishtar Gate, Babylon
Pages 10–11: John Lydgate and pilgrims leaving Canterbury
Pages 82–83: Ramses I flanked by Anubis and Horus
Pages 118–119: Sudama approaching the Hindu god Krishna

CONTRIBUTORS

Dr. Greg Bailey is a reader in Sanskrit at La Trobe University in Melbourne, Australia. Greg has published books and articles on Hindu mythology, Buddhism, and contemporary Australian mythology. He teaches Sanskrit, Indian, and Religious Studies at La Trobe University, and is presently completing the translation of a mythological text about the elephant-headed god, Ganesha.

Michael Carden completed his Ph.D. in Biblical Studies at the University of Queensland in 2002. His dissertation examined interpretations of the story of Sodom and Gomorrah in Judaism, Christianity, and Islam. He has taught in the areas of biblical studies, comparative religion, and religion and contemporary studies in the Religion Department at the University of Queensland. In 1999, he introduced a course on Religion and Sexuality, the only course of its kind in Australia. He contributed two chapters—on Genesis and on the Twelve Minor Prophets—for the Bible in Translesbigay Perspective, an international project published in 2005. Outside of academia, he has had a long involvement in community work on sexuality, HIV/AIDS, and social justice issues.

Dr. Elizabeth Dimock is a Research Associate in the African Research Institute at La Trobe University, Melbourne, Australia. She has lived and worked in Africa, and her research interests have been concerned with colonial histories of Africa and African women's history. Recently she has been involved with the history of African communities in Victoria, Australia, and settlement problems faced by Africans after migration.

Christine El Mahdy is an Egyptologist. She became fascinated with the subject at the age of seven, and was reading hieroglyphs before she was nine. Today she is the Professor of Egyptian Studies at the British Centre for Egyptian Studies, a distance learning pro-vider, which she founded in 2000. She has written and broadcast material on ancient Egypt for more than 30 years, as well as lecturing widely. Over the years she has made more than a hundred visits to Egypt, taking many people to sites rarely seen. Previous books include *Exploring the World of the Pharaohs*; *Mummies, Myth and Magic*; and *Tutankhamen, Life and Death of the Boy-King*. She lives in Hampshire, England, with her twin daughters Nadine and Yasmine.

Denise Imwold is a writer and editor from Sydney, Australia, who has also worked for many years as a bookseller. She studied literature and anthropology at Macquarie University, where she received a Bachelor of Arts, as well as a Postgraduate Diploma in Editing and Publishing. Denise has contributed to a wide range of publications in fields such as travel, literature, sport, gardening, health, and spirituality. Currently she is working on her first novel, which draws inspiration from Irish mythology and history. Her interests include reading, walking, animals, and traveling, and she finds special joy in visiting sacred places.

Hugo McCann was born in Ireland in 1937. He was educated in Belfast and Tasmania, after immigrating to Australia. He taught in high schools in Ireland in the sixties and, in the next two decades, taught literature for children and general literature to education students. At the same time, he taught philosophy to teachers. Hugo has been a lecturer in drama in Australia and worked in theater in Ireland. He is now retired and living in Tasmania.

Dr. Alice Mills is an associate professor of literature and children's literature at the University of Ballarat located in the Australian state of Victoria. One of the many interesting subjects that she teaches is Myth and Mythmaking. She began learning Latin when she was just 11 years old, then classical Greek when she was 12, and has had a lifelong interest in the mythical stories and characters that underlie contemporary Western culture. Dr. Mills has published many scholarly articles on the topics of children's literature and fantasy, and has edited several anthologies of children's literature including the Random House *Treasury of Children's Literature*. She is also a Jungian psychotherapist, and she brings Jung's ideas about the human psyche to bear on her understanding of the ancient myths of Greece and Rome.

Dr. Antone Minard received his Ph.D. in the subject of Folklore and Mythology from the University of California, Los Angeles, in 2002, with an emphasis on folkloric material as it appears in the literature of medieval Europe. He has also done research into ethnicity and identity, especially his own family's experiences as Italian-Americans. While he was Stott Fellow at the University of Wales's Centre for Advanced Welsh and Celtic Studies in Aberystwyth, Wales, he worked on an atlas of Celtic Studies, a multidisciplinary resource designed as an introduction to Celtic Studies with data from archaeology, history, linguistics, and literature.

Dr. Peter Orton was born in Leicester, England, and completed his Ph.D. thesis at the University of Exeter on the transmission of Old English verse-texts. He taught at University College, Dublin, for several years, following a series of temporary appointments at the University of Leeds, during which he first began to study Old Norse. He has also lectured in Old English, Old Icelandic, and the history of English at the University of London. Special research interests of his are the Old English elegies, on which he has been extensively published, and the meter and style of Germanic alliterative verse. He is also particularly interested in the possible correlations between Old Norse and Old English mythological, poetic, and epigraphical traditions.

Simon Roberts was born in Hobart, Tasmania (Australia), in 1964. His interest in mythology was ignited when, as a child, his father read him the Greek myths and brought them to life. More recently he fell in love with the Icelandic sagas and developed an avid interest in the mythology of northern Europe. He worked as an Air Traffic Controller for six years before graduating with a Bachelor of Law in 1995. He currently works for the Tasmanian Department of Police and Public Safety. Simon has previously written entries for *Trees and Shrubs* (Global Book Publishing, 2000). A keen traveler, Simon has settled back in Tasmania about a hundred meters from the hospital in which he was born.

Dr. Paul Rule completed an honors degree in history at the University of Melbourne located in Victoria, Australia, and a doctorate in Asian Studies at the Australian National University in Canberra. Until 2002 he was the Senior Lecturer in History at La Trobe University in Melbourne, and formerly he was Director of the Religious Studies program at that same university. He taught courses on Chinese and Aboriginal religions, religious theory, and modern Catholicism. Paul's research and publications include *K'ung-tzu or Confucius? The Jesuit Interpretation of Confucianism* as well as books and articles on Christianity in China, other Chinese religions, Australian Aboriginal religion, and peace and justice issues. He has been Editor for the Australian Association for the Study of Religions and a member of the Australian Catholic Social Justice Council. From 2000 to 2004 he spent part of each year at the Ricci Institute for Chinese–Western Cultural History at the University of San Francisco as EDS–Stewart Distinguished Fellow working on a history of the Chinese Rites Controversy.

Dr. Rudolf Simek was born in Austria in 1954. He completed his Ph.D. in Vienna in 1980, a Masters in Theology in 1981, and a PhilHabil in 1990. His main fields of research are pre-Christian Germanic religion, Viking Age Culture, and Medieval Scandinavian non-fictional prose literature. Rudolf has worked at numerous universities in Europe and internationally and has had guest professorships and academic exchanges with educational institutions in Bergen, Catania, Cagliari, Kraców, Durham, Krems, Reykjavík, and Rome. As well as lecturing around the world, Rudolf has had research stays in cities as far afield as London, Reykjavík, and Sydney. He currently teaches in the German Department at the University of Bonn.

Dr. Elisabeth Stuchbury spent three years in the northwestern region of the Himalayas. The resulting anthropological fieldwork, which took place in a small Tibetan hermitage, was the basis for her extensive academic research. She received a Ph.D. from the research School of Pacific and Asian Studies at the Australian National University located in Canberra, and continued her research with a Post-Doctoral Fellowship from the Australian Research Council. She has taught in several different universities throughout Australia and has presented the results of her research internationally in lectures and publications. During her time in the northwestern part of the Himalayas, Elisabeth also began her engagement with the practice of Vajrayana Buddhism. Chögyal Namkhai Norbu, a renowned Dzogchen master of the Tibetan tradition and Professor Emeritus from the University of Naples, Italy, continues to inspire and guide her. She has a prominent position within his international following.

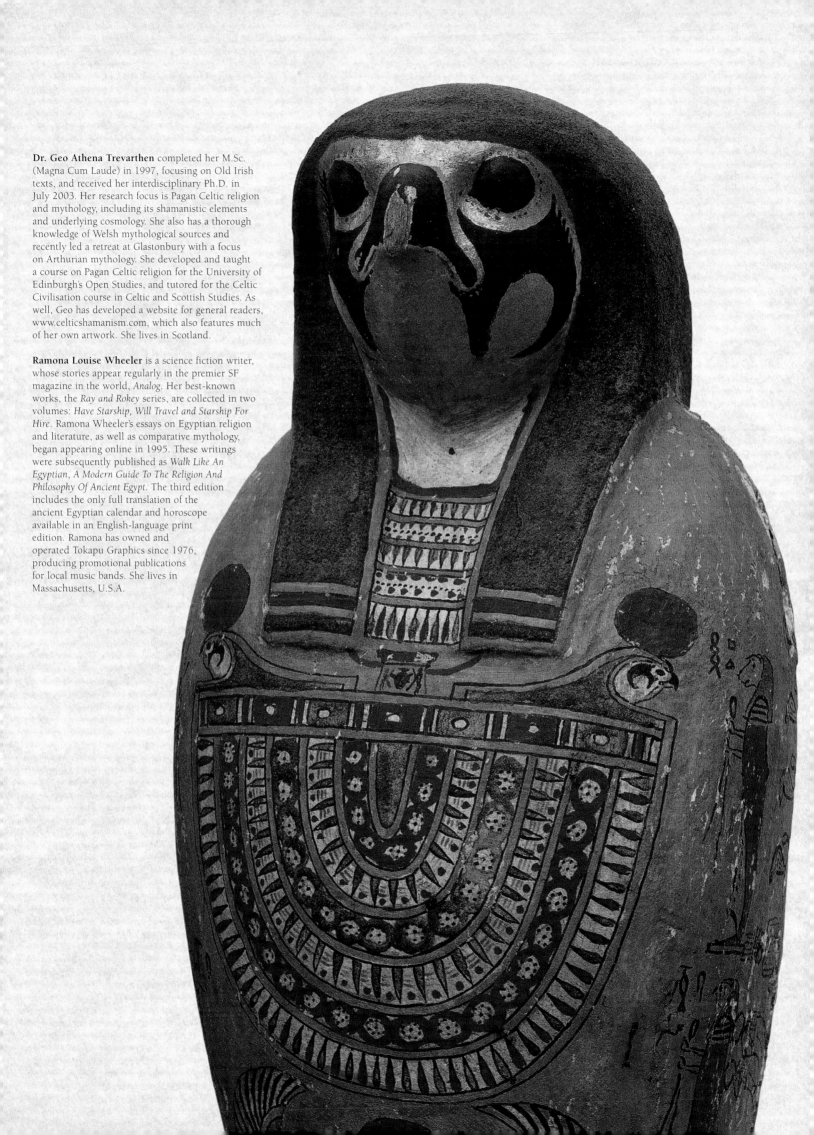

Dr. Geo Athena Trevarthen completed her M.Sc. (Magna Cum Laude) in 1997, focusing on Old Irish texts, and received her interdisciplinary Ph.D. in July 2003. Her research focus is Pagan Celtic religion and mythology, including its shamanistic elements and underlying cosmology. She also has a thorough knowledge of Welsh mythological sources and recently led a retreat at Glastonbury with a focus on Arthurian mythology. She developed and taught a course on Pagan Celtic religion for the University of Edinburgh's Open Studies, and tutored for the Celtic Civilisation course in Celtic and Scottish Studies. As well, Geo has developed a website for general readers, www.celticshamanism.com, which also features much of her own artwork. She lives in Scotland.

Ramona Louise Wheeler is a science fiction writer, whose stories appear regularly in the premier SF magazine in the world, *Analog*. Her best-known works, the *Ray and Rokey* series, are collected in two volumes: *Have Starship, Will Travel and Starship For Hire*. Ramona Wheeler's essays on Egyptian religion and literature, as well as comparative mythology, began appearing online in 1995. These writings were subsequently published as *Walk Like An Egyptian, A Modern Guide To The Religion And Philosophy Of Ancient Egypt*. The third edition includes the only full translation of the ancient Egyptian calendar and horoscope available in an English-language print edition. Ramona has owned and operated Tokapu Graphics since 1976, producing promotional publications for local music bands. She lives in Massachusetts, U.S.A.

Contents

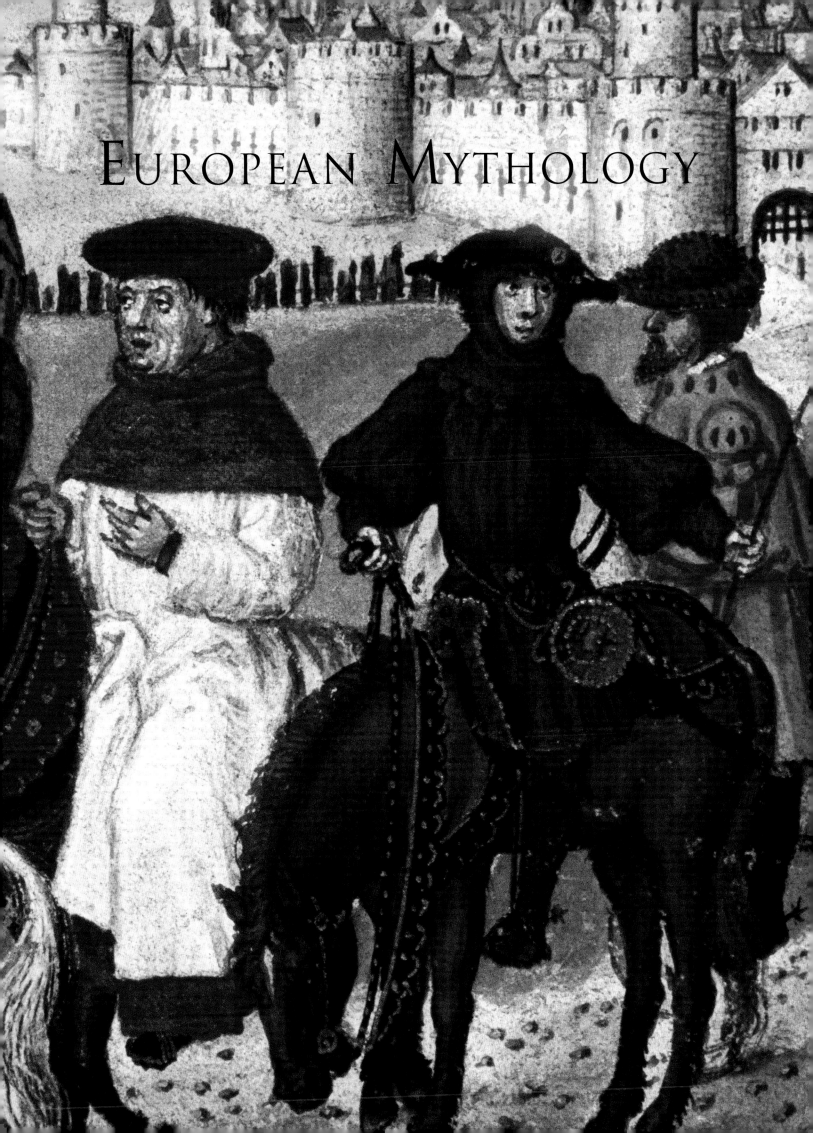

European Mythology

CELTIC AND IRISH MYTHOLOGY

Above *Ossian's Lament* by K. Kisfaludy (1788–1830). This painting was inspired by *The Tale of Ossian* from the third century A.D. These stories by the warrior and poet Oisin recount the exploits of his father, Finn MacCool, and the Fianna.

Right **Statue of a god with a lyre, from Paule Saint Symphorien, France.** One of the typical features of all Celtic peoples is their love of music, and people skilled in song and verse were highly valued.

Celtic-speaking peoples have ranged over much of Europe and Asia Minor over a period of more than 3,000 years—from 1400 B.C. to the present. By the sixth century B.C. they had spread from their probable homeland in what is now western and central Germany, across much of western and northern Europe and over into the United Kingdom and Ireland. By the end of the millennium, they had moved as far east as the Black Sea, the Ukraine, and western Turkey. Although of the same race, the Celts were made up of individual tribal groups and were not politically united.

The various language groups give us an outline of the different Celtic tribes, and the recorded Celtic languages may be divided into two categories: continental Celtic and insular Celtic. Continental Celtic, in possibly three or four different forms, was spoken by Celtic tribes across Europe: in central, north, and northwestern Iberia (now Spain and Portugal); in Gaul (France); in the valley of the Po, south of the Alps; and a possible fourth in the middle Danube valley.

Insular Celtic has been spoken in Britain, Ireland, and Brittany until the present. This language divides into two main branches: the Celtic that forms Welsh, Cornish, and Breton; and the Celtic spoken in Ireland, Scotland (highlands and islands), and the Isle of Man, off the English coast.

The Celts did not leave written records, unlike other ancient cultures such as the Egyptians or Greeks; instead, they preferred and valued an oral tradition of storytelling, and this has had an impact on how we form an understanding of them and their beliefs. What does exist of Celtic origin is largely restricted to Celtic inscriptions, coins, and place names, which can offer only a limited insight into their values and beliefs. In particular, little remains of the myths of the continental Celts, who most greatly felt the force of the Roman Empire. The insular Celtic myths are more intact, precisely because the Celtic culture remained alive to be recorded. Indeed, from Ireland, Scotland, and Wales, we have a rich store of related and interconnected myths and legends.

However, the majority of our knowledge of the ancient Celts comes from non-Celts, those conquering peoples who came into contact with the Celts as a consequence of either war or religion. These ancient writers, among whom are military opponents such as Julius Caesar (100–44 B.C.), left many records, much of which can be useful in drawing a fairly detailed picture of these long-ago people. Caesar noted that the Celts were brave in battle, some fighting naked, while the Greek Diodorus Siculus (c. 90–21 B.C.) gave the following description: "The Celts were tall of body, with rippling muscles, and white of skin, and their hair blond." The women "are not only like

IMPORTANT FEASTS OF THE CELTIC YEAR

The Celts celebrated four lunar festivals that marked important passages in the year.

Samhain, November 1, Celtic New Year. Samhain, or "end of summer," coincides with Halloween and the slaughter of stock before winter. Rituals are conducted in honor of the the dead as well as to seek protection from them over the harsh months of winter.

Imbolc, February 1, Brigid's Feast. Little is known about Imbolc, however, it probably included rituals that centered on the ewes coming into milk, heralding the arrival of spring. This later became St. Brigid's festival.

Beltane, May 1, Belinus, the God of Fire. This feast included rituals such as the driving of animals, especially cows, between two fires, suggesting it may have been connected with purification and rebirth rituals. Its timing marks the beginning of summer.

Lughnasa, August 1, Anticipation of the Harvest. The Lughnasa feast in Ireland was a harvest feast, and the rituals appear to have centered on the marriage between the earth goddess and the sun god Lugh. Many contests of skill and strength took place and betrothals were made at this time.

the men in their great stature but they are a match for them in courage as well."

Taken together, these early writings suggest a society that was essentially tribal, each tribe being led by a chief or king. The society was divided into nobles (who had horses), druids (priests), bards who told memorable tales, commoners or freemen, and slaves. Women, at least the aristocratic ones, seem to have played an active part in society. While the tribes were fiercely independent, to the degree where it appears that much of their time was spent in battle with each other, a number of common features can be discerned. Chief among them is a great love of story, decoration, and of music. In these areas their talented bards excelled, creating a universe of mighty warriors, powerful gods, headstrong women, shape-changers, wailing banshees, and leprechauns.

CELTIC BELIEFS AND RITUALS

Though the names of deities appear in the surviving myths, we know few details about the actual forms of worship followed. The druids were wise men and philosophers, extremely learned, who also divined future events from a variety of sources. Animals were sacrificed throughout Celtic regions, as was done elsewhere in the world. Human sacrifice is thought to be a part of their rituals, which is supported by the recovery of bodies of executed people from European and insular bogs. European archaeological evidence, as well as Irish and Welsh myths, indicate headhunting in war, where victims were decapitated and the heads kept as trophies and parts of shrines.

Of Celtic origin is the terrible wicker man—a huge construction of woven branches in the form of a human being, which contained prisoners who were then burnt alive. Julius Caesar wrote of this practice, as did others, though their comments were often only hearsay. Not much is really known, and hints about it in the myths may be more symbolic than actual.

Left *Human Sacrifice* by Stephen Reid (1873–1948). A Celtic mother sacrifices her child under the watchful eye of a druid, trusting that the gods will bestow milk and corn in exchange. Celtic sacrifice has caused much debate, though human remains seem to support the idea. The Lindow Man, recovered from a bog, from the second century B.C., was killed in a three-step process: strangled, hit on the head, then throat cut. This may have been ritual sacrifice or execution.

THE CELTIC COSMOS

Celtic peoples over time and place appear to have had many gods, and there is evidence for over 360 names of gods across the Celtic world, but only around 20 or so appear more than once. These include names like: Lugos, Cernunnos, Esus, Sequana, Brigantia, Epona, and Matrona. However, as many Celtic gods had a variety of names, many of the gods may be one and the same. Our knowledge is sometimes sketchy: duties for the male gods included war, oratory, and the youthful savior. Female roles were related to the earth and fertility, and included the earth mother, as well as goddesses of springs, lands, and the tree fruit. These deities existed side by side with people and were very real. It was not a case of the gods being worshipped so much as that they were present and had to be respected.

Only two gods can be identified almost everywhere: the god Lugos (Irish Lugh, Welsh Llew), whose name we find from Germany to Spain and probably even further east, and the mother goddess Matrona (the Welsh Modron). She is also known as Noreia, Sequana, Brigantia, and, probably, also Eriu and Boand.

Below **Mater (mother goddess), Gallo-Roman statuette, Alésia, France.** Many of the Celtic female deities were worshipped as mother goddesses, strong figures that were linked to areas such as fertility, fire, inspiration, and healing. They were also often active in war and could take the form of ravens, the sign of coming death.

The Otherworld

The Celtic-speaking peoples appear to share a common view that there are several layers to reality: the ordinary world, and another reality where other beings exist that might easily erupt into everyday life. It is possible to cross from the ordinary world into the Otherworld, a feature seen in both Irish and Welsh myths, such as in legends of the hunt, where creatures and gods move freely from that world to this. The Otherworld could be a place where the dead live well, enjoying feasting and music, and where warriors live to fight again, or it could be a dark, somber, and dangerous place, especially for a human who visits it before death. Celtic stories often take great pleasure in this shifting reality, using animals and birds to indicate the supernatural.

The Celts and the Natural World

The Celts observed nature closely. Water was vital and there were specific springs, lakes, rivers, and bogs that were considered sacred. Animals such as horses, bulls, boars, and stags were worshipped variously for their speed, ferocity, fertility, courage, and beauty. The Celtic god, Cernunnos, is frequently pictured as having stag antlers. When they hunted, the Celts appear to have respected their prey, and the death of such animals required acts of propitiation.

The flights of birds were read by Celts and their druids to divine possible futures, and were also seen as an allegory of the human soul. Ravens and doves were listened to as voices telling of coming events. Water birds linked sky and water. In Welsh stories, the birds of the goddess Rhiannon lull the sick to sleep. Crows and ravens—considered scavengers—were associated with impending death.

In Celtic myths there is no impenetrable frontier between the human and the animal worlds. There is also a belief in the ability of humans to shape-change, or be transformed, into animals, and many Irish and Welsh myths involve people being transformed into animals, or animals dispensing wisdom to humans. Magic and shape-changing, often as much as bravery and valor, affect the outcome of Celtic stories.

Gods and Goddesses of the Insular Celts

The two branches of insular Celts—those peoples from Wales, Cornwall, and Brittany; and those from Ireland, Scotland, and the Isle of Man—believed that the gods and goddesses all descended from a mother goddess called Don in Welsh and Danu in Irish. The descendants were thus called the Children of Don in Wales and the Children of Danu (Tuatha De Danaan) in Ireland. Among the Children of Don were the sons Amaethon, god of agriculture; Gwydion, god of the arts; and Nudd. The only daughter was Arianrhod who, with Gwydion as the father, gives birth to Llew (Irish Lugh), known as "the Bright One."

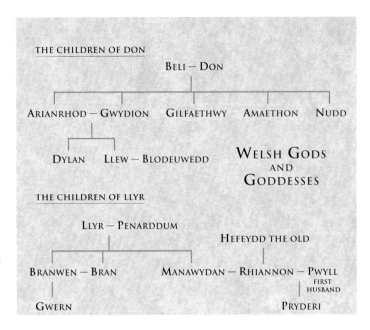

WELSH GODS AND GODDESSES

THE CHILDREN OF DON

BELI — DON

ARIANRHOD — GWYDION   GILFAETHWY   AMAETHON   NUDD

DYLAN   LLEW — BLODEUWEDD

THE CHILDREN OF LLYR

LLYR — PENARDDUM

HEFEYDD THE OLD

BRANWEN — BRAN   MANAWYDAN — RHIANNON — PWYLL
FIRST HUSBAND

GWERN   PRYDERI

In Welsh myth there are also the gods, possibly connected with the goddess Don, that are the descendants of the god Llyr, god of the sea and king of the ancient Britons. Llyr has two sons, Bran and Manawydan, as well as a daughter Branwen. These two male gods appear in Irish myth as Bron and the more familiar Manannan Mac Lir. While there are similarities between them, there is much that differs, and they are involved in different exploits.

WELSH MYTH

Existing Celtic myths come predominantly from Wales and Ireland. These oral stories were collected and written down in the Middle Ages by writers who were deeply influenced by Christianity. Hence, apart from the long delay in time, there is also the bias of the writers themselves to bear in mind.

Many of the Welsh myths come from a collection of stories known as the *Mabinogion*, which was given its name by Lady Charlotte Guest who translated what are essentially Welsh medieval stories between 1838 and 1849. These medieval tales come from two main sources, themselves collections of earlier stories: the *Red Book of Hergest*, a fourteenth-century manuscript kept at Jesus College, Oxford, in England; and the *White Book of Rhydderch*, an incomplete set of the tales, also from the fourteenth century. The stories were probably first drawn up in their present shape toward the end of the twelfth century, but the stories are of much greater antiquity, some belonging even to the time of Celtic paganism and to the period of unity between Wales and Brittany.

Lady Charlotte Guest's *Mabinogion* contains eleven tales in all, though the term applies really to just the first four, which recount the tales of the children of the Welsh gods Don and Llyr. The title derives from the Welsh word *mab* meaning "youth," and the tales of the gods' youthful exploits may have been be intended as instructive.

Early Sources of the Arthurian Legends

The second part of the *Mabinogion* includes four tales that feature King Arthur, and while they reveal more about medieval themes and concerns than they do pagan Celtic beliefs, they do shed some light on the ancient Celtic origins of those stories. These tales are also related to the well-known story of Tristan and Iseult, which connects Wales, Cornwall, Brittany, and Ireland, the remaining medieval sites of the Celtic speaking world. Tristan and Iseult is one of the great Celtic love stories, and it has parallels with Irish stories such as that of Deirdre and Naoise.

Above *Tristan Abducting Queen Iseult*, from *Le Roman de Tristan*, fifteenth-century manuscript. A love potion, intended for Iseult and her betrothed, King Mark, sets this tale on its tragic course when it is accidentally drunk by Iseult and Tristan. They separate, Tristan heading to France and marrying, but his heart remains faithful. Finally, he is fatally wounded and calls for Iseult. She comes but Tristan's jealous wife tells him otherwise. He dies grief-stricken, as does Iseult when she arrives. They are buried together and two trees grow from their graves, their branches forever intertwined.

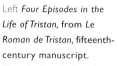

Left *Four Episodes in the Life of Tristan*, from *Le Roman de Tristan*, fifteenth-century manuscript. Though the tale is perhaps best known through the medieval Arthurian tales, it still retains some traces of its Celtic past, such as the use of a magic love potion. It may have its roots in the real-life figure of Drustan, son of Cunomorus, whose name is recorded on the famous "Tristan Stone," a sixth-century grave marker in Cornwall, England.

PWYLL IN THE OTHERWORLD

In Episode One of the story of Pwyll, told in the first book of the *Mabinogion,* Pwyll, Lord of Arberth and Prince of Dyfed, meets Arawn, Lord of Annwn (the Otherworld) one day when Pwyll was out hunting stags. Pwyll is about to take Arawn's kill when he is surrounded by Arawn's shining white hunting dogs with red ears—colors typical of Otherworld beings. Pwyll can redeem himself only by changing places with Arawn for a year, at the end of which he must fight and kill Arawn's Otherword enemy, Hofgun, if he is to return to his world. Arawn warns Pwyll to strike Hofgun only once because, if Hofgun is struck twice, he will recover and become stronger. Pwyll keeps his pledge and, at the appointed time, meets Hofgun. He deals Hofgun a mighty blow, and Hofgun pleads for Pwyll to finish the job. Pwyll resists and thus defeats Hofgun. Pwyll returns home, and from that time on is called Lord of the Otherworld. When he dies his son, Pryderi, maintains the family friendship with King Arawn of the Otherworld.

Pwyll and the Goddess Rhiannon

The second part of the story relates Pwyll's meeting with the goddess Rhiannon. While at the magical meeting place for his court, the Mound of Arberth, Pwyll spies a beautiful young woman dressed all in shining gold and riding a shining white horse. Pwyll is entranced and rides after her, but though her horse seems to move at a leisurely pace, and though Pwyll urges his horse forward, he cannot catch up with her. Pwyll calls to the shining woman who reveals herself as Rhiannon. The pair swear their love but she is betrothed to Gwawl. Only through trickery is Pwyll able to win her hand.

In the third year of her marriage to Pwyll, Rhiannon gives birth to a son, Pryderi, who is surrounded by supernatural

mystery. When he reaches his first birthday he is stolen while his watchwomen are asleep. To avert blame, the women accuse Rhiannon of his murder.

The story then moves from the castle of Arberth to the house of Teynrnon Twyl Liant, Lord of Gwent Is-Coed. Teynrnon has determined to find out why, on every May eve, his mare has a foal, usually a fabulous colt, which disappears.

Hiding in wait, he sees a giant claw seize the foal and drag it away. He hacks off the claw and finds a baby boy. Teynrnon and his wife decide to foster the child, who develops at such speed that after three years the boy is given the foal saved on the night he arrived. His foster parents note a strong resemblance to Pwyll and realize that the boy must really be Pryderi. The boy is then returned, to the great joy of Pwyll and Rhiannon.

GODDESSES OF THE HORSE

Horses were very important to the Celts, both practically and symbolically, who used them for riding from around 800 B.C. They also used horses to pull wagons and, more importantly perhaps, to pull their two-horse war chariots into battle against the Romans. The horse was revered for its beauty, speed, bravery, and sexual vigor. The nobles of Celtic society were linked with the horse, and legends suggest that kings were ritually wed to Epona, the greatest of the horse deities. Worshipped throughout Gaul, Epona was later adopted by the Roman cavalry. The Welsh goddess Rhiannon and the Irish Macha may also be some kind of horse goddesses.

Right **Epona, limestone
statue, Alésia, France.**
Epona is usually shown riding sidesaddle, and it was said that she rode with the soul of the dead on its final journey. The horn of plenty often accompanies her, symbolizing abundance.

BRANWEN AND BRAN

Matholwch, the King of Ireland, seeks the hand of the lovely Welsh Branwen, daughter of Llyr, king of Briton. Her brother Bran agrees, and the wedding takes place at his court. However, Efnisien, a half-brother on her mother's side, objects to the marriage and during the wedding festivities, mutilates Matholwch's horses while they are stabled at the court. Bran attempts to appease Matholwch by presenting him with various gifts, the greatest of which is a magic cauldron that was made in Ireland. Its power is such that it can revive dead warriors, though without the power of speech.

Matholwch accepts the offer, and he and Branwen sail to Ireland, but he resents his treatment in Wales and he treats his new queen like a servant, making her work in the kitchens where she is roughly treated by the butcher.

In desperation, Branwen trains a starling to carry a message back to Bran, who immediately sets out to attack Ireland and avenge his sister. An enormous man, he wades across the Irish Sea, appearing to the Irish as a mountain coming toward them. The Irish position themselves behind an impassable river and destroy the bridge. Bran, however, lies down across the river and his army advance to the other side, soon defeating Matholwch's army. Peace follows, but it doesn't last. When fighting breaks out again, once more partly due to the actions of Efnisien, Bran is wounded by a poisoned spear and only seven of his men survive. He commands the men, who include Pryderi of Dyfed and Manawydan, his brother, to cut off his head and carry it around the country, before burying it in London at the White Mount, facing east, guarding against foreign invasion of Britain. The journey to London is a wondrous saga in itself, taking 87 years. The head remains alive and telling of wonders, until its final interment.

Meanwhile, Branwen dies of a broken heart at Aber Alaw, lamenting that through her, the two great islands are at odds with each other.

Left **Celtic stone head, from Dorset, England.** The head was regarded by the Celts as the center of spiritual power, and images of the head in art had a protective function. In the story of Branwen and Bran, the wounded leader puts his people first, instructing that his head be cut off and buried facing France. As long as it remains there, Britain will be safe from attack.

MANAWYDAN AP LLYR AND THE ENCHANTING OF DYFED

The third book of the *Mabinogion* is set after Pwyll's death. When Pryderi and Manawydan return from burying Bran's head in London, Manawydan marries Pwyll's widow, Rhiannon. With Pryderi and his wife Cigfa, Rhiannon and Manawydan go to Gorsedd Arberth in Dyfed. Although unharmed themselves because they are on the magic Mound of Arberth, the four see Dyfed fall under enchantment: all the inhabitants and houses vanish, and the countryside is covered in a magical mist.

With nothing left in Dyfed, the four are forced to head to England where Manawydan and Pryderi set up as skilled craftsmen making saddles and shoes. Wherever they go, the skills of Manawydan incite the envy and malice of the local craftsmen, so the four

> *And by force of strength, fierceness, and by the magic of Gwydion, Pryderi was slain.*
>
> LADY CHARLOTTE GUEST (1812–1895)
> THE *MABINOGION*

return to Dyfed where they make a living by hunting. On one hunting expedition, Manawydan and Pryderi encounter a huge boar, dazzling white (a sure sign that it comes from the Otherworld).

The boar lures their dogs toward a strange castle. Despite Manawydan's warnings, Pryderi follows the dogs to the castle. He sees a golden bowl and touches it, then becomes fixed to the spot and is struck dumb. Rhiannon follows Pryderi and she also suffers a similar fate. Manawydan and Cigfa, bereft of their families, and without hunting dogs, turn to wheat growing. The crops flourish, but just before harvest two fields are destroyed by armies of mice. Manawydan lies in wait for them when they come to waste the third field. All but one, a pregnant mouse, escapes. Manawydan sets about hanging this mouse, despite the pleas of passersby. Finally a bishop interrupts the proceedings and tries to redeem the mouse.

Manawydan has recognized the bishop as a fellow magician, and refuses to yield until Rhiannon and Pryderi are restored and the 700 farmsteads of Dyfed are released from the enchantment. The bishop then reveals himself to be Llwyd. He claims that he cast the spell over Dyfed to avenge the wrong done by Pwyll to Gwawl, Rhiannon's first suitor, when Pwyll married Rhiannon and took her from him.

The pregnant mouse is really Llwyd's wife. She and her women were transformed into mice and sent to destroy Manawydan's wheat. Manawydan's magic proves stronger, however; Dyfed is restored, and the mice return to human form.

MATH AND HIS TWO NEPHEWS

The convoluted story of Math Ap Mathonwy, Lord of Gwynedd in the North, forms the fourth book of the *Mabinogion*. As with many of these tales, it involves deception and magic, and slips easily back and forth between this and the Otherworld; it is a magical tale, in which the wrong are punished, but only just.

When Math, a magician, is not out surveying his lands or at war, he has to set his feet in the lap of a virgin. His two nephews, sons of the goddess Don, Gilfaethwy and Gwydion, desire the virgin footholder, whose name is Goewin.

The brothers, who have been trained in the art of magic by Math himself, plan to distract their uncle by starting a war with Pryderi, Lord of Dyfed in the South. Gwydion tricks Pryderi out of his magic white pigs and, as planned, war breaks out between the towns Gwynedd and Dyfed. While Math is at war,

Below *Rabbits, Hare, Boar, and Mouse* from *Bestiary*, manuscript, *c.* A.D. 1300. As with objects with magical properties, animals in the Celtic world were often more than what they at first seemed. In the hunt, they can be understood as symbolizing the search for wisdom, particularly in their capacity to connect with the Otherworld.

The Birth of Llew Llaw Gyffes, the Bright One

Arianrhod, the sister of Gwydion and Gilfaethwy, applies to Math for the vacant position of virgin footholder. She fails the purity test, however, giving birth to two sons when she steps over Math's magic staff. Arianrhod curses the second boy three times: he shall have no name unless she agrees to name him; he will bear no arms unless she gives them to him; and he shall have no mortal wife.

Gwydion takes pity on the boy—some stories suggest he is the boy's father—and, disguising himself and the boy as cobblers, Gwydion tricks Arianrhod into giving the cursed son a name: Llew Llaw Gyffes ("the bright one of the skillful hand"). He next tricks her into arming him, then Math and Gwydion conjure a wife for Llew—a beautiful, mystical creature created from flowers of meadowsweet, broom, and oak. She is called Blodeuwedd ("woman made from flowers").

Despite his beginnings, Llew is charmed. He cannot be killed inside or outside of doors, not on land or water, neither clothed or unclothed. Only a spear made at a time when work is forbidden can kill him.

The Faithless Wife

Blodeuwedd, born without roots, is faithless. She takes Gronw Pebyr as her lover and they plot to kill Llew. Blodeuwedd first finds out how the spear can be made and contrives to have Llew reveal how he may be killed. When Llew shows her, the hidden Gronw spears him. Llew is transformed into an eagle and flies into an oak tree.

Here Gwydion finds him and entices him through song back to earth where he restores Llew to human form. Blodeuwedd, in contrast, is turned into an owl, shunned by other birds and forced to hunt by night.

Left *Blodeuwedd and Gronw Pebyr* by Ernest Wallcousins. Though the wife of Llew, Blodeuwedd asks Gronw Pebyr into her home, forming the classic Welsh three-sided affair. The two plot to kill Llew but this is not easy: some versions say Llew can only be killed at twilight, draped in a fish net, with one foot on a cauldron of water and the other on a goat, and only with a specially made spear.

Below **Boar-shaped votive figure, first century** B.C. Like many animals in Celtic mythology, the boar can act as an agent of the Otherworld. As befits an animals of great strength, dreams that feature boars are usually connected with warriors. In some tales, boars can be eaten, to be magically reborn.

the brothers rape Goewin, then return to the battlefield. Gwydion next kills Pryderi, by using his magic.

When Math returns, his anger at discovering their treatment of Goewin leads him to punish the two brothers. For three consecutive years he turns them into pairs of animals: a stag and a hind; a boar and a sow; a wolf and a she-wolf, forcing them to take on their nature. The brothers alternate between male and female each time, and every year they produce an animal offspring. At the end of this time, Math forgives the brothers and restores them and the offspring to human form, but they retain animal names.

CULHWCH'S IMPOSSIBLE TASKS

One of the most popular tales from the *Mabinogion* concerns Culhwch and Olwen. Culhwch is of royal blood, indeed he is the cousin of Arthur. His birth is unusual: before he was born, his mother, Golenddyd, developed a violent antipathy to pigs. While passing a herd of pigs she is frightened by them and gives birth to a child whom she abandons. A swineherd later restores him to his parents.

Golenddyd dies and her husband Cilydd remarries. The new wife has a daughter whom she wishes Culhwch to marry. But he demurs, claiming that he is too young. The queen curses Culhwch, proclaiming that the only woman he will ever marry is Olwen, daughter of Ysbaddeden, the Chief Giant. On hearing her name, Culhwch falls passionately in love with her.

Culhwch decides to ask Arthur for help in finding this maiden. He leaves in great splendor, fully armed with battle ax, golden sword, and a hatchet that "can make the air bleed." He has an ivory horn, two gray hounds, and is mounted on a great horse.

When Culhwch reaches Arthur's court the gatekeeper attempts to stop his entry. Culhwch threatens to utter three shouts that will make women barren and the pregnant abort. He duly passes and meets Arthur, who is persuaded to help him in his search for Olwen. Scouts search for a year, with no luck. Eventually, they assemble a team of the best knights, each blessed with remarkable traits. They include Kay, whose sword gives wounds no doctor can heal;

Bedwyr, the swiftest of all knights, and Gwalchmai, who never returned from a quest with it unfulfilled. After more searching, Olwen is finally found.

She returns Culhwch's love but explains that her father Ysbaddeden is fated to die when she marries. Olwen advises Culhwch to accept without complaint any demands that Ysbaddeden may make of him.

Culhwch approaches the Chief Giant and is given a long series of "impossible tasks." The most daunting of these is the recovery of the scissors, razor, and comb from between the ears of the great destructive boar Twrch Trwyth. However, Culhwch accepts all the tasks willingly.

Culhwch and Arthur further enlist the help of Mabon, the hunter who has been kept prisoner in a castle after being stolen from his mother, Modron. By the time he is freed, he is called "the young," although he is the oldest of all creatures.

Mabon, Culhwch, and the knights are helped by magical animals: the Eagle of Gwernabwy, the Blackbird of Kilgory, the Stag of Rhedynvre, the Salmon of Llyn Law, and other enchanted beasts. One of Arthur's men, Gwrhyr, can speak to each in its own language. After a long pursuit through South Wales, Cornwall, and Ireland, in which the evil boar lays waste to much of the land, and with Mabon's help, Twrch Trwyth is finally overcome and driven into the sea. The razor, scissors, and comb are delivered and Culhwch and Olwen finally marry.

IRISH CELTS AND THE TUATHA DE DANAAN

It is not known when the Celts came into Ireland. Although they have beliefs in common with other Celtic peoples, and their mythology has various similarities with Welsh myths, there are also many variations. Many of the myths come from manuscripts transcribed by monks in the twelfth century, such as the *Book of Leinster* (A.D. 1150), although various myths are mentioned in an eighth-century manuscript known as the *Book of Dun Cow* (supposedly because the fabric it is written on actually came from St. Ciaran's cow). The myths themselves are surely much older.

The story of the Tuatha De Danaan is the foundation myth of Irish lore. Meaning "the tribe or children of the goddess Danu," the Tuatha were a beautiful, golden-haired, godlike race—people of the light—who came down to earth from the heavens on a cloud. Their horses were sleek and fleet-footed, decorated in gold and silver. They were said to be descendants of the great mother goddess Danu (also known as Anu or Aine), whose two chief consorts were Echdae, the sky horse, and Manannan, a god of the sea.

There were three levels in Tuatha society, each having different functions: the chiefs (*tuatach*), the gods (*de*), and the gifted people (*dan*), which included healers, artists, and druids.

THE DAGDA

The Dagda, which means "the good god," was the son of the goddess Danu and a major personage of the Tuatha De Danaan. A great and benign patriarch, he was the Lord of Perfect Knowledge. He is associated with feasting and sexuality—important attributes of a chieftain. He was romantically linked with the gentle Boann, goddess of the sacred River Boyne in Ireland, as well as the fiery war goddess Morrigan, who he coupled with each year at Samhain.

> *I hope to make the old stories as familiar to Irishmen at any rate as are the stories of King Arthur and his Knights to all readers of books.*
>
> W.B. YEATS (1865–1939)

There are three magical objects associated with the Dagda: an enchanted club that had powers of both destruction and restoration; a harp that could play wonderful melodies by itself; and a cauldron that produced a never-ending supply of food, and was so large that it needed a chariot to transport it.

In the second of the Tuatha De Danaan's three earthly battles, it is told how the Fomorians, enemies of the Tuatha De Danaan, forced the Dagda to consume a gigantic bowl of porridge, threatening to kill him if he did not finish it. The porridge was enough to feed an army, and even contained live sheep and goats—not even Dagda's cauldron could contain it. But his legendary appetite was so gargantuan that not only did he eat the entire meal, he made love with a young woman afterward.

When the Tuatha were forced underground by the Milesians, the Dagda settled his people into *sidhe*, or "fairy mounds." As befitting a god of his stature, his home became the large burial mound at Newgrange in the Boyne Valley. At the winter solstice, a beam of light shines through the main passage of the tomb.

Above **Exterior of the megalithic passage tomb, c. 3000 B.C., Newgrange, County Meath, Ireland.** This mound is said to be one of four underground palaces of the Dagda, mighty ruler of the Tuatha. An all-powerful figure, his titles include Earth God, God of Magic, and High Druid. At the same time, however, he is often shown as a rotund figure dressed in a short tunic that exposes his buttocks.

NUADA AND THE FIRST BATTLE OF MAG TUIREADH

The Tuatha fought three major battles during their time above the ground. The first was the Battle of Mag Tuireadh (also known as Moytura, the plain of the towers), fought against the Fir Bolg for control of Ireland, and is said to have taken place in today's Connemara region of County Galway. The Fir Bolg, or "bag men," were slaves that had come from Greece and who were forced to carry bags of soil. The bags were made into boats that brought them to Ireland. These people were dullwitted and no match for their brilliant rivals, the Tuatha De Danaan, who quickly forced them into retreat.

Nuada was the Tuatha De Danaan king who led the battle against the Fir Bolg. Though owner of a magic sword, Nuada's arm was severed during the battle and the kingship went to Bres. This was in keeping with Tuatha law, which stated that a king must have no physical flaws. But Bres was an unpopular monarch, partly due to the fact that he had Fomorian blood, and also because he demanded heavy taxes and was not very sympathetic to bards and harpers.

Bres did not stay ruler for very long, however. Nuada enlisted the help of Dian Cecht, the god of healing, who fashioned an arm out of silver for the king, thus restoring him to health and to the throne. He was given the name Nuada Airget-Lam, or "Nuada of the silver arm." Dian Cecht's skills in herbal medicine also helped many warriors wounded in the battle. After the Fir Bolg were defeated, the Tuatha banished them to the Aran Islands off Galway.

LUGH AND THE SECOND BATTLE OF THE MAG TUIREADH

In this second battle, so central to Irish mythology, the Tuatha De Danaan struggled yet again for control of the land, this time against the fearsome forces of the Fomorians. The Fomorians are often depicted as one-legged, one-armed, ugly sea monsters, and they were indeed malicious and grotesque.

The ruler of the Fomorians was Balor, a repulsive Cyclops with an evil eye whose mere look would kill anyone who gazed upon him—a fate which befell Nuada, the Tuatha king. When Nuada died, the leadership fell to the celebrated Lugh.

Lugh, the Bright One, was a sun god lauded for his many talents. He was a craftsman, musician, poet, sorcerer, and warrior. He was also, it turned out, the grandson of the evil Fomorian Balor. Before Lugh's birth it had been prophesied that Balor would be killed by his grandson. Balor tried to get rid of Lugh, without success, however, because the sun god was protected by powerful magic.

After Nuada's death, Lugh took it upon himself to slay the evil-eyed monster. As Balor was falling asleep,

Lugh attacked him with a stone from an enchanted slingshot, shooting it with such force that it drove the monster's eye out of the back of his head, thus turning his evil gaze toward his own army. Balor was killed, and the Fomorians returned to the sea. Lugh was given the title Lugh Lamfhada ("Lugh of the long arm"), and the summer harvest festival Lughnasa (August 1) is named in his honor.

Morrigan, the war and fertility goddess, assisted the Tuatha De Danaan in their battles against both the Fir Bolg and the Fomorians, taking up arms, or transforming herself into a raven or crow to startle the enemy.

DEFEAT OF THE TUATHA DE DANAAN

The third and final battle of the Tuatha was heralded by the arrival of the Milesians on the southwest coast of Ireland on the feast of Beltane in 1000 B.C. Also known as the Sons of Mil, they came from Spain, and were said to be the descendants of the biblical Noah and ancestors of the present-day Irish. They are also attributed with naming the country Eriu.

When the Tuatha De Danaan saw the Milesians approaching the coastline of Ireland, they sent a magic wind in an attempt to drive them away. However, the Milesians had their own vital magic, in the form of the poet Amhairghin, who calmed the wind with his chanting so that the invaders were able to land. He sang:

I am an estuary into the sea.
I am a wave of the ocean.
I am the sound of the sea.
I am a powerful ox.
I am a hawk on a cliff.
I am a dewdrop in the sun.

Left *Lugh, the Sun God* by Ernest Wallcousins. When Lugh arrived at Nuada's door, he was initially barred entry. He first stated he was a carpenter, but they had plenty of those. Each craft he chose, they had—poet, blacksmith, hero, warrior. Finally, he asked if they had one man with all those gifts. They didn't and so Lugh entered, owner of all those talents.

BRIGID: GODDESS AND SAINT

Brigid (or Brigit), meaning "greatness," was the daughter of the Dagda, the good god of the Tuatha De Danaan. She was also the wife of Bres, who ruled over the Tuatha De Danaan after Nuada's injury. Because Brigid's virtues and skills were so many and varied (she was the patron of poetry, fertility, healing, and childbirth), it is thought that she may even be an aspect of the Great Mother deity Danu. Her dedicated festival is Imbolc, the lambing time when ewes' milk comes in, signifying nourishment and the end of winter.

With the arrival of Christianity, many qualities of the goddess were attributed to St. Brigid who, along with St. Patrick and St. Kevin, is one of Ireland's best-loved saints. St. Brigid founded a convent in Kildare in the sixth century A.D., and was renowned for her hospitality and great kindness to the poor. Her feast day on the Christian calendar is February 1, which coincides with Imbolc. Both Celtic goddess and Christian saint are associated with purification by fire, and are the keepers of the flame.

Above *A Banshee* from *Dictionnaire Infernal* by C. de Plancy (1794–1881). The banshee, as a portent of coming death, has a long history in Irish folklore. In an eighth-century poem, the goddess Morrigan is depicted washing the entrails of the soon-to-be dead. It is believed that if a banshee is caught, she will divulge the name of the doomed person.

Right *Cuchulainn Carries Ferdiad Across the River* by Ernest Wallcousins. According to legend, the valiant Ferdiad was forced by Medb to wage battle with his foster-brother Cuchulainn. For three days they fought until the magic spear of Cuchulainn ended the battle. Grief-stricken, he carried his friend back to the Ulster camp rather than leave him with Medb.

At the battle of Teltown in County Meath, the Milesians defeated the Tuatha De Danaan with their great iron weapons. Not intending to go down without a fight, however, the Tuatha cast a spell, destroying the Milesians' crops. The Milesians were so impressed by the Tuatha's magical prowess, however, that they came to an arrangement. They allowed the people of Danu to go beneath the earth and occupy the hillocks and mounds (*sidhe*). Other Tuatha migrated to Tir Na Nog, the land of eternal youth.

Still others were changed into banshee (the *bean sidhe* or "woman of the fairies"). The banshee can manifest itself as a fair young maiden or as an old hag—both having long flowing tresses and eyes red from crying. The appearance of the banshee is always a frightening occurrence, as it takes place just before someone's death, accompanied by lamenting and wailing in a strange language.

The talented and handsome sun god Lugh went underground and became a craftsman, and was called "little stooping Lugh," or Luchorpain. His companions became known as leprechauns and are depicted in popular folklore as tricksters, shoemakers, and the keepers of hidden treasure and pots of gold.

And so the powerful and magnificent Tuatha De Danaan became the fairy folk of Irish mythology, occasionally making brief sojourns above ground at such times when the veil between the Otherworld and the ordinary world was lifted, such as at Samhain and Beltane.

CUCHULAINN: HERO AND WARRIOR

Cuchulainn is perhaps the best-known and loved of all the ancient Irish heroes. Belonging to the Ulster Cycle of stories, Cuchulainn is the archetypal Celtic tribal leader. He was conceived from an Otherworldly affair between the sun god Lugh and Dechtire, said to be the daughter of the druid Cathbad or of the chieftain Conchobar. At Cuchulainn's birth, it was predicted that his life would not be long.

From the time he was a small child, Cuchulainn was charismatic, handsome, and courageous. He was first given the name of Setanta, meaning small, but he became known as Cuchulainn (Hound of Culann) after he killed the vicious dog belonging to Culann, the local smith, at the tender age of seven. He then took over the duty of guarding Culann's property.

Cuchulainn was sent to learn military skills under the tutelage of Scathach, the famed warrior woman on the Isle of Skye. And Scathach was an extremely generous mentor. Not only did she give Cuchulainn the *gae bolga,* an enchanted javelin, she also sent her daughter Uathach to train him in the art of love.

When Cuchulainn went into battle, his mind and body would undergo a dramatic transformation that was known as "battle frenzy" or "warp spasm." His limbs contorted, his face became like a bright red

Right *Macha Curses all Ulstermen* by Stephen Reid (1873–1948). Macha embodied the apparent opposites of earth mother and slaughterer of men. She was one of the three war goddesses, and warriors drew their inspiration from this formidable creature.

bowl, one eye was sucked back into his head while the other protruded, and a fountain of red-black blood came out of his head. When he was in this altered state, he was unable to tell friend from enemy and his battle cry was so shrill and discordant it would send people mad. Only by being dipped three times into a vat of water could he be calmed.

Lover and Father

As well as having a reputation as a fierce warrior, Cuchulainn was known to have an extremely powerful effect on women. Emer, the woman who would become his long-suffering and jealous wife, would only marry him if he first proved himself as a warrior, and could perform certain superhuman tasks, such as stay awake for an entire year. Cuchulainn succeeded, won the heart of Emer, and was married.

When Cuchulainn was apprenticed to Scathach, she enlisted his help in fighting her rival Aoife, a fierce warrior from the land of shadows. Cuchulainn conquered Aoife as well as her heart, and when he left her she discovered herself pregnant. About 15 years later, a fiery-tempered youth named Connla arrived in Ulster and challenged Cuchulainn to a fight. After Cuchulainn killed the boy with his javelin, he noticed that Connla was wearing the gold ring that he had given Aoife years before, and realized, too late, that Connla was his son.

Cuchulainn also fell in love with Fand, the beautiful fairy woman who was married to Manannan Mac Lir. When Emer and Mac Lir discovered the infidelity, they arranged for a druid to wave a magical cloak between the pair so that they would never see each other again. Cuchulainn was heart-broken, but Emer had the druid give Cuchulainn a potion of forgetfulness that destroyed all memory of Fand.

WARRIOR GODDESSES

The three Celtic warrior goddesses—Badb, Macha, and Morrigan—are all aspects of the triple goddess "The Morrigana" (the great queens). These goddesses of both war and regeneration are inextricably linked to the Cuchulainn story.

Badb appears either as a wild, red-haired woman or as a crow. In either guise, she is a harbinger of death, and a terrifying presence on the battlefield.

Macha is the archetypal fertility goddess and sorceress. Her mortal husband Crunnchu made a bet that his pregnant wife could win a race against the Ulster king's horses. The effort of winning the race brought on the birth of the twins, and she cursed all Ulstermen: at their time of greatest need they would suffer labor pains. Their need arose during the Cattle Raid of Cooley, leaving Cuchulainn to fight alone.

Morrigan is the supreme sex and fertility goddess and oracle, and is strongly identified with the land. Because Cuchulainn rejected her amorous advances, she did not assist him in his final battle; rather she transformed herself into a crow and flew onto his shoulder at the time of his death.

Below *Finn Encounters Otherworldly Creatures* by Stephen Reid (1873–1948). Many of the exploits of the great warrior Finn are concerned with the Otherworld, and involve magic. A giant of a man, it is said that he built the Giant's Causeway as stepping stones to get to Scotland.

The Cattle Raid of Cooley

Considered the grandest epic poem in the Irish language, The Cattle Raid of Cooley (*Tain Bo Cuailnge*) was written in the eighth century A.D. It tells the story of the greedy and manipulative goddess and warrior-queen Medb (Maeve) of Connacht and the heroic death of Cuchulainn against cowardly forces. Medb was obsessed with the desire to own the brown bull of Cooley, in order to upstage her husband Ailill, the owner of the great white-horned bull.

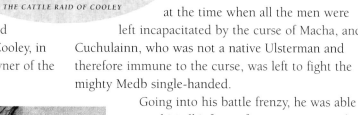

*Dismay of battle riseth
For there was never found
One like unto Cuchulainn*

TRANSLATION BY J. DUNN (1914),
THE CATTLE RAID OF COOLEY

The brown bull was owned by the Ulster chieftain Daire, and Medb, who was famous for her powers of seduction, "extended him the friendship of her upper thighs" (so the epic goes) in exchange for the beast. Daire refused, and Medb summoned an army to help her steal the bull. She chose to invade Ulster at the time when all the men were left incapacitated by the curse of Macha, and Cuchulainn, who was not a native Ulsterman and therefore immune to the curse, was left to fight the mighty Medb single-handed.

Going into his battle frenzy, he was able to repel Medb's forces for some time until a fatal wound to the stomach finally overcame him. Cuchulainn fastened himself to a pillar stone so that he could remain upright and continue fighting. His death was signaled by crows landing on his shoulder.

FINN MACCOOL

The equally popular tale of Finn MacCool (Finn Mac Cumhaill) is part of the Fenian Cycle of myths that tells of the adventures of Finn and his son Oisin. (It is sometimes referred to as the Ossianic Cycle.) Finn was a great military leader, visionary, and poet but, unlike Cuchulainn, he was a wandering hero rather than a tribal leader. His father was the warrior Cumhaill and his mother, "Murna of the white neck," was a descendant of the godlike race, the Tuatha De Danaan.

Demne (which was the name Finn was first given as an infant) was sent away to be fostered by two wise warrior women to hide him from the man who murdered his father. Like Cuchulainn and other mythical heroes, Demne was a very gifted child, with a great understanding of the natural world. He was renamed Finn, meaning "fair" or "shining."

The Salmon of Knowledge

When Finn was a bit older, he was sent to continue his education with Finegas, a noted bard and wise man. For seven years, Finegas would go every day and patiently sit by the River Boyne, waiting for a certain salmon to appear. It was said that the person who caught and ate this special fish (who was known as Fintan) would receive the gift of second sight, and "nothing would remain unknown to him."

One day, a jubilant Finegas caught the salmon, a large orange and gold creature, and told his young apprentice to cook it while he went to collect more wood for the fire. Finegas gave strict instructions for Finn not to eat any of the fish because Finegas wanted the gifts all for himself.

Finn accidentally burned his thumb on the salmon and, in a reflex action, immediately put the thumb in his mouth, tasting the oil of the fish. The teacher was disappointed but philosophical, realizing that it must have been the young boy's destiny to eat of the salmon. From that time on, Finn would only have to put his thumb in his mouth to receive the wisdom. With this knowledge, Finn was now ready to fulfill his destiny and he set off to find the Fianna.

The Fianna

The Fianna was an elite band of mighty warriors that supported and protected the High King at the royal seat of Tara. Every year at Samhain (November 1), the underworld demon Aillen Mac Midna would wreak havoc on Tara, putting everyone to sleep with his enchanted music, then burning down the palace. The High King, Cormac MacAirt, was so tired of this annual occurrence that he asked for helpers to try to rid the palace of the demon. Finn MacCool accepted the challenge, but requested the leadership of the Fianna, the king's warriors, in return for killing the demon. Because Finn had magical weapons, he was able to resist the enchanted music, and beheaded Aillen with his spear. Cormac MacAirt granted Finn his wish, as agreed.

Under Finn's expert guidance, the Fianna grew in strength and excellence. His requirements were very stringent, and he demanded a high level of physical prowess, honor, chivalry, and literacy. It is thought that some aspects of the King Arthur and the Knights of the Round Table legend have been patterned on the Fianna. The modern-day Irish political party known as "Fianna Fail" has taken its name in honor of its ancient predecessor.

Sabd and Oisin

One day when Finn was out hunting, he came across a gentle doe. Finn's hounds did not attack her; rather they played with her very affectionately and Finn was rather bemused to find the doe following him home.

The next morning the doe had vanished and a beautiful maiden

greeted Finn instead. The young woman, called Sadb (Sava), was the granddaughter of the god Dagda, and she had been changed into a doe by an evil wizard. Finn's kindness and healing touch had transformed her back into her human state.

They fell in love, and lived together for many happy months. However, Finn was eventually called away on Fianna business, and when he returned a week later, Sadb had disappeared, lured away by the sorcerer.

After a long, fruitless search, Finn eventually gave up. Several years later, when hunting around Ben Bulben in County Sligo, he came across a strange little boy who had a tuft of deer hair on his forehead. Finn recognized the boy as his son. He named him Oisin ("little fawn") and the boy grew up to be a Fianna warrior and poet.

Above *Finn MacCool Aids the Fianna* by Stephen Reid (1873–1948). The Fianna was a military elite founded around 300 B.C., responsible for guarding the king. Before Finn was leader, they were unruly; he introduced a code of honor and made them into champions of the people.

Left *The Druid Warns Medb about Cuchulainn* by Stephen Reid (1873–1948). Medb used all her skills and magic to kill Cuchulainn. According to legend her own demise came at the hands of King Conchobar's son Furbaide, who hit her with a piece of cheese, flung with such force that it killed her.

TRAGIC LOVE STORIES

Among the saddest tales in Irish mythology are those of Deirdre of the Sorrows and of Diarmuid and Grainne. They share several common traits: both have strong magical components; they both tell of a love triangle between a beautiful woman and two men (one young and the other much older); and in both, the woman actively pursues the younger man, a noted characteristic of Celtic tales. But most of all, the stories are about the fragility of the human heart when denied true love, and the endurance of love beyond the grave.

Deirdre of the Sorrows

Written versions of the story date back to the ninth century. It is part of the Ulster Cycle and, as in the great Cuchulainn legend, it begins with a bleak prophecy from Cathbad, King Conchobar's chief druid. Before Deirdre was born, Cathbad predicted that she would be a great beauty, but would bring destruction to the king and to all of Ulster.

When the Ulstermen heard this prediction, they wanted the child destroyed at birth. But King Conchobar decided to let her live, raising Deirdre in a remote castle under his watchful eye, and planning to marry her as soon as she came of age.

When Deirdre grew up, she had a dream that she would fall in love with a man with hair as black as raven's wings and pale skin with rosy cheeks. She soon learned of a handsome, talented, young warrior known as Naoise who had those attributes. From her castle keep, she heard a man singing and was captivated by his voice. When she discovered that the singer was Naoise, she immediately decided that she would marry him.

DRUIDS

Druids were an intrinsic part of the religion, politics, and myths of Celtic Ireland. They were believed to have been descended from the Tuatha De Danaan, and therefore were afforded godlike status.

The responsibilities of the druid were many and varied. Depending on the situation, they could be called upon to act as priest, bard, healer, sorcerer, oracle, or sage, and serve as mediator between the physical world and the spirit realm. King Conchobar's druid, Cathbad, was skilled as a prophet, and the Tuatha sun god, Lugh, enlisted the help of a militaristic druid to defeat the Fomorians. As the holders of ancient lore, and the teachers of noblemen and bards, they controlled knowledge in the tribe.

Ceremonies were held in places of great natural beauty and energy (such as on the Hill of Tara) or in secluded groves. Druids had the power to cause storms or earthquakes and could predict the future, but they could not change the course of fate. To train as a druid was not to be taken lightly—it took 20 years to qualify.

Above *An Arch Druid* from *Costume of the British Isles* by Meyrich and Smith (1821). Mystery surrounded the druids and still does. The early Christians did their best to destroy their knowledge and power and, as the druids passed on their lore by word of mouth, little information survives that is not secondhand.

Although Naoise was captivated by Deirdre's wondrous charms, he was frightened off by the prophecies. His brothers Ainle and Ardan tried to dissuade him from Deirdre, but to no avail—she was a woman obsessed. Eventually Naoise and Deirdre married, and the couple, along with Ainle and Ardan, fled across the sea to Alba, now Scotland.

Because Naoise and his brothers were such excellent warriors, the Ulstermen convinced the king to grant them a pardon. Conchobar agreed, and the brothers were summoned back to Ireland. The night before their journey, Deirdre received a message in a dream that Conchobar's offer of peace was a false one, and pleaded with Naoise not to return. However, Naoise and his brothers chose to ignore her, and all three of them were killed on their return.

Deirdre became Conchobar's prisoner, and she never smiled again. One year later, while Deirdre and Conchobar were traveling in an open carriage, they passed by Naoise's tomb. Deirdre was inconsolable at the sight of it and, rather than continue her hateful life, she threw herself out of the carriage, smashing her head on a rock and killing herself. Two yew trees grew on that very spot, their branches becoming intertwined for eternity.

Diarmuid and Grainne

Grainne, the striking and spirited daughter of the High King Cormac MacAirt, was promised to the ageing leader of the Fianna warriors, Finn MacCool. At the couple's engagement feast, Grainne set eyes on Diarmuid, a young Fianna officer, and fell instantly and tragically in love.

Diarmuid's loyalties were with the Fianna, and he initially rejected Grainne's advances. Eventually he succumbed to her seductive powers, and the pair eloped. Finn was furious to have been so betrayed, and relentlessly pursued the lovers for many years. Several times when the Fianna were close to catching them, Diarmuid and Grainne were assisted in their flight by Aengus, a god of love and Diarmuid's foster father. He gave them a cloak of invisibility so they could avoid being caught by Finn, and Finn never saw them when he was chasing them.

Finn finally gave up the chase, and accepted the loss of Grainne. Diarmuid and Grainne made a home, but Diarmuid came to miss his friends from the Fianna. So, when Finn invited Diarmuid to join him in a boar hunt at Ben Bulben, as an apparent token of good will and forgiveness, Diarmuid accepted, even though he had been warned in his youth that

he would be killed by a boar. The prophecy proved true: Diarmuid was mortally wounded by the boar, and when Finn came across the dying man, he refused him a drink of water, even though he knew that, as he had the power of healing, it would have saved Diarmuid's life.

Grainne was heartbroken to have lost her true soul mate. But the magical Aengus came to their assistance again. He transported Diarmuid's body to an enchanted spot in the River Boyne, and there the unhappy lovers could communicate with one another.

Left **Stone votive offering, Alésia, France.** Although Celtic life revolved around the tribe, Irish tales are full of deeds by individuals, often in the name of love.

Below *A Farmer Rescues His Wife from Fairies* by Henry J. Ford (1860–1941). The fairies of the Tuatha live in a blessed land, but do visit the world of mortals; they have been known to take humans back with them .

FANTASTIC VOYAGES

There is a genre in Irish mythology known as the imram story, which tells of perilous sea voyages to the mysterious "blessed islands," or to "phantom islands," thought to be located in the Atlantic Ocean west of Ireland. The tales of Bran and Mael Duin were subsumed into the Christian adventure of St. Brendan the Navigator, while the legend of Oisin, perhaps one of the most captivating of all, has inspired several plays, films, and poems.

The Voyage of Bran

One day Bran encountered a stunning, seductive woman who presented him with a silver bough laden with magnificent white blossoms. The woman told of her Otherworld home, the "island of women" (Tir Inna mBan), which was described as a true paradise: endless food, endless love, a never-ending summer, and eternal youth.

Bran recruited a crew of 26 men and headed west in search of this enchanted isle. When he crossed a crystal bridge and arrived on the island, he found it was all that he had hoped it would be and much more; he became the lover of the beautiful goddess. There was only one catch: the goddess had put a spell on the men and warned that they could never return home.

For a year, everyone was happy. Then some of the men began to miss Ireland and their families, and persuaded Bran to take them back. When their ship was approaching Irish soil, the men on the boat began to wave eagerly, but no one on shore recognized them. In his excitement to be home, one man jumped ashore, and as soon as his feet touched the land, he crumbled into a pile of ashes. Bran and his remaining crew turned and headed west, never to return.

Mael Duin and the Amazing Islands

Mael Duin was the son of Ailill, a warrior who was brutally killed in battle. As soon as he was old enough, Mael Duin swore to avenge the untimely death of his father. A druid warned him that he would have to travel to an island far across the sea if he wanted to find the murderer.

The druid also warned him to carry only 18 men on the boat, and not a single person more, otherwise misfortune would occur. Mael Duin duly obeyed the druid's instructions. But just as he was departing, his three foster brothers climbed on board, determined to make the voyage.

After several days, the men neared the island home of Ailill's killer. But a ferocious storm blew the boat off its course and into the enchanted waters of the Otherworld, where they encountered many weird places and saw many wonderful creatures.

On one island there was a palace filled with food, drink, and precious jewels. One brother stole a necklace there, and was promptly destroyed by a giant magic cat. The second brother landed on the

island of his father's murderers. With all resentment and malice gone from his heart, Mael Duin made friends with the people there who, in turn, hailed him as an explorer and hero.

Oisin and the Land of Eternal Youth

Niamh of the Golden Hair was a lovely fairy woman and daughter of the sea god Manannan Mac Lir. She had heard good stories of the poet and warrior Oisin (son of Finn MacCool) and was drawn to earth to seek him out for her husband.

Niamh found Oisin hunting near misty Lough Leane, one of the lakes of Killarney. She enticed him into the lake, which was a portal into the Otherworld known as Tir Na Nog, "the land of eternal youth." Tir Na Nog was indeed a paradise: breathtakingly beautiful, alive with birds, color, and music, and where love was always fresh and new. Its inhabitants were blessed with eternal youth, oblivious to such concepts as time, rules, or work. The days fled, and Oisin led a blissful life with Niamh.

But as humans do, he became homesick—for his father, for the Fianna, and for Ireland—and told Niamh he wanted to go home. Niamh gave him a handsome white horse and told him he could return to Ireland, but under no circumstances should he get off the horse and set foot on the soil.

When Oisin arrived in Ireland, he discovered that 300 years had passed. Everyone he knew had departed, but what was even worse, all the old ways and beliefs had disappeared, and even the legendary deeds of Finn MacCool had become just a distant memory. Thus dispirited, he forgot Niamh's warning and dismounted. Immediately he became a withered, blind, and decrepit old man.

Some versions of the story say that St. Patrick found Oisin and took care of him, encouraging him to tell the stories of Finn and the days of old, which were recorded for posterity.

Isle of Weeping where he was forced to remain for all eternity crying. Then they visited the Isle of Women, where they were lured by dreams of immortality and love. Mael Duin enjoyed his stay there for a while, but eventually decided to head home. On the return journey, the last brother set foot on the Isle of Mirth where he still lives with the laughing folk to this day.

With the loss of his foster brothers, Mael Duin was back on course, and eventually came to the

Left **The Journey** by **Stephen Reid (1873–1948).** Niamh of the Golden Hair takes Oisin to her father's land. According to some versions of this story, the lovely Niamh had been watching Oisin for some time before approaching him. When they arrived at her land, she waved her hand and the mist parted to reveal a shining castle.

Above **Votive ship from Broighter, Derry, first century B.C.** This model represents a real ship, intended for the high seas. It was probably a votive offering, possibly to Manannan Mac Lir, King of the Sea, to ensure a safe voyage. He used mist to shroud his land and he gave the Tuatha the gift of invisibility and sanctuary in the underground mounds.

GERMANIC AND NORSE MYTHOLOGY

Below *Representation of the Valkyrie* from *The Ring Cycle* by Richard Wagner (1813–1883). Germanic mythological figures are perhaps best known to us today through much later works such as Wagner's operas, with the swooping Valkyries, or via Tolkein's stories. Early compilations of the oral traditions reveal a complex world of gods, giants, and heroes, pitted against each other and against the elements.

This section covers the mythologies and religious perceptions of the various Germanic tribes that emerged from the dark of prehistory in Northern Europe during the early Iron Age, that is, sometime before 500 B.C. The origins of these tribes is still a matter of scholarly discussion, but there were well-defined groups among them by the time they came into their first contact with the Roman Empire in the last centuries B.C. Among these tribes were the Angles, Saxons, Jutes, Danes, and Swedes in the north, the Franks in the northwest, the Suebi in the southwest, the Vandals in the northeast, and the Goths in the east. They spoke different languages to each other and the tribes were not always a single group—each could be made up of smaller tribes.

The Alemanni, for example, probably belonged to, or broke away from, the Suebi, and their language, Alemanic, is the dialect of High German that is spoken in Swabia (from Suebi), which is Germany today.

Lo now, Allfather, wouldst thou have me toil for ever, nor win the wages due?

ANON. VÖLSUNGA SAGA C. 1300

During the course of the first millennium A.D., and especially as the Roman Empire weakened, the Germanic tribes—many of whom remained semi-nomadic—spread and settled large parts of Europe. The Goths, who were divided into the Ostrogoths and Visigoths, moved south following the attacks of the Huns, eventually moving into Spain. The Franks moved into Gaul (France) and the Vandals moved south and west into Spain and then Africa, from where they sent an army to sack Rome in A.D. 455. The Saxons moved south and along the coast of Gaul, and eventually into Britannia (England). The Lombards, also from the north, moved through Hungary and Austria, and the Alemanni and Burgundians settled areas of central Europe. Thus, the Germanic peoples were spread from Iceland and Britain to Spain and west to the Black Sea.

Broadly speaking, the Germanic peoples were pagans who worshipped many gods, though little is known of their religion. Naturally, migrating over such an extensive area, their religions developed differently, depending on local experiences and also as a result of exposure to foreign influences (mainly pagan Roman and Christian, but also Slavonic and Celtic). Consequently, there does not appear to be a unified Germanic mythology. Except for a number of runic inscriptions or pictures on stones, writing as a means of recording historical events had not been developed. Their myths were instead passed down by oral tradition, especially by poets and minstrels, or *skalds* as they were known in the Scandinavian countries. Therefore, Germanic mythology, to a large degree, was recorded by others.

CHRISTIANITY AND ITS IMPACT

Christianity came to the various tribes at different times. By the time information about their beliefs was recorded, much had been lost as the tribes had dispersed or moved to new lands. The mostly Christian writers worked with fragments and local memory, and with a Christian interpretation that did not wish to show paganism in a favorable light.

While the Goths were already Christians in the fourth century A.D., the Germanic tribes to the very north remained somewhat isolated from the developments in central Europe, and retained more of their original mythology than elsewhere. The Old Norse peoples, today's Scandinavians—the countries of Denmark, Sweden, Norway, and Iceland—only converted to Christianity in the course of the tenth and eleventh centuries, with paganism being alive and well in Sweden as late as A.D. 1100.

This uneven development of the tribes, combined with varying contact with the other groups, means that the sources available for the myths are also very uneven in their quality and distribution. The richest sources of the traditions are preserved in the Norse corpus of works, especially in Icelandic works from the thirteenth century known as the poetic *Edda,* and the slightly later prose *Edda* written by Snorri Sturluson (1179–1241).

This Norse corpus of mythology is more uniform and extensive than that of both central and eastern Germany. Previously, most Scandinavians, like all the Germanic peoples, were polytheistic pagans who worshipped a variety of gods and goddesses, many of whom were familiar to all other Germanic tribes under different names. The best known of the Norse deities were Odin, Thor, Freyr, Freyia, and Niord; but although we know their names, as elsewhere, we have very little reliable information about how they were worshipped. Archaeological evidence of pagan activity exists, but much of it is very uncertain in its implications. Scandinavian place names sometimes

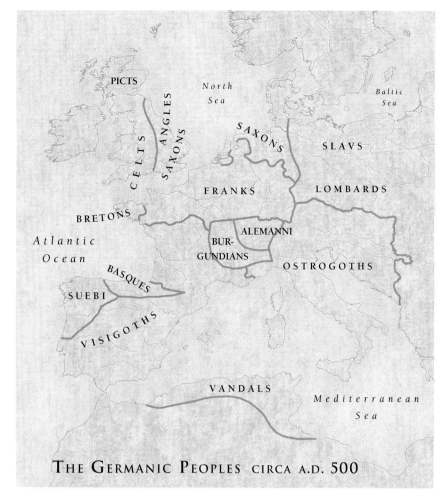

THE GERMANIC PEOPLES CIRCA A.D. 500

incorporate the names of pagan gods or goddesses, indicating their worship in parts of Scandinavia; but they tell us virtually nothing about pagan practices and rituals in any detail.

Later, from the thirteenth century onward, the Icelandic sagas in the two *Edda* contain retrospective accounts of pagan activity, but the late date of these sources—getting on for 300 years or so after Iceland's conversion to Christianity around A.D. 1000—means that their evidence cannot be relied upon too heavily. They bear the stamp of typical Icelandic storytelling through their medieval Christian authors, and these sources may give a picture of pagan mythology that is rather too systematic and learned, the stories reflecting literary rather than religious qualities. There is some evidence—including allusions in the preserved poems of pagan Norse poets of the ninth and tenth centuries, pictorial sources such as stone engravings and, very rarely, old runic inscriptions—that corroborate these medieval Icelandic stories, but some care is required when assessing their validity as sources for the wider Germanic pagan mythology.

Above **Principal Germanic peoples.** Incursions against the Romans by the Goths, Saxons, Franks, and others had been occurring since the third century A.D. This took on greater urgency with the arrivals of the Asiatic Huns around A.D. 350. By the fall of the Roman Empire 100 years later, various distinct Germanic empires had established themselves across Europe.

Left *The Gods of Northern Europe* from *Historia Gentibus Septentrionalibus* by Olaus Magnus (1490–1557). The three gods shown here are Frigg, the wife of Odin; Thor, their son; and Odin. Many of the different Germanic tribes believed in the same gods, despite their differences in geography and language.

SOURCES OF MYTH AND HISTORY

Right *Mannus, the First German King, from The Origin of the First Twelve Old Kings and Princes of the German Nation, 1543.* According to the writings of Tacitus, Mannus is the father of the three German tribes: the Ingaevones, the Herminones, and the Instaevones. In popular oral tradition, the god Heimdall created the three classes of society after spending one night each with three different couples. The children borne from this union were slave, freeman, and noble.

Most of the specific information scholars possess about Old Norse pagan mythology derives from a relatively small number of written sources. One is the collection of heroic and mythological poems that are known as the poetic *Edda.* This was compiled from various sources by unknown writers, probably sometime during the early thirteenth century. The second source is the prose *Edda,* written by the Icelandic politician Snorri Sturluson (1179–1241), a little after the poetic *Edda* was completed. Sturluson lived an adventurous life as a political leader, gaining great wealth and influence. His prose *Edda* is a guide to the conventions of traditional Icelandic poetic composition, written for the benefit of aspiring poets. Of its four parts, the two most important sources of mythological information and narratives are *Skaldskaparmal* (poetic diction) and *Gylfaginning.* In *Gylfaginning* a fictional king, Gylfi, goes in disguise to Asgard, the city of the gods, to find out about the gods and to learn all of their wisdom. Odin comes to King Gylfi in three guises and tells the history of the stories of the gods. Snorri Sturluson clearly drew heavily on the poetic *Edda* for some of the myths he records in his prose *Edda.*

Only occasionally are we given brief glimpses of Germanic mythological tales outside Scandinavia, but here too we must be aware that they were normally either written down by Roman authors with only limited knowledge of conditions in the Germanic areas, or else by Germanic authors who had converted to Christianity.

Tacitus

One of the most ancient references to Germanic myths is given by the Roman historian Gaius Cornelius Tacitus (who lived approximately A.D. 56–120). He wrote a brief ethnography of the Germanic peoples living outside the Roman Empire at that time, called *Germania.* The problem of recording another culture with only limited knowledge can be seen in his discussion of various goddesses.

In Chapter 9 of *Germania,* for example, Tacitus concludes that the Suebi venerated a goddess who was similar to the Egyptian goddess Isis because ships appeared to be a part of the ritual. This goddess is more likely Nehalennia, who was intensely venerated, especially by the Frisians in the third century (living mostly on the Frisian islands off the northwestern coast of Germany). Nehalennia is named on votive stones as far afield as Cologne, in western Germany. Some of the inscriptions explicitly mention her assistance in trading voyages, which depict her as a goddess of seafaring Frisian merchants. The Suebi lived far from the coast, and probably would have had very little to do with a goddess related to seafaring.

Tacitus, however, provided much other useful information, and this mention of the goddess, even if misleading, is valuable for its rarity.

GERMANIC CREATION MYTHS

One of the oldest references to Germanic myths is given by Tacitus. In his *Germania,* he mentions that in "ancient songs" the Germanic tribes celebrate the origin of mankind as going back to a certain "Tuisto, a god born from the earth, and his son Mannus, as the forefathers and founders of the nation. To Mannus they assign three sons, after whose names so many people are called: the Ingaevones, dwelling next to the ocean; the Herminones, in the middle country; and all the rest, Instaevones." That is, these three sons were seen as the forefathers of the principal Germanic peoples, living in the east, center, and west of northern Europe.

Although these mythical Germanic forebears are referred to only in Tacitus, the name "Mannus" clearly refers to Germanic "man." The Norse creation myth, as presented through sources like the two *Edda,* is different, though there are some similar concepts.

Below **Yggdrasill, the Mundane Tree or World Tree.** The great tree of the world extends through all levels of the universe: the heavens, earth, and underworld. The Bifrost Bridge, which humans see as a rainbow, links the real and supernatural worlds. Near the roots of the tree dwell the *norns*—fate.

Old Norse Tales of the Cosmos

Unlike the myth of Tuisto and the first father of the middle Germanic tribes, as given by Tacitus, the origins of the cosmos, according to Norse stories, were supposed to lie in obscure but dynamic interactions between water, ice, and fire. A number of distinct subworlds were the result, many of them inhabited by specific types of being. The Norse sources do not, it is true, present an entirely consistent or systematic vision of the universe's structure, but some aspects of it are fairly clear. Midgard, conceived as a central landmass surrounded by sea, is where the gods and humankind live. Within it lies Asgard, the city of the gods, presided over by Odin, the lord of all the gods. Underneath it is the world of the dead, which is ruled by the goddess Hel. The giants have their own world, located rather vaguely on the fringes of the cosmos, perhaps beyond the encircling sea. Finally, dwarves live in the rocks and caves below the earth. All the various subworlds in the Norse myths are dominated by the world tree Yggdrasill, which towers over all while its roots are buried in each of the three worlds—Asgard, Midgard, and the Underworld.

As the various Old Norse myths explain it, the earliest of all living creatures were the giants. All beings came from the "protogiant" Ymir, who had a son, Buri, begotten by Ymir's two legs with each other, who in turn had a son called Burr. This son conceived three sons with a giantess, namely the gods Odin, Víli, and Vé. The gods evolved from them, and created the first man and woman from two logs that they found washed up on the shores of Midgard.

The body parts of the dead protogiant Ymir were used as the basis for the principal features of the universe: his blood became the sea, his cranium the round vault of the sky, his brains the clouds, and his bones the rocks.

Despite the difference in their names, the three descendants of the protogiant Ymir—Odin, Víli and Vé—appear to be the forefathers of the main tribes across the Germanic lands, as described in the Tuisto myth. This suggests common origins of the myth, especially as Odin is widely named as a mythical ancestor of the western Germanic tribes and of royal houses from Scandinavia to Britain and Lombardia. In the case of the three "peoples" Tacitus mentions, it may be possible to see links here, too. The ancestors of the Ingaevones may be identified in Scandinavian tradition as Yngvi, a name that is assigned to the god Freyr, who was the protector of the Swedish royal dynasty of the Ynglings.

Two Families of Gods

In this world created out of Ymir, there were two distinct families of gods, the Vanir and the Aesir. In the long-ago history of the universe they had fought each other, but by the time in which most of the myths are set their differences are forgotten and they live harmoniously together in the realm of Asgard. The chief members of the Vanir are Niord and his children—the goddess Freyia and her twin brother Freyr. All the Vanir are closely associated, in both religion and myth, with love, fertility, and material wealth. All the other most prominent deities—Odin, Thor, and Tyr—are Aesir, though the distinction between the two races is rarely noted in the sources.

Below *Hel, Daughter of Loki and Goddess of the Underworld* by Johannes Gehrts (1855–1921). It is said that Hel was born after Loki ate the heart of a giant witch known as Angerbotha. Hel was cast into the lowest level by Odin, to emerge again only at the final battle. Her hall was Elvidnir, or Misery, and her realm, Niflheim (Hel).

OF GODS AND GIANTS

The gods and the giants are traditional enemies, and many of the myths tell of skirmishes between them. Thor, with his hammer, is a warrior god, the enemy most feared by the giants. The myths state that one day this enmity will boil over into a final war, known as the Ragnarok. The whole universe will be destroyed in this war, along with most of its inhabitants. However, the sources hint at a new dawn: a few gods and men will survive and together they will begin the work of rebuilding and repopulating a better and more peaceful world.

Above **Thor's hammer Miollnir, amulet, tenth century A.D., Sweden.** Associated with a thunderbolt, Thor's hammer was used to defend the gods and their world. It always returns to his hand after being thrown. This amulet would have been worn as a protective charm and is decorated with the staring eyes of Thor.

A Giant Builder

The following story comes from that part of Snorri Sturluson's prose *Edda* called *Gylfaginning,* which refers to the tales told to King Gylfi on his visit to the city of Asgard. It illustrates the dishonesty of the gods in their dealings with the giants, and some see this moral flaw in divine society as leading ultimately to the gods' destruction at the Ragnarok.

The myth is set in an early part of the mythical past, after the gods have established Midgard, and built there the great hall Valhalla. A builder visits them and offers to make them a fortification that will be proof against attack by mountain giants and frost giants, even if they force entry into Midgard itself. As payment, he asks for the goddess Freyia as his wife, as well as the sun and the moon.

The gods accept, on the condition that he completes the work within a single winter without help from any man; otherwise he forfeits all payment. The builder agrees, but asks that his stallion Svadilfoeri be allowed to help him, and this is granted on the advice of the mischievous god Loki. The agreement is sealed with solemn oaths on both sides. The builder begins the work. Svadilfoeri, who works during the night hauling stones, has twice the builder's strength, and by the time summer approaches it looks as though the work will be finished on time. The gods now wake up to the terrifying prospect of losing not only Freyia, but also the sources of all light in the world. They

Right *Thor Fights the Jotunes* by Martes Winge (1825–1896). Thor leads the fight against the giants, (the Jotunes or Jotun). The sound of thunder accompanies his chariot, which is drawn by magical goats. His power is aided by his Girdle of Strength and he often wears iron gauntlets at his wrists, which enable him to wield his hammer.

blame Loki for his bad advice and force him to devise a way of preventing the builder from finishing the job on schedule. Loki's solution to the problem is simple: he transforms himself into a mare. That very evening, as the stallion begins its work, he entices it away. The two horses disport themselves in the wood all night, and work on the fortifications is held up. The builder, faced with the loss of his fee, goes into a rage so terrifying that the gods realize that he is not really a man but a mountain giant. Forgetting their agreement, they summon Thor, who raises his hammer, Miollnir, and shatters the giant's skull. Thus the story ends, though there is an epilogue: Loki, in the form of a mare, has mated with the stallion and gives birth to a remarkable foal with eight legs, which grows up to be Sleipnir, the best of all horses and the chosen mount of Odin.

ODIN, RULER OF THE GODS

The god Odin was by far the most widely known of the Germanic gods in the first millennium A.D. Known to the Anglo-Saxons as Woden, to the Alamanic and Saxon tribes as Wodan, and to the Langobards as Godan, he was seen as the mythical ancestor of many of the Germanic tribes as well as several Anglo-Saxon royal families of

the early Middle Ages. Much earlier, however, he was seen in general as a god of healing, magic, runes, and knowledge, as well as the god of death, war, and fate. However, his followers were also well aware of the ambiguities of this multifunctional god, as they knew that in battle he could give victory as well as death to those who were dedicated to his worship.

ODIN AND THE RUNES

An Icelandic poem, the *Hávamál,* which in its preserved written form was only compiled in the twelfth century, along with the prose *Edda* from the thirteenth century, gives us a poetic but remarkably powerful version of how the god Odin became the first to obtain knowledge of the runes, that is, of the power and uses of writing. In both works,

Odin himself talks, declaring how he won the runes by hanging "on the wind-swept tree, for nine nights in all, wounded by a spear and dedicated to Odin, given myself to myself." As a result of this nine-day fast, he gained insight into the nature of the runes.

This scene, known as Odin's self-sacrifice, has similarities, even if only superficial, to Christ's sacrifice through both the hanging from a tree and the wounding by a spear. Some say it suggests a very early adoption of the central Christian myth by the ancient Scandinavians, possibly by way of the British Isles. Similar forms of self-sacrifice, however, are also found in the initiation rites of numerous archaic cultures, and its origins may more accurately be seen in the context of shamanistic initiation rites into the knowledge of poetry and magic.

Above **Viking picture stone from Gotland, Sweden, eighth century A.D.** This stone features the god Odin (Wodan) on his horse Sleipnir, assisted by Valkyries. The greatest of all horses, Sleipnir has eight legs, and it is he who bears the valiant dead to Valhalla.

Left **Rune stone, Uppsala, eleventh century A.D., by Gamla Torget.** Germanic mythology invested great value in writing, which was in the form of runes. This knowledge was not gained without suffering, however. Odin, the father of the gods, underwent nine days of fasting and pain in order to gain understanding.

POETIC MEAD: THE ORIGIN OF POETIC INSPIRATION

This myth comes from the part of Snorri Sturluson's prose *Edda* called the *Skaldskaparmal* and is very complex, with several episodes together forming a cycle (that is, several tales together forming a complete narrative about a person or event). The myth tells of poetry as a product of divine inspiration, and gives us an idea of the value placed upon poetry and the prestige of poets in the Scandinavian world.

Following an early war between the Aesir and the Vanir, a truce is declared, symbolized by both sides spitting into a vat. The gods make a man, Kvasir, out of the accumulated spittle. Kvasir was born fully grown, omniscient, and filled with the knowledge of both the Aesir and Vanir.

In Midgard, where mankind dwell, Kvasir became renowned for his ability to answer any question, no matter how learned the questioner. Those in need of advice knew they had only to send for him, and he would come. On one such trip he meets two dwarfs, Fialar and Galar, who invite him to a meal deep within their caves. There, they murder him and drain off his blood into two crocks and a kettle. They mix it with honey to produce a mead that turns anyone who drinks it into a poet or scholar.

The dwarves tell the gods that Kvasir has died, after choking on his own great learning because he could find no one who was able to compete with him in knowledge.

The two dwarves next invite Gilling, a giant, and his wife to their dwelling. They take Gilling rowing, but their boat strikes a rock and capsizes. Unable to swim, Gilling drowns, though the dwarves were able to right the boat and return home to tell the giantess of her husband's death. The dwarf Fialar asks her if it would ease her grief to look out to sea in the direction of the drowning, but this is a

Left *The giant Baugi, persuaded by Odin, drills into his brother Suttung's chamber.* This illustration shows the giant Baugi making a hole into the cave where the mead is hidden. The drill has magical powers, getting longer and longer the more it is used. No depth is too great for it.

trick: as she passes out through the doorway, Galar kills her by dropping a millstone on her. When the giants' son, Suttung, learns of what has happened, he seizes the two dwarfs and maroons them on an island that is covered at high tide. They beg for mercy, offering Suttung the mead as compensation for his parents' death. Suttung agrees, takes the precious mead, and hides it inside a mountain called Hnitbiorg, setting his daughter Gunnlod to guard it.

Odin's Search for the Mead

The story now turns to Odin's efforts to obtain the mead from Suttung. Dressed as a farm hand, Odin sets out on his mission. One day, Odin comes across nine serfs mowing hay. He carries a whetstone as part of his normal equipment, and he sharpens the serfs' scythes with it. The serfs are so impressed by the result that they offer to buy the whetstone from Odin, which he agrees to on condition that the price is right. He then throws the whetstone up into the air and in their eagerness the serfs all struggle for it; in the melee they all manage to cut one another's throats with their scythes.

Odin takes lodging with a giant called Baugi, who is Suttung's brother; but Odin conceals his true identity, giving his name as Bolverk. The nine serfs had worked for Baugi, who now faces the task of finding new workers to mow his hay. Odin offers to do the work of all nine men in return for one drink of Suttung's mead. Baugi is doubtful if his brother will surrender any of the mead, but agrees to help Odin to get hold of it once the work is done. Odin completes the mowing, and he and Baugi approach Suttung, but he refuses to part with any of the mead. Odin produces a drill called Rati and tells Baugi to bore a hole through Hnitbiorg to get at the mead. Baugi deliberately drills short of the cave where the mead is kept, but Odin forces him to extend the hole as far as the cave.

After changing himself into a serpent, Odin slithers through the hole. Baugi, in a last attempt to thwart him, stabs with the drill at the snake's tail as it disappears, but misses. Once inside the mountain, Odin seduces Gunnlod, who guards the mead, and spends three nights with her. He persuades her to give him three drafts of the mead for each night he spends with her. This is all Odin needs to drain all three of the containers in which the mead is kept. Then he

RUNES

The Germanic peoples had an alphabet made of twenty-four "letters," or staves, called runes. The earliest evidence of runic inscriptions comes from the second century A.D., but it is likely they were in use earlier than this. As the Germanic peoples did not have parchment, runes were carved into wood, stone, and bone, and this may account for their angular shape. They also appear on ornaments, swords, armor, and coins.

It has been suggested that the runes may have developed from Latin, after contact with the Romans, but there is no clear evidence of this. The word "rune" in Old Norse means mystery or secret, and so runes have often been associated with magic. However, there is no direct link between runes and magic, even in pre-Viking Age Scandinavia, although runes were occasionally used for magic, as well as for religious and secular purposes.

Above **Rune stone of Rok, Sweden, ninth century A.D.** This stone was carved by Varin for his dead son Vemod, and contains an ode to Theodoric, King of the Goths. Runes have meaning as single units, as combinations, and through their ordering. In the myths, eighteen runes were initially revealed to Odin.

transforms himself into an eagle and flies off toward Asgard. Suttung sees him escaping and follows, also in the shape of an eagle. Seeing Odin appear, the Aesir put out containers in Asgard's courtyard as instructed. Odin disgorges the mead, but Suttung is in close pursuit, and he inadvertently excretes some of the mead. This is not collected, but left for anyone who wants it.

The collected mead was given by Odin to the gods, and anyone who drank it became a skilled poet; but anyone who tasted the excreted mead produced only doggerel. As for Suttung, some versions of the tale say the sun's rays touched him just as he reached the walls of Asgard, robbing him of his eagle cloak, and he fell to the ground. In others, the gods built a fire, which singed his wings, again causing him to fall to his death.

Left **Pendant or amulet, ninth century A.D., Sweden.** The figure, possibly a priest of the cult of Odin, holds a sword and two spears and wears an adorned helmet. Odin is highly complex: god of battle, he is also god of wine and inspiration. Yet some see in his many sides a common thread: a loss of the self, be it through death or intoxication.

Above **Angel, on an altar of the Lombard King Rachis, eighth century** A.D. The Langobards (or Lombards) were originally from southern Sweden but settled in Italy, and gave their name to the region of Lombardia. Early tales explain how, when the numbers of the Winnili grew too big, they divided themselves into three and drew lots. The group led by Ibor and Aio lost, so they departed in search of a new homeland.

DESCENDED FROM THE GODS

Many of the Germanic tribes had myths linking their authority with the gods. Often this was Odin, the most powerful of the gods. One of the better known and oldest of the Germanic myths of origin comes from the Langobard historiographers of the sixth and seventh centuries A.D. They relate an old tradition that describes a battle between two Germanic tribes, the Wandali (Vandals) and the Winnili. The Wandali prayed to their chief god Godan (Wodan/Odin) for victory. The Winnili, however, were led by Gambara, the wise old mother of their leaders Ibor and Aio, who prayed to Godan's wife, Frea (Frigg).

Frea advised the Winnili warriors to position them-selves in the east on the morning of the battle and for the women to stand with the men on the battle lines, arranging their long hair around their faces. Godan planned to give victory to the first army he saw in the morning. The next morning, on looking out his favorite window to the east, he spied the Winnili gathered, and called out, "Who are those Langobards (long-beards)?" Having named them, Frea said he had to grant them victory, and under that name they carved out their kingdom in what would later become known as Lombardia, in northern Italy.

In their description of this legend the authors reveal some influences from their understanding of the Classical couple that ruled the gods, Zeus and Hera, but the undoubtedly old story shows that even in the middle of the first millen-nium A.D., Wodan/Odin and his wife Frigg were already the powerful ances-tral deities from whom Germanic royal families, as well as whole tribes, wished themselves to be descended.

Despite the fact that it was mainly Odin who featured as a divine ancestor in the genealogies of Germanic royal families, in Sweden at least it was the god Freyr who was widely celebrated, both as the ancestor and as the guardian and protector of the royal house of the Ynglings, the house from which even the Norwegian royal family later deduced their ancestry. Although Freyr was often seen as a god of fertility, mostly because Viking Age statues and pocket talismans show him with an erect phallus, he was really mainly perceived as the powerful and opulently rich epitome of Swedish kingship, as represented by the kings of Old Uppsala (a seat of power in Sweden in the sixth century and later, and still a religious and cultural center). His distinc-tive virility was surely part of this image of a young and powerful king, as was Freyr's attribute, the boar, which is another symbol of aggressively dangerous strength, and also of wealth. The soldiers of the Swedish royal guards of the seventh and eighth cen-turies, for example, wore helmets that were crowned with a metal boar. The connection with the house of the Ynglings was even reflected in a by-name given to Freyr when he was called Yngvi-Freyr, which |may possibly be a very old name going back to the Germanic tribes mentioned by Tacitus who called themselves the Ingaevones.

Freyr and the Giantess Gerd

The story of Freyr, Gerd, and Skirnir is told in its fullest form in the Eddaic poem *Skirnismal.* Snorri Sturluson recounts a shorter more romanticized version of it in *Gylfaginning.* The story begins in Asgard. Freyr, god of wealth and fertility, sits in Hlidskialf, Odin's house, from where there is a view over all the other worlds in the universe. Looking down into the world of the giants he spots Gerd, a beautiful giantess, in the courtyard of her father's estate, and immediately falls in love with her. He languishes.

Freyr's servant Skirnir is sent to ask what is troubling him. Freyr explains, but feels his passion is doomed to remain unfulfilled. Skirnir offers to travel to Giantland and woo Gerd on his behalf. He borrows Freyr's magic sword and horse and, after negotiating mountains and a ring of fire around Giantland, arrives at Gerd's house but finds access to her prevented by savage guard dogs. Gerd, however, decides to receive him in her bower.

Skirnir communicates Freyr's love to her, offering as inducements golden apples and Draupnir, a magic self-reproducing gold ring, but Gerd has plenty of gold and spurns these gifts. Then Skirnir threatens her (and her giant father, Gymir, as well if he should he try to intervene) with death by Freyr's sword, but still Gerd resists. Skirnir describes in graphic detail the consequences of a curse that he will impose on her if she persists in rejecting Freyr's generous offer of love.

The curse will be carved in runes on a "taming wand." Under its terms, Gerd will be condemned to a veritable living death in Giantland. Skirnir describes her life under the curse as a burlesque of the life she would enjoy with the gods were she to accept Freyr's hand. She will live on the edge of her world, like Heimdall does, the gods' watchman in Asgard; but whereas Heimdall is guarding his world against attack, Gerd will instead be a prisoner, staring outward and longing for the escape that only death can bring. Her only drink will be the urine of goats, a severe enough prescription, but made even more piquant by the reminder it will bring that the gods extract an excellent mead from the udders of the goat Heidrun, who grazes on the leaves of the world tree. Gerd will be regarded by others in this nightmare world as a freak and be stared at; and if she chooses to marry, the best she can hope for is a three-headed giant called Hrimgrimnir. Her days will drag horribly, as she is constantly persecuted by the trolls who constitute her only company. She will be assailed by tears, and desire will attack her with uncontrollable force.

Gerd caves in only when Skirnir begins to carve the runes that will turn this terrifying vision into her reality. She agrees to meet Freyr nine nights hence in Barri, a place described as a "calm grove." Skirnir returns to Freyr with this news, and the poem ends with the god complaining now about the delay Gerd has imposed on their union.

Different interpretations of this story are possible, but a symbolic reading of it as an agricultural fertility myth probably makes the best sense of it. Thus Freyr, established elsewhere in the mythology as a god of fecundity, represents the sun; Gerd is the unfertilized earth; and Skirnir, the go-between, whose name means "the shining one," represents the beams of the sun that bring about the germination of crops.

Left **Fro, fertility statue, Sweden, eleventh century A.D.** The principal Norse gods of fertility were Freyr (Fro) and his sister Freyia. They came to Asgard with their father after the defeat of the Vanir by the Aesir. It is said that at the Ragnarok Freyr will be the first to fall, as he gave his magic sword to Skirnir in thanks for aiding his marriage with Gerd.

Below *Wild Boar and Wolf* by Friedrich Gauermann (1807–1862). In Norse mythology, many gods are associated with particular animals. Freyr's chariot is drawn by two boars: Gullinbursti, whose coat shines in the dark; and Slidrugtanni. In battle, Norse boar-cult warriors would fight in a wedge formation, their two champions at the front forming the *rani* (snout).

THOR AND HIS HAMMER

Thor was the god about whom the majority of myths from old Scandinavia were told, and who functioned as a cosmological protector of man and gods alike. As such, he was closely modeled in many of the stories on the Greek and Roman hero Heracles/Hercules, although in the Germanic translations of the Roman weekday names, he was even considered as equivalent to Zeus/Jupiter, the leader of the gods in classical mythology. Thor seems to have been very widely venerated as a god of thunder and lightning, as well as the weather generally. His popularity can be seen in the extremely frequent use of his name in the formation of many Scandinavian personal names, such as Thorleifr and Thorlakr. He has also survived in many of the Christianized folktales of St. Peter walking on earth. In southern Germanic areas he was known as Donar, the Anglo-Saxons called him Thunor, and in Viking Age Britain (in the eighth to eleventh centuries A.D.) he was usually called Thur or Thor, closely following the Scandinavian form of the name. In the tenth and eleventh centuries in Sweden, Thor and his hammer became pagan symbols that were used in opposition to Christ and the cross, and it can be seen that a number of grave stones from these late pagan times either show the hammer or invoke Thor to "hallow these runes."

THOR'S EXPEDITION TO UTGARD

This is the longest of the myths told by the Aesir to King Gylfi in Snorri Sturluson's *Gylfaginning*, and one of the most entertaining.

Thor and Loki are on an expedition in Thor's chariot, pulled by his two goats. They pass the night with a peasant family and repay their hospitality by slaughtering the goats and making a meal of them. Thor spreads out their skins on the floor and tells the peasant family to throw the bones onto the skins when they have eaten the meat off them but not to damage them. During the meal, Thialfi, the son of the family, splits the bones of one of the goats to get at the marrow. In the morning, Thor blesses the goatskins with his hammer and the goats stand up alive again, though one of them is lame in the hind leg. Thor is furious, but is mollified by the peasants' remorse, and he accepts the two children, Thialfi and Roskva, as his bondservants in compensation. Leaving his goats and chariot with the peasant couple, Thor, Loki, and the two children set off on foot toward Giantland in the east, with Thialfi, a fast runner, carrying Thor's knapsack. They cross the sea and then enter an extensive forest. They look for a place to spend the night, but can find only a large deserted building. In the middle of the night the travelers' sleep is disturbed by an alarming shaking of the earth.

Skrymir the Giant

They search the interior of the building for a place to defend themselves and find a side chamber halfway down one wall, which they occupy. A great rumbling and groaning is heard. At dawn, Thor goes outside to find a huge giant sleeping on the ground. His footsteps and snoring were what had woken them in the night. Thor prepares to kill the giant with his hammer, but before he can do so the giant awakes, rises to his feet, and introduces himself as Skrymir. He knows who Thor is, and jocularly accuses him of stealing

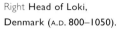

Right **Head of Loki, Denmark (A.D. 800–1050).** The thorn in the side of the gods at Asgard, Loki is mostly depicted as driven by jealousy of the gods, and of Thor in particular, but some of his escapades do end well for the gods. Thor's hammer is one such example, made by dwarfs in a bet with Loki.

Below **Dead giant, detail of a marble statue, 170 B.C., Pergamon.** In Norse myths, giants are the chief enemies of the gods, who they are destined to meet on the day of the Ragnarok. At the roots of Yggdrasill lies the "well of highest wisdom," guarded by the giant Mimir. In some stories, Odin, ever seeking knowledge, sacrifices an eye to have a drink from it.

his glove which, it now emerges, is the building the travelers had slept in. The side chamber in which they took refuge was the glove's thumb.

Skrymir obtains Thor's permission to travel with his party. The giant has with him a knapsack containing food and opens it to make his breakfast. He suggests that the whole party pool their food. Thor agrees to this, and all the food goes into Skrymir's knapsack. They resume their journey, Skrymir setting a cracking pace. In the evening they find a comfortable place to camp beneath a large oak tree.

Before he goes to sleep, Skrymir tells the rest of the party to help themselves to food from the knapsack, but so firmly has the knapsack been fastened that even Thor is unable to open it. He then becomes angry, takes his mighty hammer, and strikes at the head of the sleeping giant. His great blow has little apparent impact: Skrymir wakes up and asks if a leaf from the oak tree had fallen upon his head. Skrymir goes back to sleep and snores loudly. At midnight, Thor strikes again at the giant's head with his hammer and feels it go deep into the skull; but again Skrymir only wakes up and enquires if an acorn had fallen on him. He resumes his slumbers. Toward dawn, Thor aims a third blow at his head, this time at the temple. He feels the hammer sink in right to the handle, but Skrymir only wakes up and asks if a bird in the tree above has dropped some rubbish on his head.

Arrival at the Castle Utgard

Skrymir's journey takes him in a different direction, but before leaving Thor's party he indicates that a castle called Utgard is not far away to the east. He warns them that the castle's inhabitants are very large, and advises them to show humility in their presence if they pay them a visit. He suggests, however, that they might be better advised to go back to where they came from. With these words, he leaves them.

Later in the day, Thor and his party arrive at Utgard, a huge castle standing on open ground. The gates are shut and Thor is not strong enough to open them, so they are reduced to wriggling through the

gaps in the portcullis. We are now in a world where Thor and his companions are, in effect, miniature beings. They enter a large hall where many people, most of them immense, are sitting on benches. Their king, Utgarda-Loki, guesses Thor's identity, though he is surprised at how small he seems in view of all he has heard tell of his exploits. The king asks the visitors what feats they are capable of performing, explaining that every guest at Utgard castle must demonstrate some notable accomplishment. Loki steps forward, claiming the ability to eat faster than anyone else. The king chooses Logi, one of his men,

Above *The God Thor, on his Travels, is Teased by a Giant with Magical Illusions* from *Journal des Voyages* (1898). Unlike most adventures featuring Thor, those with the giant Skrymir leave him uncharacteristically abashed. His directness and ready strength are of no use to him in Giantland, also known as Jotunheim.

to compete with Loki. A large trencher is filled with food and set on the floor. Loki starts at one end, Logi at the other, both proceeding to eat furiously. By the time they meet in the middle, Loki has eaten all the meat off the bones; but Logi has eaten everything—meat, bones, and even the trencher itself. Loki is plainly the loser.

Utgarda-Loki then asks what Thialfi is good at. Thialfi, who has already demonstrated his ability as a runner, offers to race against anyone the king puts forward. Hugi, described as a small person by local standards, is chosen as his opponent, and everyone goes outside where there is a suitably level course for racing. Thialfi and Hugi run three races in a row and, although the king seems impressed by his speed, Thialfi still loses all three, performing ever less successfully as race follows race.

Utgarda-Loki finally turns to Thor and asks him to demonstrate just one among the many accomplishments for which he is famous. Thor decides to display his enormous capacity for consuming drink. A large horn is produced. Utgarda-Loki points out that some local drinkers are able to empty this horn in just a single pull, others take two, but no one needs more than three to drain it. Thor's first and second drafts produce very little change to the level of drink in the horn. With the third enormous gulp, under the provocation of some mild jeering from Utgarda-Loki, he manages to make quite a visible impression on the level, but the king declares himself very disappointed with Thor's overall performance.

Utgarda-Loki offers Thor a chance to prove himself in another kind of contest, though in view of Thor's evident weakness Utgarda-Loki can only suggest a game that the

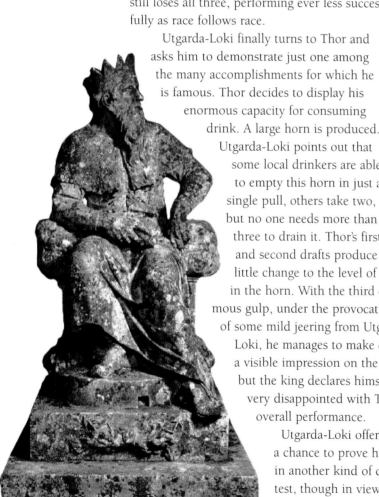

Above *Thor Enthroned* by J. Rysbraeck (1693–1770). Thor's realm in Asgard is Thrudvangr, "plains of strength." In his hall, the tables are always groaning with food, for equal to his strength is his appetite.

boys of the castle amuse themselves with: lifting his pet cat off the ground. A very large gray cat appears on the floor of the hall. Thor pushes its belly upward, but it arches its back so that he cannot reach high enough to exert much upward pressure. All Thor succeeds in doing is getting the cat to lift one of its feet off the ground.

By this time Thor, humiliated by his repeated failures, is in a fighting mood and offers to wrestle any local opponent. The king doubts if any of his people would not find it demeaning to take on such a weak opponent, but calls for an old woman called Elli, his former nurse. She wrestles with Thor and succeeds in forcing him down upon one knee, at which point Utgarda-Loki stops the fight.

Evening has come and the king makes his guests comfortable for the night. In the morning Thor and his party prepare to leave, but the king delays them with a generous breakfast to speed them on their journey. They set off, with the king, Utgarda-Loki, accompanying them for part of the way. He asks Thor if he has encountered anyone mightier than he during his expedition. Thor is frank about his sense of failure, but is most irritated by the damage to his reputation that has been done.

At this point, Utgarda-Loki comes clean about a whole series of deceptions that he has worked on Thor and his companions, and the whole story is transformed in retrospect. Thor, it now appears, was regarded as a serious threat to the giants. The giant Skrymir was none other than Utgarda-Loki himself

three races was Hugi, Thought, the speed of which no runner can hope to match. As for the horn from which Thor had drunk, its end was open and in the sea, so that Thor had no hope of draining it. His three drafts, however, had been prodigious enough to produce a new natural phenomenon: forever afterward the sea would be subject to the ebb and flow of tides. The giant cat that Thor had tried to lift was a transformation of his age-old enemy, the Midgard serpent, which lies wrapped around all the worlds of the universe. Thor did in fact manage to raise the middle part of its body to the sky, though the enchantment had concealed the magnitude of his achievement. Finally, Thor's seemingly feeble opponent at wrestling was Elli, Old Age, who brings everyone down in the end, though Thor had put up impressive resistance.

Utgarda-Loki then takes his leave of the party, warning them that any attempt to revisit Utgard will be resisted by similar tricks. Thor grabs his hammer for a last attempt to destroy the giant, but Utgarda-Loki has already disappeared, along with his castle. Thor and his party return home.

This myth was no doubt meant mostly as entertainment, though it is possible to see broader significance in some of the competitions. Perhaps the myth is meant to demonstrate human weakness in the face of natural forces and processes, for neither god nor man is able to defeat the natural power of fire (Logi), match the speed of thought (Hugi), or resist the slow onslaught of old age (Elli).

Left *Knight in Armor in Combat with Dragon* from *Historia de Gentibus Septentrionalibus* by Olaus Magnus (1490–1557). This masterpiece by Magnus was designed to bring the Scandinavian flora, fauna, history, and traditions to Renaissance Italy, which at that stage still thought of most northern folk as barbarians. This woodcut shows their pride in their fighting skills, against an ancient foe, though the warrior appears in armor more familiar to Italians.

in disguise. The provisions bag that Thor had failed to open was held by a magic wire that would defeat anyone who tried to loosen it. The three hammer blows struck by Thor at Skrymir as he lay under the oak would have killed the giant if they had in fact connected with his head; however, he placed a nearby mountain between himself and Thor's hammer in such a way that Thor failed to notice. The mountain is now dented with three square valleys where Thor's hammer fell. The defeats that were suffered by Thor and his companions in the games had all been engineered by Utgarda-Loki's magic.

Thus, in the eating competition Loki's opponent was Logi, a personification of Fire: Loki lost only because no one can consume anything as quickly as fire. Similarly, Thialfi's opponent in the

WARRIORS IN LIFE AND DEATH

The Germanic warriors emulated the fearlessness of their gods Odin and Thor, and were known to be fierce, brave, and proud fighters. Warriors followed their leaders out of choice rather than tribal obligations, according to Tacitus, and there was a strong code of honor and loyalty: "The chiefs fight for victory, the companions for their chief."

It was an honor to die in battle, giving a warrior almost godlike status: those who died of other causes went to the Underworld; while those who died in battle went to Odin's hall, Valhalla, to pass their days fighting and their nights feasting. Valkyries, fearsome and bloodthirsty female spirits, rode down through the sky on horses to bring the fallen to Valhalla, where they then served them food and mead. On the day of the Ragnarok, these warriors, called "Einheriar," would follow their leader Odin into the final battle.

Beserkers are said to be gifts from Odin, savage warriors that, in the frenzy of battle, become immune to pain, and may even turn into animals, or assume their qualities.

Left *Valhalla and Viking legends, bildstenar (engraved stone)*, pre- A.D. 1000, Gotland, Sweden. Valhalla was the greatest of the twelve halls at Asgard. Some stories report that its roof was made of overlapping shields and that it had over 500 doors.

THOR'S FISHING

Of all the cosmological myths, none is better preserved than the episode of Thor trying to catch the Midgard serpent, known as Thor's Fishing. In the most detailed version, which is the version found in the prose *Edda*, Thor leaves Midgard in the disguise of a young man. When he reaches the abode of the giant Hymir, he spends the night there and next morning accompanies the reluctant giant on a fishing trip. When he is told to find his own bait, he pulls off the head of one of Hymir's bulls. Thor rows out further than the giant wants, then fastens the head of the ox to a sturdy fishing line, and the Midgard serpent bites at once. Thor pulls on the line with such might that his feet break through the planks of the boat and, standing on the bottom of the sea, he drags the monster up to the boat. The sight of the serpent fills the giant with terror and, as Thor tries to strike the serpent with his hammer weapon, Hymir cuts the fishing line and the monster sinks back into the sea. Thor throws his hammer after it, and, as the *Edda* says, "some people say that the hammer cut off its head at water level. I believe that the truth is that the Midgard serpent is still alive and out there in the seas which surround the world." Thor then hits the giant Hymir with such strength and anger that he falls overboard and must wade back to land.

> *I warn of his tree, while seeming slight, harmfully hurled ... will slay Odin's son*
>
> VÖLUSPÁ POEM c. A.D. 1100
> (FROM THE POETIC *EDDA*)

This story was, however, known at least 400 years before it was retold in the poem called *Hymiskvitha* in the *Edda*. This was a common story recited by the Icelandic *skalds* (poets) working at Norwegian courts in the ninth and tenth centuries A.D. From around this time five separate allusions to this myth can be found, all brief, but clearly referring to a not very different version of the story. Even older still, from the eighth century, is a pictorial representation of the legend on one of the elaborate picture stones on Gotland (in Sweden), where two male figures in a boat seem to be baiting something with the head of an ox. Other, although later (but still pagan), pictures in stone in Scandinavia and Britain are partly more explicit in that they occasionally show Thor with his hammer raised and one of his feet breaking through the bottom of the boat.

Thus, the myth of Thor and the Midgard serpent was probably very widely known, not only across Scandinavia and Britain, but even throughout Germany in the fourteenth century, where the Midgard serpent (though without mentioning Thor) is referred to as being the source of earthquakes.

THE DEATH OF BALDR

One of the sadder stories from Snorri's *Gylfaginning* concerns Baldr, fairest of the gods, son of Odin and his wife Frigg. Baldr suffers from dreams foretelling his own death. The gods decide to protect him by extracting a promise from everything in the world not to harm him. Then, at assemblies, the gods amuse themselves by striking at him, or pelting him with missiles, in the knowledge that he cannot be hurt. Loki, envious of Baldr's immunity, visits Frigg in the guise of a woman. During their conversation, Frigg lets slip that the mistletoe has been excused from making the promise not to harm Baldr on account of its youth. Loki, resuming his natural shape, plucks some mistletoe and takes it to the assembly where Baldr is being pelted. Baldr's blind brother, Hod, is standing nearby. Loki encourages him to join in the fun, putting the mistletoe in his hand and pointing him in the direction of Baldr. Hod throws the mistletoe at his brother and it kills him. The gods are struck dumb with horror. Odin, Baldr's father, is especially grief stricken. Frigg asks who will go to Hel to offer a ransom for Baldr's release. Hermod, another of Baldr's brothers, offers to go. Odin lends him his horse, Sleipnir, and Hermod starts out.

An elaborate funeral for Baldr is prepared. His body is carried to the sea where his great ship, Hringhorni, is pulled up on the beach, but the ship cannot be moved. A giantess, Hyrrokkin, is summoned from Giantland. She arrives riding on a wolf, using vipers as reins. It takes four of Odin's warriors to restrain the wolf as she dismounts. Hyrrokkin launches the boat with a single touch, the rollers throw out sparks, and the ground shakes. Thor, ever ready to kill giants, becomes angry and threatens her with his hammer, but the other gods plead for her to be spared. Baldr's body is placed on the launched ship beside that of his wife Nanna, who has died of grief. The funeral pyre is lighted. Thor consecrates it with his hammer, Miollnir. A dwarf called Lit runs in front of his feet, and Thor angrily kicks him into the fire where he perishes. All the gods and goddesses, and many frost giants and mountain giants, attend the funeral. Odin places the gold ring called Draupnir on the pyre and Baldr's horse is also burnt, with all its trappings.

Opposite page *The Norse god Thor fishing for the Midgard serpent.* The Midgard serpent, Jorgamund, was a child of Loki. The serpent is usually shown circling Midgard, its tail in its mouth. On the day of reckoning, the serpent will emerge from the water for one final battle with Thor. The god will manage to kill the terrifying creature but its poison is too great: Thor will also die.

Above **Pendant, one of a pair, representing Baldr on his horse, Sweden.** Many interpretations for Loki's part in the death of Baldr have been proffered. Some have suggested that the gods, in seeking to free Baldr from death, are disrupting the natural order of things: everything must die. Loki's actions prove this.

Loki's Treachery

Below *Loki Punished* by
J. D. Penrose. For his
misdeeds, Loki is tied to
rocks below a serpent. His
wife is often shown with
him, catching the poison in
a bowl. When it fills, she
has to tip it out and the
poison falls on Loki.

Hermod, meanwhile, rides for nine nights through deep and dark valleys until he reaches a bridge over Gioll, the river of death. Modgud, a maiden who guards the bridge, comments that he does not look like one of the dead. She tells him that Baldr has recently crossed the bridge, and directs Hermod downward and northward to Hel. On reaching the gates of Hel, Hermod jumps over them easily on Sleipnir's back. He comes to a hall, dismounts and enters, and finds Baldr sitting in a place of honor. Hermod describes the gods' grief to the goddess Hel and pleads with her to allow Baldr to return to them. Hel agrees, on condition that everything in the world will weep for Baldr. Hermod immediately returns to Asgard, taking gifts from Baldr for his parents: the ring Draupnir for Odin, and a robe for Frigg.

The message goes out to the whole world to weep in order that Baldr can leave Hel. Everyone and everything begins to weep, with one exception. A giantess called Thanks, generally assumed to be the malicious Loki in disguise, refuses to weep. Baldr must remain in Hel. Loki is found hiding in a cave and is caught and chained, to remain that way until the Ragnarok.

This myth is another illustration of Loki's treachery; but it is more significant as a myth about a pagan Christ who dies but is not resurrected. The obvious inversion of the Christian myth is a clear sign of the author's exposure to the religion that eventually replaced paganism in Scandinavia.

Below *Loki Punished* by J. D. Penrose. For his misdeeds, Loki is tied to rocks below a serpent. His wife is often shown with him, catching the poison in a bowl. When it fills, she has to tip it out and the poison falls on Loki.

CONTINUANCE AND CHANGE

Although much of the mythology of the various Germanic tribes was lost as they spread across Europe and intermingled with new peoples, some aspects of their culture and heritage were retained. Over time, new cultures arose and gradually developed into nations such as England, France, and Germany. Some of the early tales survived outside of the original homeland, or were developed to keep memories of the older culture alive.

One of the best-known stories of Germanic origin concerns the adventures of the mighty warrior Beowulf. However, this legend is not found in Norse mythology but in Old English. Beowulf's adventures were recorded by unknown scribes in a tenth-century A.D. manuscript, itself a copy of earlier manuscripts. There is only one manuscript in existence, and this epic poem is now regarded as the oldest known work of English literature. The story most likely comes from the seventh and eighth centuries and may have been created to keep alive the history and culture of the Anglo-Saxons, who

THE RAGNAROK

When Heimdall, the god who guards the entrance to Asgard, blows his trumpet, it will sound the beginning of the Ragnarok. The fate of the gods was predestined: at a future time there would be a great battle, gods against monsters and giants, and humans against humans, in which most would be destroyed.

It is said that the great battle will begin thus: after a winter lasting three years, wolves will devour the sun and moon. Loki and his children, the goddess Hel and Fenrir the wolf, will be released by earthquakes. With the frost giants, they will sail to meet the gods in battle. The Midgard serpent, another of Loki's children, will swell the waves and the water will engulf the land. Warned by Heimdall's horn, the gods, with the fallen warriors gathered at Valhalla in Asgard, will advance with Odin at their head. Most will die in the battle and a great fire will sweep the earth. Only the sons of Odin and Thor, and the daughter of the sun, will survive. Baldr and his blind brother Hod will be freed from hell and the world will begin again.

Left **The god Heimdall blowing his horn before the Ragnarok.** Heimdall is the god of light and the watchman on the Bifrost Bridge, the only entrance to Asgard and also the connection with the underworld. At the Ragnarok, he and Loki will fight, and though the victor, he will die of his wounds.

had invaded England in the fifth century A.D. While Beowulf is a legendary hero, some of the tribal kings mentioned in the story are known to have existed, and Heorot, where part of the story takes place, is an ancient seat of Danish leadership.

The Story of Beowulf

The great mead hall of Hrothgar, King of the Danes, at Heorot is attacked by a troll-like monster called Grendel. No one is strong enough to kill him and he keeps returning. Beowulf, nephew of the King of the Geats, sails with his warriors from Sweden to help Hrothgar, and determines that he must fight the monster without his sword. When the monster returns to the hall, a mighty fight ensues. The hall is shaken to its foundations, but Beowulf, with his incredible grip, mortally wounds Grendel, tearing off his arm.

There is a brief time of great rejoicing, but when Grendel's mother learns of her son's death, she soon attacks the hall, killing King Hrothgar's most beloved companion. Beowulf must swim to her cavern at the bottom of a lake to kill her. When he confronts her, he finds that his sword is useless and he must fight her barehanded. The monster fights back savagely, wrestling Beowulf to the ground and sitting on him. When she attempts to stab him, only his coat of mail saves him. He breaks free, and, grasping a giant's sword that he sees on the wall of the cavern, kills her. He cuts off her head and takes it to Hrothgar as a prize, along with the hilt of the sword, the blade having been destroyed by the monster's blood. Beowulf is rewarded with much praise and treasure. He later becomes King of the Geats, and, in his last battle, dies killing a cursed dragon.

Left *Grendel and Victims,* by J.H.F. Bacon (1865–1914). The monster Grendel has abducted two youths from Heorot, the court of the Danish King Hrothgar. Some stories say that such monsters lived in shadowy, fearful places within the moors, exiled from the rest of mankind by the gods.

FINNISH MYTHOLOGY

Right *Cornelius Tacitus,* engraved by Freeman from an antique bust (1830). The writings of Tacitus offer a detailed description of the ancient Finns, however, they need to be read with care as they are influenced by his prejudices as a Roman.

The ancestors of today's Finns have inhabited the southern part of the country known today as Finland since as long ago as 5000 B.C. Some of the numerous tribes to which they belonged give their names to present-day Finnish provinces. The Estonians, from the southern side of the Gulf of Finland, and the Ugrians, from Hungary and western Siberia, are closely related to the Finns and share some of the same myths.

The earliest mention of a Finnish people is to be found in *Germania,* written by the Roman historian and politician Cornelius Publius Tacitus in A.D. 98. According to Tacitus, the Finns (Fenni) were "unimaginably barbarous and miserably poor." He reports that they had "no weapons, no horses, no houses, and nowt but wild plants for their food, skins for their clothing, and the ground for their beds." In spite of Tacitus's description it is likely, judging from their rock paintings, that the diet of the ancient Finns was not so simple, but also included elk and fish. During the Iron Age (*c.* 500 B.C. to A.D. 400), the distinctive features of their folk poetry were emerging, as well as a peasant way of life, which combined agriculture with hunting and fishing.

The early Finnish tribes spoke different languages that were dialects of the Uralic language, which spread to Finland in the period between 4000 B.C. and 2000 B.C. They did not live in towns but in family groups surrounded by neighboring races with whom they traded. Because the groups were relatively isolated from each other, a uniform set of

Above **Knife made from engraved reindeer bone, Lapland.** For the ancient nomadic Finns, hunting and fishing were important aspects of daily life. Rock paintings depict animal ceremonies that seem to indicate a belief in the souls of animals.

Opposite page *Story of Kullervo* by A. Gallen Kallela (1865–1931). The fable of Kullervo, as told in the *Kalevala,* is an epic of family feuding, revenge, and regret. It has inspired plays and musical compositions, including one by Jean Sibelius, Finnish composer (1865–1957).

ELIAS LÖNNROT (1802–1884)

The man responsible for the *Kalevala,* Elias Lönnrot, was a true polymath: explorer, doctor, poet, and linguist. He was motivated to create the *Kalevala* by the idea, associated with the German scholar J.G. Herder (1744–1803), that a nation cannot exist without a distinctive cultural identity. The Grand Duchy of Finland had been annexed by Russia in 1809 and would not achieve independence until the Russian Revolution in 1917.

Together with the *Kalevala,* Lönnrot's dictionaries and periodicals earned him great fame during his lifetime. Today he is regarded as one of the fathers of written Finnish. His birthplace, the rustic Paikkari Cottage, is owned by the Finnish National Board of Antiquities and is operated as a museum. It can be found in the parish of Sammatti about 47 miles (75 km) west of Helsinki.

beliefs did not develop. As well, due to exposure to other cultures, their ancient tales exhibit a number of outside influences—particularly from Slavic, Norse, and Germanic mythologies.

THE SONG CATCHER

The majority of what is known today about Finnish mythology comes from the many songs and poems collected by Elias Lönnrot, which were originally published in 1835. Lönnrot conceived the idea of collecting the tales of ancient Finland in 1828. He traveled the length and breadth of Finland and Karelia for the next seven years, visiting even the smallest villages to record the songs and poems of the peasantry. He then compared and arranged these tales into the heroic epic that he called the *Kalevala.* This collection continued to grow until, by 1849, it contained nearly 23,000 verses.

The *Kalevala* is, in truth, part ancient mythology and part invention by Elias Lönnrot himself. In his eagerness to create an epic that would compare with Homer's *Iliad,* Lönnrot created entirely new poems from fragments of material he had gathered on his travels. The *Kalevala* describes a struggle between two peoples: the Kaleva from southern Finland, and the Pohjola from northern Finland or Lapland.

THE KALEVALA

The entire *Kalevala* is written in an unusual, archaic trochaic tetrameter, which means that each line has four pairs of syllables with a stress-unstress pattern in each pair. The opening lines describe how singers support each other during a recital that can last several hours.

> *Let us clasp our hands together,*
> *Let us interlock our fingers;*
> *Let us sing a cheerful measure,*
> *Let us use our best endeavours,*
> *While our dear ones hearken to us,*
> *And our loved ones are instructed,*
> *While the young ones are standing round us,*
> *Of the rising generation,*
> *Let them learn the words of magic,*
> *And recall our songs and legends,*
> *Of the belt of Väinämöinen,*
> *Of the forge of Ilmarinen,*
> *And of Kaukomieli's swordpoint,*
> *And of Joukahainen's crossbow:*
> *Of the utmost bounds of Pohja,*
> *And of Kalevala's wide heathlands.*

ENGLISH TRANSLATION BY W.F. KIRBY (1907)

Väinämöinen, the protagonist of the *Kalevala*, is a remarkable character, the greatest of sages and magicians. His mother was the divine mother Luonnotar, and the first part of the *Kalevala* describes how Väinämöinen carves the land of Kaleva from the primordial chaos. It is told that he spent 30 years in his mother's belly and, as a result, was wise from birth. As well, he was known as a warrior and an unrivaled musician and singer. When he played his kantele, a five-stringed harplike instrument that he made from the bones of an enormous pike, all the animals drew near to listen to his wondrous tunes.

IN SEARCH OF A WIFE

Despite his gifts, Väinämöinen was unlucky in love. The *Kalevala* tells how he and the blacksmith Ilmarinen seek a wife—a search that takes them to the land of Pohjola, Kaleva's mysterious northern neighbor.

In return for her daughter's hand in marriage the Mistress of Pohjola requires a "many-colored" sampo (a talisman usually identified as a type of mill) that brings unlimited riches to its owner. Ilmarinen duly forges the sampo and marries the daughter in a wedding of great magnificence.

Above *Ilmarinen Ploughing the Field of Snakes* by Joseph Alanen (1885–1920). In Finnish mythology, Ilmarinen is the primeval smith: forger of the sky, sun, and moon. He taught mankind how to work with metals and brought them fire. He is also the patron of travelers.

*Then the aged Väinämöinen
Went upon his journey singing,
Sailing in his boat of copper,
Sailed away to loftier regions,
To the land beneath the heavens,
There he rested with his vessel,
Rested weary with his vessel.*
ENGLISH TRANSLATION BY W.F. KIRBY (1907)

ORIGIN MYTHS AND PRACTICAL ADVICE

In addition to recounting the many adventures of Väinämöinen, Ilmarinen, and Lemminkainen, the *Kalevala* describes in detail the origins of, among other things, iron and fire. These "origin myths" are in the form of incantations that confer mystical power upon the character that recites them.

The *Kalevala* also provides practical advice for readers and listeners. An entire section (Rune) of the *Kalevala* is devoted to advice for brides.

*Hear, O maiden, what I tell thee,
What I say, and what I tell thee,
Do not go without thy clothing,
Nor without thy shift disport thee,
Move about without thy linen,
Or without thy shoes go shuffling,
Greatly shocked would be thy bridegroom,
And thy youthful husband grumble.*
ENGLISH TRANSLATION BY W.F. KIRBY (1907)

Bad Blood

Soon after the wedding Lemminkainen, a petulant and proud young man also from Kaleva, takes time-out from his favorite pastime of seducing girls to make his own expedition north in search of a wife. His excursion is rather less successful and, after incurring the wrath of the people by killing one of their chiefs, he is chased out of Pohjola.

Largely as a result of Lemminkainen's efforts, relations between the people of Kaleva and Pohjola deteriorate into open conflict. When Väinämöinen discovers the prosperity that the sampo has brought to his northern neighbors he, together with his countrymen Ilmarinen and Lemminkainen, decides to retrieve it. Väinämöinen lulls his enemies to sleep with the aid of his kantele and they steal away with the sampo. As he sails home, the Mistress of Pohjola summons a terrible tempest; the sampo is smashed into many pieces and lost overboard. Väinämöinen is able to retrieve some of the fragments, and with these he brings fertility and prosperity to his people.

The Punishment of Pohjola

The Mistress of Pohjola does not take the loss of the sampo lightly. She brings a number of scourges down upon the people of Kaleva, culminating with her stealing the sun and moon and hiding them in a great mountain. Väinämöinen protects his people and retrieves the sun and moon by using his magic, skill in fighting and hunting, and great knowledge. With this achievement, however, Väinämöinen gets ready to depart. In the closing canto the aged, god-like Väinämöinen anoints his successor and sails away with his kantele for a well-earned rest.

ANCESTOR WORSHIP AND SHAMANISM

The ancient Finns believed in a tripartite world. Above were the heavens, where the gods lived, while the living inhabited an island surrounded by a great river. On the other side of the river was the kingdom of the dead, Tuonela.

The family unit was considered to include both its living members and those that had crossed over to the kingdom of the dead. Death did not relieve an individual of his or her familial duties; the deceased continued to take part in the lives of the offspring in a number of ways. In return, the living were required to observe faithfully the ancient rites and continue their ancestors' work. This practice lay at the heart of ancient Finnish understanding of family life.

If these rites of passage to Tuonela were not properly performed, the dead could become restless souls, known as *sijattomat sielut,* who haunted the house of future generations of their family, rather than become integrated into the larger family unit.

The Kingdom of the Dead

This land is not seen as a place of punishment in Finnish mythology. While it is darker than other lands, the sun does shine and plants grow. Its rulers are the king, Tuoni, and his wife, Tuonetar. Their two daughters are terrible to behold and cause all manner of disease and illness.

The ancient Finns believed that it is actually possible to travel to Tuonela although the attempt would be likely to end in a terrible death, if not in the thick dark forests on the way, then almost certainly at the hands of the inhabitants of Tuonela. Lemminkainen, as a young man, travels as far as the bank of the black river that surrounds the kingdom of the dead while pursuing a beautiful swan; he is tossed into the river and torn to pieces. It takes all his mother's skills as a magician to bring him back to life.

Väinämöinen alone is able to visit the kingdom of the dead and live to tell the tale. He travels to Tuonela in search of an incantation that will allow him to finish his magic copper ship. He is offered a horrible brew of frogs and worms by Tuonetar and told that he will never be allowed to leave. However, that night he changes into a type of snake and escapes.

Shamans

A family could communicate with their ancestors in the kingdom of the dead via a shaman who would contact the dead by beating his magic drum. A shaman might also eat certain types of mushroom to achieve the trancelike state required to communicate with the dead.

Successive neighbors and occupiers of Finland regarded the shamans with suspicion and fear. In the Middle Ages, the Norwegian kings prohibited their subjects from traveling to Finland to consult with the shamans. In the sixteenth and seventeenth centuries the Swedish authorities tried to render the shamans impotent by confiscating their drums (*quodbas*).

Left **Eighteenth-century drum from Lapland.** The magic drums of ancient Finland, *quodbas*, were sacred objects, used by shamans to contact the spirits. To the Swedes, however, they were pagan objects that impeded their "civilizing" efforts.

Left *Swan of Tuonela* by I.J. Belmont (1885–1964). This illustration, inspired by ancient Finnish tales and a musical composition of the same name by Jean Sibelius, evokes the eerie movements of the swan as it glides over the black waters of Tuonela.

ANIMISM

Care must be taken when using the *Kalevala* as a source for ascertaining the beliefs of the ancient Finns. While the songs are primitive in origin, they were collected in the nineteenth century and exhibit a number of external influences.

Analysis of the *Kalevala* has caused much discussion about the place of the Finnish gods in respect to their shamans. One commentator says: "The dead were the guardians of morals, the judges of customs, and they maintained the order of society. In this respect not even the god of the upper regions could compete with them." *The New Larousse Encyclopaedia of Mythology* (Hamlyn: London, 1968) observes that "shamanism … is scarcely compatible with the idea of gods who are essentially superior to humanity,

We are doomed to be eternal sentinels, our periods of rest have not been long.
ANON., FINNISH POET

because the shaman is capable of subduing everything with the magic of his spells."

It is now generally accepted that the gods of the *Kalevala* are too nebulous to have formed the basis of a "religion," and that it is probably more correct to suggest that the ancient Finns' beliefs resided somewhere between the worship of nature itself and the divinities that inhabited natural phenomena.

A Living World

The ancient Finns believed that every object had an "essence" or soul that was known as the *haltijat*. This essence is not like the Christian soul that lives on after the death of its host; the *haltijat* is inalienably linked to its physical form and dies along with the object that it inhabits.

The Finns understood even inanimate objects to have a type of life. There were spirits of the house and yard, the threshing shed, and of the cowshed. As long as these spirits were treated with adequate reverence and not "killed," they would watch over the activities of the people that lived and worked in these buildings. Hence, when Finns drew water from a well they would pour a little back in deference to the spirit of the well.

A Bond between Opponents

The souls of animals were believed to survive as long as the animal's bones existed. The *Kalevala* describes an intriguing "bear feast." After the bear had been killed and eaten, its bones were placed in a tomb with various objects. The dead bear was then treated like a friend and asked to tell other bears about the honors that humans had paid to it. As late as the seventeenth century a similar rite was described with some disdain by the Lutheran Bishop Isak Rothovius: "When they kill a bear they hold a feast, drink out of the bear's skull and imitate its growling in order to ensure plenty of game in the future."

FINNISH GODS

The creation myth in the *Kalevala* describes how Luonnotar, a virgin, grows tired of her lonely sterile life in the heavens and allows herself to fall from the celestial plane onto the surface of the void. She floats there for seven centuries until an eagle appears, builds a nest on her knee, and incubates its eggs. The eggs

Below *The Enormous Oak Tree is Cut Down* by Joseph Alanen (1885–1920). The *Kalevala* tells how the gnome of the plowland, Sampsa, is sent by Väinämöinen to find wood for his boat. He finds an oak tree with a "girth nine full fathoms," which he fells with his axe.

eventually drop from Luonnotar's knee—the yolk is transformed into the sun, the whites the moon, and fragments of the shell, the stars.

The heroes of the *Kalevala,* including Luonnotar's son, Väinämöinen, are left with the task of taming the wild lands that she creates.

Finnish mythology does not establish a detailed hierarchy of gods although some invocations name Ukko as the head of the pantheon. He is sometimes described as the "god of the sky and air" and other times, more narrowly, as the god of thunder. Indeed he gives his name to the Finnish word for thunder, *ukkonen.* In addition to thunder, he seems to be responsible for almost all natural phenomena that emanate from the sky: clouds, rain, snow, and hail. His wife was the divinity Rauni.

Other gods include Paiva (the sun), Kun (the moon), and Ilma (the divinity of the air whose daughter Luonnotar is named in the creation myth). Lesser divinities include Pellervoinen (the fields), Atho (water), Mannu (earth), and Metsola (forest).

There are numerous other Finnish deities. Even common activities such as dyeing and weaving are imbued with their own divinities (Sinettaret and Kankahattaret). As one commentator has observed: "Every deity, however petty he may be, rules in his own sphere as a substantial, independent power, or, to speak in the spirit of the *Kalevala,* as a self-ruling householder. The god of the Polar-star only governs an insignificant spot in the vault of the sky, but on this spot he knows no master."

HASTY ASSUMPTIONS

When Tacitus described the Finns as "unimaginably barbarous and miserably poor," he was unaware that their riches lay in their mythology. The *Kalevala,* with its poetic and vivid account of Väinämöinen's heroics, compares favorably with the best mythic tales of the Finns' neighbors.

The *Kalevala* was written to be recited rather than read in silence. Fortunately for lovers of the ancient Finnish tales, parts of the *Kalevala* are still performed by Finnish folk music ensembles today, although rarely, if ever, in English.

Above *Witches Sell Winds* from *Historia de Gentibus Septentrionalibus* by Olaus Magnus (1490–1557). The title of Magnus's work on the Nordic peoples means "History of the People below the Big Dipper, or the Plough." It consists of 22 books and describes how the harsh elements shaped both the people and their mythologies.

FROM FINNISH TO ELVISH

J.R.R. Tolkien (1892–1973) was Professor of Linguistics at Oxford University for 34 years. He had a genius for language, however, he is more famously known as being the author of *The Hobbit* and *Lord of the Rings.* Even as a child he was fascinated by words and was inventing languages. Later, his great "hobby" was to develop a complete language. Sound and the rhythm of the language was always very important to him; words should sound beautiful, as well as sound like the thing they describe. Tolkien was thrilled when he discovered Finnish which, for him, was filled with just such beautiful sounds. Elvish, or *Quenya,* one of the principal languages later used in the *Lord of the Rings,* was based on the sound of Finnish.

To develop a "real" language, not just one of invented words, Tolkien needed a mythology of the peoples who used it. Texts such as the *Kalevala* and the Icelandic *Edda* would have helped guide the way.

Also, just as the early Finns believed the forest was alive and venerated trees as well as animals such as the bear, the forests live in Tolkien's books. There is the wild man Beorn in *The Hobbit,* with his ability to turn into a bear. Tom Bombadil from *Lord of the Rings,* a character who sings constantly and has command over the trees, perhaps contains elements of Väinämöinen; and the Ents, the ancient forest beings Tolkien created in *Lord of the Rings,* could almost have walked out of ancient Finnish forests.

SLAVIC MYTHOLOGY

Right **Targitaj fighting a monster, bronze chariot ornament.** Slavic peoples cannot be considered a single group, though they share a common mythology. This piece was made by the Scythians, nomadic tribes who inhabited the Black Sea steppes from 500–300 B.C.

Below **Dragon of Krakow, Poland** from **Cosmographia Universalis** by Sebastian Munster (1489–1552). A long time ago, the town of Krakow was terrorized by a dragon. The wise Krakus smeared a sheep with sulfur, and gave it to the dragon to eat. The sulfur burnt the dragon, who drank water until it burst.

The Slavic peoples do not share a common ancestry, their bond is their culture, which has at its core a rustic mythology that has been passed between generations in folklore.

Probably originating in or near the Carpathian Mountains, and growing to incorporate tribes throughout eastern Europe, the Slavs were not recognized as a distinct people until the sixth century A.D. Today, the Slavs are arranged in three great blocs: south, west, and east, stretching from the Balkans to Russia. These blocs are divided into numerous ethnic enclaves including Russians, Poles, Czechs, Ukrainians, Belorussians, Serbians, Croatians, Macedonians, Slovenians, Bulgarians, Kashubians, and Slovakians. Although each of these groups has its own individual language, speakers of one Slavic language can generally understand much of what is said in another Slavic language.

OPPOSING FORCES

Slavic mythology does not provide a coherent system of gods, priests, and religious rites. It is best viewed as an attempt to make sense of the capricious forces of nature—storms, floods, and droughts—against which the ancients, gathered in small family groups, were largely defenceless. The myths are dominated by the opposing forces of chaos and malevolence on the one hand, and benevolence and order on the other.

Chernobog is the bringer of destruction. His name is a mix of the word *cherny* meaning "black," and *bog* meaning "god." He lives in shadows and the night. Conversely, Byelbog, from *byely* meaning "white," is the god of light and creative forces. He only reveals himself during daylight hours and is usually represented as a kindly old man with a white beard who protects those in peril from harm.

Dualism and Animism

The two forces of Byelbog and Chernobog were later to be infused with the character of God and Satan inherited from Christianity, but in their original form they did not represent good and evil in the Christian sense. On the contrary, Slavic mythology established a kind of dualism that was opposed by Christianity, so much so that most records of the ancient gods, including writings and carvings, were destroyed after the arrival of the Christian evangelists such as the Saints Cyril and Methodius, as well as Orthodox missionaries from the east. For example, a statue of the god Dazhbog towered over Kiev until A.D. 988, when Vladamir I converted to Christianity and instructed that it be thrown into the Dneiper River, together with statues of other pagan gods. Nevertheless, many of the ancient Slavic stories were preserved in legends, tales, songs, and proverbs.

Slavic stories also describe a pantheon of animist spirits—sometimes playful, occasionally cruel—that inhabit the earth, sun, wind, and water. These spirits are so rooted in the Slavic psyche that even today on the eastern fringes of the Slavic world, there still exists a mix of Christian and animist beliefs, which is known as *dvoeverie* or "double-faith."

GODS OF THE ELEMENTS

The ancient Slavs believed that the unseen hands of the gods guided all natural phenomena.

The Slavic sky god was Svarog. He had two sons, Dazhbog, who was the personification of the sun, and Svarogich, the god of fire. According to myth, Svarog, after reigning over the world for countless years, passed his power to his children, and Dazhbog ultimately became the Slavs' supreme deity.

It is easy to understand how the gods of sun and fire came to be at the head of the Slavic pantheon. The Russians suffer some of the harshest winters of any people in the world. Fire and sun, as providers of warmth and light, were not just comforts but lifesavers. It is largely for this reason that Dazhbog also became synonymous with happiness and justice.

Dazhbog was said to live in a golden palace in the east, in a land of plenty where summer never ended. Every morning he would emerge from his palace on a diamond chariot, drawn by fire-breathing white horses, and traverse the sky. He was attended by two beautiful virgins, the morning and evening stars, and was counseled by seven judges (the planets). The comets acted as his messengers.

In some myths Dazhbog is represented as being born every morning, growing to become a handsome young man at midday, and dying each evening.

THE CYRILLIC ALPHABET

The lack of any records written before the ninth century by Slavic peoples led some historians to suggest that the ancient Slavs had no written language. It now seems more likely that records of the early gods, written in ancient Slavic runes, were destroyed after the arrival of Christianity. In the ninth century, the saints Cyril and Methodius created the Cyrillic alphabet by combining Slavic runes with the Greek alphabet. With some modifications the Cyrillic alphabet is still used by most Slavs today although some, such as the Poles, have adopted the Roman alphabet.

Below **Roman mosaic of the Saints Cyril (A.D. 826–869) and Methodius (A.D. 825–885).** These early evangelists of the Byzantine Empire traveled to Greater Moravia in A.D. 863 to spread Christianity.

The Quarrelsome Family

While the ancient myth relating to the sun god varies only slightly between the different ethnic groups, the god of the moon, known as Myesyats, is by turns represented as either a balding old man who waits patiently for Dazhbog to return from his daily adventure, or as a beautiful young woman who is married to Dazhbog. The legends which represent Dazhbog and Myesyats as husband and wife can be viewed as a way of explaining a number of natural phenomena through the vagaries of their rather tempestuous relationship: for instance, tremors or earthquakes are caused by their arguments and the barren winters by their separations.

Above **Bronze votive figurine, from Strakonice, the Czech Republic, first century** B.C. Though Slavic mythology seems to suggest a world ruled by violent elemental forces, these forces could be appeased by giving due respect to the gods.

Opposite page *Baba Yaga, the Witch* by Dimitrii Mitrokhin (1883–1973), from Arthur Ransome's *Old Peter's Russian Tales*. Renowned children's author, Arthur Ransome (1884–1967) traveled to Russia to report on the Revolution of 1917. While there, he compiled a collection of 21 fairy tales.

Right **Anaitis, goddess of hunting, bronze statue, Romania, 700–600** B.C. This statue belongs to the Scythians, a hard-living group of fierce warriors. They believed that their wealth could be taken with them into the afterlife, and their burial sites have borne many treasures.

The Temperamental Winds

The ancient Slavs recognized at least three wind gods: north, west, and east. They were said to live on the island of Buyan and their tempers were reflected in the nature of the wind that they inhabited. For example, the west wind, Dogoda, was kind and gentle. *The New Larousse Encyclopaedia of Mythology* (Hamlyn: London, 1968) records the following spell, which would be uttered by a man experiencing difficulty wooing the woman of his affections: "On the sea, the ocean, on the isle of Buyan, live three brothers, the Winds: one is the North, the second is the East, the third is the West. Blow ye Winds, blow unbearable sadness to … [such and such a girl] so that she cannot live a single day, a single hour without thinking of me!"

Respect for the Earth

The Slavs also revered the earth beneath their feet, which was believed to be possessed by Mati Syra Zemlya or Moist Mother Earth, to whom great respect was given. Unlike other deities, Mati Syra Zemlya was always worshipped in her natural form, and was never represented as having human features.

In early spring the earth was considered to be pregnant and no one was allowed to strike Mati Syra Zemlya with a hoe or plow until the vernal equinox. If treated with adequate reverence she would reward the household with great bounty in spring, some of which she would expect to be returned to her by the pouring of wine into a hole or the burying of bread.

Sacred oaths were sworn while holding a piece of Moist Mother Earth, sometimes in the mouth. Wedding vows were taken with a small clump of earth placed on the head.

Mati Syra Zemlya was also considered to be a type of oracle. Peasants would dig a hole in the ground, speak into it, and listen for her reply. In fact, until the early years of the twentieth century, if no priest could be found, sins were told to Mati Syra Zemlya, and her forgiveness sought before death.

BABA YAGA AND THE CYCLES OF DEATH AND INITIATION

Baba Yaga, as she is called in Russia (from *baba* meaning "old woman," and *yaga* meaning "hag"), is a witch with the gifts of shape-changing and prophesy. She is known by other names outside Russia: Jezda in Poland and Jazi Baba in the Czech Republic.

Although most often depicted as a bony old crone with long sharp teeth, Baba Yaga is a highly complex character containing a number of facets. In addition to being the personification of death, Baba Yaga is also regarded as having an important role in relation to fertility and fate. Just as the ancient Slavs faced disease and death without warning or explanation, so Baba Yaga can fly into fits of rage on the smallest pretext, to the degree that she is wont to eat people that offend her or do not fulfil their duties.

Baba Yaga's house is one of the most evocative creations in the tales that involve her. It sits upon four chicken's legs—one in each corner—which allow it to turn and move about. Baba Yaga herself is often depicted inside at a spinning wheel (originally spinning thread from the innards of the dead). Some legends say that her teeth, nose, and breasts are made of iron and that her hair is a knot of writhing snakes.

Baba Yaga also has the gift of prophecy and can impart great wisdom. Those that wish to benefit from these gifts must undertake an arduous journey to Baba Yaga's house, which is in the most remote and inaccessible part of the forest. They must then survive Baba Yaga's demanding tasks and tests. The fence surrounding her house is made of the bones of those who failed to ask the right questions or satisfy her ruthless test of motives. Each picket is adorned with a skull.

Throughout eastern Europe, many tales involving Baba Yaga survived the advent of Christianity and continue to be the subject of great fascination. Despite years of analysis by academics, Baba Yaga continues to be an enigma. As one commentator has said, "Baba Yaga hails from the place where fear and wisdom meet, she straddles the gap between life and death and holds the secrets of both."

In the Christian era some myths that recorded Baba Yaga's unpleasant habits were altered to make them less gruesome. Some later legends even confuse her with Mary, Mother of Jesus—very strange to anyone who knows the original tales.

BABA YAGA AND VASILISA

Below *The Witch Baba Yaga* by Ivan Bilibin (1872–1942), from *Vasilisa the Beautiful*. Baba Yaga is found in stories and fairy tales throughout Russia and Eastern Europe. She is often shown flying in a mortar, steering with the pestle, and sweeping away her traces with a broom.

Vasilisa is a young girl when her mother becomes ill. Before she dies, her mother gives her a tiny doll. She tells her daughter that this doll will guide her; all she needs to do is ask, and the doll will answer.

Vasilisa is distraught when her mother dies. After a short time, her father remarries a woman with two daughters of her own. The stepmother and her children greatly resent Vasilisa. They torment and mistreat her when her father is away. Vasilisa says nothing of these abuses to her father, for she is too kind.

One day, when the father is away, the stepmother foolishly allows the fire to burn out. Without the fire there can be no food, no heat, and no light. Vasilisa's step-family entreat her to travel through the forest to the hut of Baba Yaga to fetch a flame with which to relight their fire. Although hesitant and fearful, the good Vasilisa agrees and sets off with her mother's doll in her pocket. The stepmother and her two daughters rejoice wickedly, since they believe that the fearsome Baba Yaga will devour the good Vasilisa, ridding them of the child that has become a constant reminder of their own shortcomings.

As she walks down the road through the darkness, Vasilisa consults the doll in her pocket. The doll gives her directions to Baba Yaga's hut by jumping up and down when Vasilisa guesses correctly. On her way three horsemen pass her, one dressed in white, one in red, and the last in black, rushing toward Baba's home.

When she arrives, Vasilisa sees that Baba Yaga's house is surrounded by a fence adorned with skulls that spew tongues of flame. Although terrified, she remembers her promise to complete the task, swallows her fear, and forges ahead. She is greeted by the repulsive hag, Baba Yaga, who flies down to confront the young girl.

Baba demands to know what the girl wants and Vasilisa replies that she has come for fire. Baba then asks the girl why she should grant her request. Vasilisa is speechless, and once again consults the doll. She replies as the doll suggests: "Because I ask it." Baba is surprised and tells the girl that this is the correct answer; she allows Vasilisa inside the hut. Baba Yaga says to the child that she must perform the tasks asked of her and that if she fails, she will be eaten.

Days go by, and the tasks become ever more difficult to perform until, finally, they

seem impossible. Nevertheless, with the doll's help and reassurance, Vasilisa meets every challenge.

Baba Yaga is impressed, and one night at dinner allows the girl to ask some questions. Before the girl speaks, Baba warns her that too much knowledge makes a person old before their time. Vasilisa asks about the three horsemen, and is told that they are Day, the Rising Sun, and Night. They live within the hut, going forth each morning to bring day to the world. The child thinks to ask more questions but the doll stops her. When Baba Yaga inquires if she wants to know anything else, Vasilisa replies that too much knowledge will make her old. This answer pleases Baba Yaga, and she asks how the child came to be so wise at such a young age. Vasilisa touches the doll in her pocket, and replies cryptically: "By the blessing of my mother."

"No blessings in this house!" shouts Baba Yaga, and pushes the girl outside. Before Vasilisa leaves Baba Yaga hands her one of the posts topped by a flaming skull as payment for passing the trials. It is dark, and the skull casts an unearthly glow across the frightening forest as the child races homeward. She becomes frightened and thinks to toss the skull away but the skull speaks to her and assures her that everything will turn out fine.

Vasilisa returns to her home, to her shocked stepmother and sisters. They thought her dead because she had been gone for so many days. She enters the house feeling triumphant, for she had survived her dangerous journey and brought fire back to her house. The skull watches the stepmother and her daughters quite closely that day, noticing the terrible way they treat Vasilisa. That night the skull burns into the stepmother and her daughters, turning them to ash before morning's light.

CHRISTIAN INFLUENCE ON THE VASILISA TALE

The influence of Christianity upon the Baba Yaga legend can be seen in the fact that later versions of the Vasilisa tale emphasise the redemptive power of charitable works rather than the mystical power of a doll and skull. The version included in *Old Peter's Russian Tales* (Jonathan Cape Ltd: London, 1916) begins similarly but quickly diverges.

In this version, the stepmother wraps a little stale bread and some kitchen scraps in a handkerchief

for the girl's journey to the hut of Baba Yaga. When the girl arrives she notices a servant of Baba Yaga's is standing in the front yard, crying bitterly and wiping her eyes with her petticoat. The girl unties her handkerchief and shakes it clean. She puts the remaining morsels of food in her pockets and gives the cloth to Baba Yaga's servant, who wipes her eyes on it. Next to the hut is a wretched dog. Reaching into her pocket for her kitchen scraps, the girl offers them to the dog that eats them as if it had not eaten in a long time.

These creatures have never experienced such acts of kindness before and later they help the girl to escape. When the girl arrives home she tells her father that his new wife sent her to Baba Yaga's hut and he drives the stepmother out of the house.

Above *Three Women and Three Wolves* by Eugene Grasset (1814–1917). Fairy tales throughout Eastern Europe contain elements inspired by the Baba Yaga tale—the forest, and the creatures it held, had a particular potency to the ancient imagination.

Left *Firebird* by Dimitrii Mitrokhin (1883–1973), from Arthur Ransome's *Old Peter's Russian Tales*. There are various versions of this tale, one featuring a peasant girl Maryushka, who was turned into the firebird by a rejected suitor. In all versions, the feathers of the firebird are valued for their magic qualities.

SPIRITS OF THE HOUSE, YARD, FOREST, AND FIELD

There are no more curious spirits than those that
inhabited the houses of the ancient Slavs.

One popular spirit is the Domovoi, from *dom*
meaning "house." Members of the household often
affectionately referred to him as "grandfather." He
was a rather forlorn character whose stifled sobs
could be heard in the creaking and groaning of
the house at night. Legend has it that
a number of Domovoi had revolted
against Svarog soon after the beginning
of time and had been banished from the
heavens. They fell to earth, down the
chimneys, and into the stoves of
houses, where they now dwell.

The Domovoi was rarely seen.
He was usually depicted
as a small old man so
entirely covered in hair
(even on his palms and the soles
of his feet) that his eyes were
hidden. He may also have had
horns and a tail. Some drawings depict
him as resembling a bundle of hay. His
wife, Domovikha, lived in the cellar.

The Domovoi and Domovikha were said to warn
the inhabitants of a house about coming disaster.
When someone in the household was about to die,
the Domovoi could be heard crying at night. He was
also said to pull a woman's hair to warn her that her
husband was about to beat her. His wife,
Domovikha, would tickle lazy children
to wake them during the night. In
contrast, the gentle furry touch of the
Domovoi at night was a good omen.

Traditionally, peasants were highly
respectful of the Domovoi and, for example,
would not sleep in an area that would inhibit
his noctural wanderings, such as near the
stove. When changing house, peasants would
acknowledge the Domovoi of the new house
before they moved in.

The Slavs also recognized spirits of the yard
(Dvorovoi), the bath (Bannik), and the barns
(Ovinnik), which were generally less benevolent
than the Domovoi and his wife. Dvorovoi was
considered to be responsible for the death of
animals in the yard, especially those with white
fur for which he reserved particular dislike. After
washing it was necessary to leave some water behind
for Bannik to bathe. If this ritual was not observed,
or a person entered the washhouse while the spirit

himself was bathing, Bannik would take a terrible revenge. Interestingly, no Christian icons were placed in Slavic bathhouses, for fear of offending Bannik. Ovinnik, or barn spirit, was often depicted as a black cat sitting in the corner of a barn, and would set it alight if angered—sometimes with the owner in it.

Vodyanoi was a malevolent spirit who lived in an underwater crystal palace in lakes and rivers. From there, he would drown any careless maiden who trespassed on his territory. Once drowned, the maiden would become a water nymph known as Ruskala.

Leshy was the spirit of the forest. He amused himself by disorienting unfortunate travelers, making them stumble around in circles, sometimes for days, before finally releasing them. When forests were cleared, the resulting fields were inhabited by Polevik, who liked to punish drunkards and idlers.

VAMPIRES

The vampire may have lost much of his power to strike fear into us today but for the ancient Slavs, in whose mythology he originated, tales of his grizzly deeds must have been terrifying.

Bram Stoker based his famous 1897 novel *Dracula* upon the legend of a corpse, the *vampir,* which returns to life at night to suck the blood from the living. The victim then becomes a vampire himself. Stoker adopted a number of elements from the *vampir* legend, including the ability of Dracula to change into a bat or wolf.

The origin of the Serbian word *vampir* is uncertain. Some suggest it is related to the Turkisk word *ubir* meaning "undead," while other sources relate it to a fantastical creature from peasant Russian mythology, Upir, who himself was a type of vampire or werewolf.

Bram Stoker's book also drew upon elements of the story of the fifteenth-century prince, Vlad Tepes (1431–1477), known as Vlad the Impaler, a name bestowed on him by his subjects because of the fearful punishment he inflicted on his enemies. Living up to his title, he would bind his victim's hands and feet to four posts and rock them back and forth until they were gradually impaled on a sharpened stake. Ruling the area known as Walachia, south of Transylvania, Vlad's other name Dracula ("son of the devil") comes from his father, Vlad Dracul.

RISING FROM THE ASHES

The gods and spirits described here provide only a sample of the ancient mythology of the Slavic people. Recent studies have commented on the impact of Christianity on the culture, effectively suppressing the mythology before it had a chance to fully develop.

What remains gives us a tantalizing glimpse of what Slavic mythology once was, and what it might have become, if given the opportunity to mature. In the last decade there has been an upsurge of interest and research into Slavic history and mythology, deepening the knowledge and understanding of the myths, and restoring, if not their original power, then their significance in Slavic cultural history.

Above *Vlad the Impaler (Vlad VI of Walachia),* German school, sixteenth century. This portrait does not reflect the terror that Vlad Tepes, also known as Dracula, inspired among his subjects. One story tells of how he invited the needy to his castle, fed them, then locked them inside and set the castle on fire. He did this, he said, to solve the problem of beggars in the town.

Left *The End of a Vampire* from *Les Tribunaux Secrets* by Paul Féval (1817–1887). Vampires have fascinated people for centuries, and a detailed mythology has built up around them. Of the various ways to kill a vampire, driving a wooden stake through the heart is the most famous method, though in this picture a red-hot iron is used.

ROMANCE MYTHOLOGY

"Romance" is a many-layered word: it is a set of languages, a type of story, a form of courtship, and an outlook on life. All of these notions are related to each other, bound up in the narrative traditions of the Middle Ages (approximately A.D. 500–1500). The word originally referred to the Romance languages, those spoken languages that developed from Latin including French, Spanish, and Italian. The language of the Roman Empire, Latin, continued to be used in an official capacity throughout the medieval period for education, government, law, and religion. The languages of everyday life, however, were the vernaculars that had developed from it, and the two carried on, each in their own spheres, until modern times. "Romance" also came to be applied to the heroic tales, legends, and adventures that were recorded in these everyday languages, unofficial works meant for entertainment. Later, the title was applied to the courtly ideals and the knightly ethos recorded in them.

Romance mythology is not like ancient Greek or Roman mythology, where people speaking the same language shared tales about heroes and a pantheon of gods and goddesses. After the coming of Christianity, the nature of religion and religious narratives changed. The Bible was the ultimate reference for religious knowledge, and even though there were some disagreements about exactly which books formed the Bible or how best to translate them, a text-based religion meant that the basic religious narratives were codified and unchanging. Traditional tales about gods and heroes no longer formed the basis of religious beliefs as they had in pre-Christian times. Folk narratives continued to circulate, however, and continued to be important vehicles for expressing and shaping people's ideas of the world around them. Ancient stories, themes, tales of heroes, and even gods remained alive in oral tradition. Within Christianity, a new mythology arose to help the religion adapt to its new setting in post-Roman Europe, explaining inconsistencies and incorporating pre-Christian traditions.

Above *The Castle where a Dragon is Imprisoned,* from *Dioscorides Tractatus de Herbis.* This fifteenth-century French manuscript reveals how medieval tales incorporated a wide range of creatures—from human figures such as saints and pilgrims to mythical beings like dragons and unicorns.

Right *Lovers in a landscape* by Marco dell'Avogardro. This illustration, taken from the fifteenth-century illuminated *Borso d'Este Bible,* is said to be the most sumptuous work of its kind. While handwritten bibles replaced oral traditions in the medieval age, they, too, would soon be replaced, due to the invention of the printing press.

For the medieval period, the only records of that oral tradition are occasional references in historical documents and depictions in art and literature. The literature closest to oral tradition and most directly inspired by it, epic and chivalric literature, began to be written down in the High Middle Ages, from the twelfth century onward. Much of this material has also survived in the form of folklore in the modern Romance countries, and together they paint a clear portrait of medieval beliefs and legends.

EPIC NARRATIVES

As with Homer's earlier epic poems, the *Iliad* and *Odyssey,* the most important medieval narratives come down to us in the form of an epic, or cycle of epics (epic poems that form a complete history or story). New forms of old tales arose for the heroes of Classical tradition, but new heroes developed as well, often based on historical figures. Two of the

most enduring are the cycles surrounding the great Frankish king, Charlemagne (*c.* 742–814), and the Spanish hero warrior El Cíd (*c.* 1043–1099). These cycles are often expressed as conflicts between Islam and Christendom, probably under the influence of the persuasive language used during the time of the Crusades.

In France, these epics were written as *chansons de geste,* literally "songs about deeds." They are long poems recounting the adventures of a hero, most probably sung or chanted to an audience by a *jongleur* or wandering minstrel. The oldest and most famous is *The Song of Roland,* written around 1125–1150, but known to be much older. It chronicles the adventures and untimely death of the noble and brave Lord Roland, Charlemagne's nephew, at Roncevaux in the Pyrenees mountains in the year 778. The story pits Christians against Muslims, but the historical basis for the story was probably an attack on the Franks by the Basques, in whose territory the real events took place. Originally composed in Old French, the story spread across Europe and remains popular today.

The Song of Roland

The story opens with the revelation that Ganelon, Roland's stepfather and one of the twelve Peers of the Realm, is jealous of Roland and is plotting his destruction. He gets his opportunity when Charlemagne's army is sent to fight Marsile, the Saracen King of Saragossa (northern Spain). Roland is captain of the rear guard, which Ganelon treacherously enables the Saracens to attack. Roland's friend and companion, Oliver, asks Roland to sound his elephant-tusk horn, Olifant, and call for help from the main army. Roland insists that it is better to die than suffer the shame of calling for assistance. They fight the Saracens bravely, but they are overcome. Only at the very end does Roland sound the horn, so that Charlemagne may find and avenge them. The effort of blowing the horn kills him. A thunderstorm and an eclipse of the sun signal Roland's death in France, suggesting that, like the heroes of Classical mythology, his death is significant on a cosmic level. Despite the tragic death of Roland, Charlemagne goes on to capture the city of Saragossa and conquer Spain. Ganelon's treachery is revealed, and he is punished by death.

Above *The Battle of Roncevaux,* fifteenth-century manuscript. While the real Roland has been largely forgotten by history, the noble Roland of legend became a figure so popular that it is said the song of his exploits was sung to the troops of William of Normandy in 1066 on the eve of battle.

Below *Death of Roland de Roncevaux,* from *Entre d'Espagne.* This epic has links to many cultures; the Danes sing *The Song of Ogier the Dane,* about a knight who died alongside Roland. In it, Morgan la Fée, better known from Arthurian myth, is featured.

El Cíd

In Spain itself, the most enduring medieval epic tale is that of El Cíd, based on the eleventh-century historical figure of Rodrigo Díaz de Vivar. The story of his deeds survives in just one manuscript from the fourteenth century, though again the story is older. The title "Cíd" comes from the Arabic word *Sayyidī*, meaning "lord, sir," and, in fact, the historical El Cíd served with the Moorish ruler of Saragossa for a time. However, the narrative is set in terms of the conflict between El Cíd's Christian overlord, King Alfonso VI of Castille and Léon, and the Moors of southern Spain. As with the story of Roland, the adventures of El Cíd center on the concept of honor. El Cíd is portrayed as the ideal vassal, doomed through lack of "a good overlord." Like Charlemagne, Alfonso makes poor decisions and therefore reveals himself to be a bad and weak king.

The story begins when Alfonso exiles El Cíd, on the unjust advice of his vassals. Undaunted, El Cíd tricks moneylenders into giving him 600 marks, which he uses to build his own army. He defeats the Moors in battle after battle, capturing Castejón, then Alcocer, all the while sending princely gifts back to Alfonso.

Won over by El Cíd's generosity and great military prowess, he forgives him and, to make up for his earlier mistake, arranges to marry El Cíd's two daughters to the two brothers Carrión. Like Roland's stepfather Ganelon, these young lords are cowardly and perfidious, qualities that contrast with El Cíd's bravery and heroism. When El Cíd's pet lion escapes, the two brothers run and hide. Later, in battle, El Cíd receives a good account of their bravery, but it turns out to be false— they had really hidden during the fighting. On their way home with the two daughters, the brothers Carrión stay with El Cíd's Moorish friend, Albengalbón. He

welcomes them hospitably and gives them horses and other fine gifts. More impressed by his wealth than anything else, they plot to kill him and steal his riches. Luckily, they are overheard by a Spanish-speaking servant, and Albengalbón sends them away in disgrace. El Cíd's daughters mock their husbands' base behavior, and in return are beaten within an inch of their lives and abandoned. The women are found by their cousin, and the brothers are brought to trial and killed. The daughters are then remarried to the Spanish princes of Navarre and Aragón.

MIXING MYTHOLOGIES

Romance mythology incorporated a number of mythical beings from the pre-Christian mythologies of Europe. Another epic centering on Charlemagne is the later medieval story of Renaud de Montalban and his three brothers, and includes characters from Celtic, Germanic, and Classical tradition. At one time, Renaud and his brothers were vassals of King Charlemagne, who gave them a magical flying horse, Bayard. Though it resembled

a normal horse, it could also expand to hold all four of them, if necessary. Bay comes from the Celtic word for "yellow," and similar horses are found throughout Celtic folklore, the horse being revered by the Celts. Swayed by wicked councilors, Charlemagne acts unjustly toward the brothers, and as a result they wage guerrilla warfare on him. Their cousin, the sorcerer Maugis, uses his magic powers to procure the sword Flamberge for them. It was first forged by Wayland the Smith, a god from Germanic mythology. When the Devil kidnaps Bayard, Maugis pursues him via Mount Vulcan, widely believed to be the Mouth of Hell in the Middle Ages. It takes its name and imagery from the Roman god Vulcan, the god of fire and metalworking who dwelled under Mount Etna in Sicily. Eventually, the conflict moves to the Holy Land, where Renaud and Maugis fight the Sultan of Persia for control of Jerusalem. They are ultimately successful, but rather than assume the kingship they elect to return to Europe, where they become holy men. Renaud de Montalban is still recognized as a saint in Cologne and other parts of Germany and France, and many miracles have been attributed to him.

THE UNICORN

The medieval world of Europe was peppered with supernatural beings of all sorts. One of the most important of these was the unicorn, both for its practical uses and its religious symbolism. It was normally depicted as a white horse with a single spiral horn on its forehead. Drinking from a unicorn's horn would protect the drinker from poison and epilepsy, and because of this protection the unicorn was seen as an exceptionally pure beast. The tusk of the narwhal (a type of whale) was pressed into service as a unicorn horn. This fabulous beast, known from Classical sources, developed its own mythology during the Middle Ages.

Medieval tales of the unicorn describe it as a ferocious fighter that could only be captured if a chaste virgin were left alone in its territory. The beast would lay its head in her lap and fall asleep, at which point unicorn hunters would capture it.

Below *Unicorn,* from *Histoire des Juifs* by Flavius Josephus. The horn of the unicorn was considered a precious treasure, desired by medieval rulers.

Above *The Lover Standing before a Richly Dressed Lady* by Robinet Testard, from *Romance of the Rose*. Begun by Guillaume de Lorris, and continued by Jean de Meung, this poem (1487–1495) was highly influential to all who aspired to the ideals of courtly love. Ostensibly an allegorical romance, it also addressed all aspects of medieval life, from how a women should sit at table to the Church.

Right *The Nun's Priest* from the *Ellesmere Chaucer Facsimile* (1410). This hugely popular tale by Chaucer is itself based on another by Marie de France. The tale, told by "the nun's priest," concerns the rooster, Chaunticleer, which is carried off by a fox. Through his quick wits, Chaunticleer manages to free himself and escape.

COURTLY LOVE

Later in the Middle Ages, a new ideal arose featuring knights and warriors that centered not on their great prowess in the field of battle, but in the adventures they undertook for the sake of romantic love. Because marriages at the time were arranged and women were given over to men, often much older men, on the basis of their guardians' economic or political needs, neither young women nor young men of the ruling classes had much opportunity to choose a partner. These knights and ladies between them created and sponsored the notion of "courtly love," a love that transcended the bounds of marriage. The powerful stories told of the natural and supernatural obstacles men and women would have to overcome to be with each other.

One of the greatest storytellers of the tradition of courtly love was the poet Marie de France. Although she probably lived in England and claimed to be translating her material from Breton (the language spoken in Brittany, northwest France) tradition, she wrote in Old French and evidently came from Île-de-France, a small region that included Paris and was then considered to be the country of France. One of the greatest female

writers of the pre-modern world, Marie's stories are simple and elegant, and contain an enticing blend of the supernatural with the prosaic. Although adultery is often celebrated in her stories, it can also be condemned, as in the following tale. The overriding ethic is one of faithfulness and constancy to love, whether inside or outside of marriage.

Bisclavret the Werewolf

Marie's story of Bisclavret is known as a *lay*, as it was told in poem or song form. It is unexpected in that the hero is a werewolf, a young married knight in the service of the king. His wife, though she loves him, is concerned with his unexplained weekly absences. At last he admits to her that he is a werewolf, and that if his clothes were to be stolen, he would have to remain a wolf. His wife is repulsed, and takes a lover. Between them they plot to steal Bisclavret's clothes, which they do successfully, and with her husband's disappearance, the wife marries again. In time, the werewolf finds the king, who is so impressed by the beast's noble behavior that he adopts him as a sort of royal pet. The only time the wolf misbehaves is when he sees his former wife and angrily bites off her nose. The court nobles defend the beast's actions, and eventually the truth comes out. The werewolf is given clothes and a changing-room, and is restored to a human state, while the wife and her lover are exiled. Many of their female descendants are born without a nose, a condition well known in the Middle Ages as an effect of leprosy.

The tale expresses the medieval ethics of love, fidelity, and honor, with both positive and negative examples. It also showcases, however, the darker elements of medieval mythology, such as the belief that a disease like leprosy is a punishment for your own or your ancestors' sins.

PILGRIMS, SAINTS, AND WANDERERS

Travel was an often difficult and dangerous undertaking in the Middle Ages, but one of crucial importance. Pilgrimages, whether long or short, were conducted for a variety of reasons: to make amends for a sin, to atone for a crime, or to venerate a site or relic. Pilgrimage sites ranged from local holy wells dedicated to popular saints, to whole cities such as Rome or Jerusalem. Pilgrimages were often social journeys, as well; pilgrims banded together for safety and comfort, and as a consequence shared news and stories.

The fourteenth-century Italian literary work *The Decameron* by Giovanni Boccaccio (1313–1375) exemplifies both the stories travelers told and the circumstances under which they might be spread. Ten noblemen and women of Florence retire to the country to wait out an attack of the bubonic plague that was ravaging the city. With nothing to do, they spend the ten-day period telling each other stories, including a mix of material from legendary and folktale traditions. *The Decameron* was one of the inspirations for the *Canterbury Tales,* by Geoffrey Chaucer (*c.* 1340–1400), and contains a mixture of piety and humor, bawdiness and courtliness. The following tale is an example of a humorous piece.

Brother Onion

Frate Cipolla (or "Brother Onion") comes to the town of Certaldo, and offers to exhibit a relic from the Holy Land, a feather from the Archangel Gabriel. Two tricksters decide to steal this feather—really just a parrot's tail-feather—and see what happens when the friar is forced to explain its disappearance. They substitute coal for the feather in the casket in which it is stored and blend into the crowd. After much fanfare, the box is opened, but the quick-thinking friar is not in the least put out. He recites a long-winded speech about his travels "through the kingdom of Algebra and through Bordello, eventually reaching Bedlam," and lists the marvelous relics he saw, including "a phial of Saint Michael's sweat when he fought with the Devil" and "holes from the Holy Cross." He explains that he keeps his relics in small caskets, all alike, and that the coal he has by mistake is the coal from the fire over which Saint Lawrence was roasted. He then uses it to draw crosses on the foreheads of the faithful. The tricksters own up to their deed and return the feather, congratulating the fraudulent friar on his quick-thinking audacity.

Below *The Storytellers of the Decameron by Boccaccio (1313–1375),* painting by Francesco Podesti (1800–1895). A collection of 100 short stories, *The Decameron* is set against the threat of the Black Plague. Its stories range from simple moral fables to picaresque tales of illicit sexual adventures.

Above *Lucifer, Prince of Hell, with devils around him,* from *Livre de la Vigne nostre Seigneur,* France (c. 1450–1470). During the Middle Ages, the Devil was the subject of much attention. It was believed that the Devil and many other lesser devils were always abroad to create mischief, often appearing in the guise of an ordinary human being.

Right *Dante Alighieri, 1265–1321, Italian writer, in Hell meeting the souls damned to be torn to pieces by wild beasts.* Dante's great work, the *Divine Comedy,* is intended as an allegory of human life, using the three stages of hell, purgatory, and heaven to gradually reveal God's presence to man.

The previous tale of Brother Onion mocks the credulity of the people of a small town in northern Italy, but by doing so it also highlights the importance of saints. The Christian saints grew in fame as the Middle Ages progressed, and more and more saints were created, some simply from popular legend.

Saint Barbara

Barbara's father, a rich pagan man named Dioscorus, kept her locked away in a tower. Food and clothing were sent up to her in a basket on a rope. Unlike the folktale of Rapunzel, however, when handsome princes offered to marry Barbara, her father accepted but she herself refused. Later, when her father was away, Barbara came down from her tower and convinced some of her father's workmen to install a third window in a water cistern, as a symbol of the Holy Trinity: God the Father, God the Son, and God the Holy Spirit. Her father was very angry at this profession of Christianity, and tried to

punish her. She hid from him in a shepherd's hut, but the shepherd gave her away, and in revenge she changed his sheep into locusts and him into stone. Finally, her own father beheaded her. As the sword fell, he was stuck by lightning and also killed.

Like many medieval saints' legends, Barbara's tale had something for everyone. In addition to the drama, it highlighted the conflict between the young and their elders, and told of the power of faith.

DEVILS AND WITCHES

Strangers and outsiders were viewed with suspicion in the Middle Ages, in part because any human being was a potential danger, either as a brigand or as the devil in disguise. There are many narratives about identifying the Devil, who may inadvertently reveal his cloven hoof or his tail, and many more stories about ordinary people tricking the devil.

One Italian tale tells of a poor man who wanted to become rich. His neighbor, a rich man, said that he would give him all his wealth if he could only strike the devil in the back with three stones. On his way to see the Devil, the poor man is given a series of problems to solve: a fountain that gives only bad water, a gravely ill prince, and a garden whose trees no longer bear fruit. The man befriends the Devil's

wife, a hideous witch, and she agrees to find the answers for him. He throws his stones, and the Devil cries out. His wife pretends to have hit him because she is worried by three problems, and the Devil reveals the answers. To fix the fountain, it was necessary to resurrect the custom of the procession to the Madonna; to regain his health, the prince had to drink water containing the dandruff of a horse which had been run to a sweat and then dried; and for the trees, the wall the greedy king had built around them had to be removed, as it kept out the breeze and prevented pollination. Having tricked the devil, the poor man returns home and becomes rich.

Medieval Hell

The abode of the Devil, Hell, is also greatly elaborated on during the Middle Ages. The teachings of the church made it clear that the majority of people would die in a state of sin and, therefore, go to Hell. Medieval creativity was at its most gruesome when describing the tortures of the damned. *Inferno,* which comprises one third of the book the *Divine Comedy,* by Dante Alighieri (1265–1321), epitomizes the medieval idea of Hell. In the book, the hero is given a tour through the nine circles of Hell by the Classical poet Virgil. They spiral lower and lower, until they reach the bottom, which is covered in ice. There, a winged Lucifer is in the process of devouring the three greatest sinners: Judas, flanked by Brutus and Cassius. Religious literature of the time such as the Vision of Saint Paul also describes Hell in some detail.

The Devil's Servants

A more everyday supernatural danger for the medieval man or woman was the Devil's human servant, the witch. Witchcraft trials of both men and women became increasingly common in the fifteenth century, but isolated references to witches of either sex and witchcraft do occur throughout the period. The son of Chilperic, King of the Franks, died in the year 583 as a result of witchcraft, so the chronicles report; Jeanne of Navarre, Queen of France, was reportedly also killed by sorcery in the year 1305, by Guichard, the Bishop of Troyes. Two Germans, Heinrich Kramer and James Sprenger,

ANTI-JEWISH MYTHOLOGY

Although medieval Christians knew very little about Jews, the Jews' existence held an important place in Christian mythology. Although Jews were important and productive members of European society, their existence as a minority in what was an overwhelmingly Christian and superstitious society made them prime candidates for scapegoats. The antiquity of their faith gave them a role as holders of wisdom and arcane knowledge, which made them both powerful and, to the Christian mind, potentially very dangerous.

Christians, encouraged by the Church, believed in the Blood Libel legend, which contended that the Jews engaged in ritualistic murder. Knowing little of their religion and practice, Christians suspected Jews used witchcraft and black magic, concluding that they conducted murder of Christians in order to drink their blood in a parody of the Christian mass, or for other magical purposes. The blood, or other substances, was sometimes believed to have been used to poison wells, and these poisoned wells were thought to have brought the Black Death. The rumors and legends of the Blood Libel resulted in the torture and expulsion or murder of Jews who were blamed for the deaths of Christians.

Above *Protestants and Jews Burned Alive, Accused of Heresy and Witchcraft,* German woodcut, 1493. Trials of witches existed as early as the 1300s and grew with the establishment of permanent judges.

co-wrote *Malleus Maleficarum,* "The Hammer of Witches," around 1486, and their work became a manual for witch hunters all over Europe. In order to identify witches and the practice of witchcraft, they collected the witchlore of Europe. For example, they describe how a witch will stick a knife into a wall and make milking motions, telling her familiar (a person or demon, sometimes taking the form of an animal such as a cat, who aids a witch) which cow she is milking. The milk pours into her bucket from the knife, and the farmer finds his cow dry. To steal butter, a male witch goes naked into a stream and sits with his back to the current, uttering certain words and moving his hands behind his back. He then returns with the butter.

> *Where thou shalt hear despairing shrieks, and see spirits of old tormented*
> DANTE ALIGHIERI (1265–1321), INFERNO

ARTHURIAN MYTHOLOGY

Below *King Arthur,*
the Holy Grail, and the
Knights of the Round Table.
As this fifteenth-century
manuscript, *Le Roman de*
Tristan, shows, Arthur and
his Knights embodied all
that was noble and good.
On one level, the tales of
their exploits are exciting
stories of derring-do, but
they also explore ideas of
order and harmony in the
world—between man, the
land, and the spiritual.

Arthurian myth is a unique category of mythology. Myth is usually grouped by culture, such as the Sumerian or Aztec mythology, but the Arthurian mythos has developed over at least eight centuries from the repeated cross-pollination of a number of traditions. It combines Celtic, German, French, and other European pagan mythologies with esoteric Christian elements. We can even discern in the tales influences of medieval magic and the symbolism of alchemy. The result is a uniquely Western mythos, with distinct ideas about sovereignty and the almost mystical relationship of the ruler's wellbeing to that of his realm. Courtly and divine love both feature prominently. The myths explore how these loves can overlap, for example, when Perceval weds the Grail Maiden and becomes a king, or be at odds, when Lancelot and Guinevere's love destroys Camelot.

ORIGINS IN HISTORY

It is tempting to imagine that the mythological tales of Arthur are based on a real man, though it is hard to find conclusive evidence for this. If he did exist, the Arthur of history would have lived around the sixth century A.D. The Roman legions had just departed Britain after four centuries of occupation, leaving the native Britons undefended. Pagan Angles, Saxons, and Jutes invaded, and King Vortigern of the Britons requested help from other Saxons, paying them with land in Kent. Vortigern's "allies" shortly proceeded to attempt their own conquest of Britain, using the handy base that he had given them. Chaos reigned.

According to the tales, this was the power vacuum from which Arthur came. One of the earliest mentions of Arthur is in the eighth-century *Historia Brittonum,* attributed to a Celtic monk, Nennius. In it, Arthur is referred to as a "war leader" who fought with the British kings against the Saxons in a series of battles. Famously, in the Battle of Mount Badon around A.D. 516, he was said to have killed 960 men in a single day. Whoever the historical Arthur was, he was acclaimed as a hero or leader, and has subsequently been "claimed" by the Cornish, Scots, Welsh, French, and Irish as their own.

However, what we are most concerned with here is the body of myths and lore that grew up around him. Oral traditions would have come first. We know that

folk tradition associated Arthur variously with the "Wild Hunt," a nocturnal foray made up of supernatural beings accompanied by hounds, and also with cairns (piles of stones marking a spot, such as a grave) and cromlechs (prehistoric stone circles). He was said to sleep in "hollow hills" like Glastonbury Tor, or in various Welsh hills, and would return when Britain needed him. The Celtic bards, poets trained in myth as well as verse, no doubt also played a part in developing Arthur's heroic biography, and would have spread his stories on their travels.

THE CREATION OF A LEGEND

Geoffrey of Monmouth (*c.* 1100–1155) became Arthur's first fully fledged mythographer when he included him in his twelfth-century *Historia Regum Brittaniae*. Modeled on the great classical histories of Rome, and fleshed out with scraps of Welsh legend, it created a British king who ranked with the greatest known world leaders.

The Anglo-Norman poet, Robert Wace, born around 1100, wrote a French version of this history for Henry II and Eleanor of Aquitane, and French authors and audiences embraced and embellished the tale. In the retelling by Wace, we have the first mention of the Round Table. Chrétien de Troyes, working for Eleanor's daughter, produced the first written versions of Lancelot and Guinevere's love story, as well as the first mention of the Holy Grail. Both of these "new" elements, however, have earlier parallels in Celtic myth, so though it is known who first wrote them down, their origins are unclear.

The cross-pollination became still more complex after the Norman conquest of Britain in 1066, when the tales came back across the channel in their new forms and were further embellished by the bards—drawing again from native Celtic traditions.

The archetypal qualities shared by Arthur, Merlin, Morgan la Fée, and other figures in the myths, raise a question about their nature. There is some evidence that "Arthur" and "Merlin" may not be names as much as titles. Merlin's epithet "Ambrosius" or "immortal" and his association with many periods of history, may mean that there are actually several historical figures. These figures may have become "Ambrosius," an immortal deity, housed in a number of human oracles and mythologized over time as one

person. "Arthur" may come from the Latin *artos*, the "Bear," or the Welsh *arddu*, the "Lofty Dark One," an appropriate title for a war leader or war deity.

Upholder of Truth

In ancient Celtic culture, the divine king as warrior and ruler was the upholder of truth and cosmic order. The Old Irish word for king, *rí,* may come from a root meaning "to extend." Sovereignty was seen as a guiding force that extended over the kingdom. As king and upholder of the truth, Arthur enabled everyone else to maintain their true social and spiritual roles in relation to him. He created a stable base from which other adventurers, such as Perceval and Gawain, could proceed.

This makes the myths sometimes seem less about Arthur personally (except at the beginning, when he gains sovereignty, and at the end, when he loses it), and more about the sacred base he created and held at Camelot.

Above *King Arthur on his throne, surrounded by the Knights of the Round Table.* Chrétien de Troyes (died *c.* 1183) from France left an unfinished tale of Perceval, in which he first introduces the Grail. All of his Arthurian tales are full of chivalric detail, in particular, the codes and dress of battle.

Left *King Arthur, legendary British King,* from the *Chronicle of England* by Peter Langtoft (1325). The real Arthur was possibly a military genius or a tribal leader, but he came to be known as the "Once and Future King." Here, he is standing on a shield with the crowns and names of 30 kingdoms.

THE BIRTH OF ARTHUR

As with so much of Arthur's story even his very existence came out of the actions of the mysterious sorcerer Merlin.

Arthur's father, Uther Pendragon, King of the Britons, had fallen madly in love with Igrena the wife of his enemy Gorlois of Cornwall. This desire so possessed Uther that he persuaded Merlin to help him make it real. Accordingly, they went to Tintagel in Cornwall, Gorlois's castle, and waited for a time when Gorlois was away. Using his magical powers, Merlin transformed Uther into the likeness of his rival so that he could enter the castle and be with Igrena without her or anyone else suspecting his true identity. Their son Arthur was conceived from this magically assisted union.

After leaving the castle, having satisfied his lusts, Uther learned that Gorlois had been killed in battle just a few hours before. He lost no time in pressing his suit on Igrena and ultimately he married her. In this way, although Arthur had been conceived through a magical deception, he was legitimized as Uther's heir as he was born after the marriage of his mother to the man who was, in fact, his father. We do not know whether or not Igrena ever became aware of the truth of Arthur's conception, indeed she plays no further part in his story. Although Uther and Igrena had no other children, the marriage brought Arthur older half-sisters. The youngest, a girl called Morgan or Morgan la Fée, would grow up to be a powerful sorceress, and become in time a major force against Arthur and his kingdom.

Shortly after Arthur's birth Merlin came to Uther and, prophesying that the king did not have long to live, warned him of the grave dangers that surrounded his son from the nobles who would try to seize power after Uther's death. Uther was not a foolish man. He

THE LADY OF THE LAKE TELLETH ARTHVR OF THE SWORD EXCALIBVR

agreed readily with Merlin's plan to take the infant Arthur away and hide him with a foster family where he could come of age in safety. Not long after this meeting Uther died and, as Merlin had foreseen, the country returned to a state of violence, split into warring factions vying for rulership.

THE TRUE RULER OF ENGLAND

After fifteen long years of this conflict, a strange event took place. In a churchyard, there appeared a large stone with a heavy iron block, known as an anvil, on top of it. Thrust deep through both stone and anvil was a sword with the following words inscribed on its blade: "Whosoever pulls out this sword is rightful born King of Britain."

Seeing a chance to find peace with this wonder, the Archbishop, counseled by Merlin, announced a truce to be held over Christmas. During this time there would be a tournament in London followed by a test to see who among the assembled lords and gentlemen of arms could extract the sword.

Among those who made their way to London was the family of Sir Ector, including his son Kay who would take part in the tournament. The young Arthur, whom everyone thought was Sir Ector's younger son, was acting as Kay's squire. On the day

Right *Arthur Draws the Sword from the Stone* by Walter Crane in *King Arthur's Knights*. The sword, and weapons generally, had a symbolic role in medieval times. The sword in the stone and Excalibur represent Arthur's right to rule, and other weapons revealed the owner's fate or the bearer's worth.

of the tournament, Kay left his sword in their lodgings, so Arthur set off to retrieve it. Unfortunately, the hostel was locked as everyone had gone to the tournament. As he returned he passed the sword in the churchyard and, removing it easily from the stone and anvil, took it to give to Kay. Kay recognized the sword at once, and hurried to his father, claiming to have drawn it himself. Sir Ector knew this could not be so and revealed the truth about how Arthur had been brought to him by Merlin to be raised as his own. The following day, after many others had tried their hand, Arthur demonstrated that he and no other could draw the sword from the stone, and he was recognized by all who were gathered there as the legitimate ruler of the country.

Excalibur

Arthur set about establishing his court and trying to bring the rule of law back to his kingdom. This was not always possible without recourse to arms and in one early conflict the sword was broken. Merlin then came to him and took him to the Lady of the Lake, a powerful otherworld enchantress, who gave him the enchanted sword Excalibur, which made its wielder undefeatable, as its sheath gave its wearer protection from harm.

Thus armed, Arthur continued his campaign to rid the country of outlaws and conflict. During this time he and the knights that were accompanying him arrived one day at the besieged castle of King Leodegrance. Arthur and his men quickly drove off the attackers and rescued the castle's inhabitants.

MERLIN AS SHAMAN AND SAGE

We first hear of Merlin when King Vortigern sought a fatherless boy to sacrifice at the base of his fort. Merlin was such a boy—some tales say he was born of an incubus—but he revealed that the structure wouldn't stand because a red and a white dragon, symbolic of the Welsh and the Saxons, fought beneath it. He further prophesied that the red Welsh dragon would win. When King Vortigern asked his name, he responded that he was Merlin "Ambrosius"—Immortal. Like shamans the world over, Merlin sometimes wore a feathered cape and antlered headdress, showing he had the power of both natural and supernatural worlds. He was "taken out of himself" when he prophesied, "and like a spirit, knew the history of people long past and could foretell the future." From his birth to his magical "sleep," he fulfilled the shamanic role of bridging the human and divine realms.

Right *Tournament of the Knights of the Round Table*, from *Le Roman de Tristan*, a fifteenth-century manuscript. Knighthood was a semi-religious affair in the medieval age and knights were sworn to uphold the code: "to protect the weak, the defenceless, and helpless, and fight for the general welfare of all." Tournaments were a place to prove oneself and thus were serious events.

Below *Queen Guinevere* by William Morris (1834–1896). Guinevere's character is variously depicted as temptress or unwilling participant, both in terms of her affair with Lancelot and in Mordred's later attempts to marry her. In all stories, however, it is her role to be the ultimate cause of Arthur's downfall.

THE KNIGHTS OF THE ROUND TABLE

After the battle for the castle, among those who came to thank their rescuers was King Leodegrance's lovely daughter, Guinevere, who Arthur straightaway fell in love with. Merlin, acting as advisor to Arthur as he had to his father, agreed that she would indeed make a fitting queen, but warned that her very beauty might in time become a danger. Arthur was undeterred and in a short time the two were married. As part of her dowry, Guinevere's father gave Arthur a great round table that had originally been made for Uther Pendragon.

Arthur took the table to his court at Camelot and set it up in the great hall. He then made it known throughout the land that any knight of good standing who would swear an oath to uphold the good and protect the weak and innocent would be welcome to join his company of the Round Table, where no man sat higher than any other. Part of the power of the table was that, when a knight arrived at Camelot, if he was worthy, his name would magically appear on the seat. Many knights came to see if they would be judged worthy enough for their names to appear in gold across the back of a seat at the Round Table. Soon, only one seat remained without a name, which Merlin told Arthur was kept for the most perfect knight.

Arthur's marriage to Guinevere and the establishment of the Knights of the Round Table began the golden age of Arthur's court. Many quests and adventures would begin from that magical place.

THE ARTHURIAN WOMEN

There is much discussion over the various origins and meanings of the female characters in the Arthurian tales. Many aspects of the myths may hearken back to ancient Celtic deities, and this is certainly true of the female figures. The most prominent of these is Arthur's half-sister Morgan la Fée, (literally "Morgan the Fairy"), who may relate to the Irish goddess Morrigan or "Great Queen." Morrigan, like Morgan la Fée, is an ambivalent figure, who can both heal or destroy heroes. Some analysts of mythology have seen in Morgan's enmity toward Arthur the relics of a transition between goddess- to god-based religions.

The Lady of the Lake is supernatural as well, and as is the case with many figures of Celtic myth, lives in an otherworld beneath the waters. One form of her name, Vi-Vianna, suggests a connection with the Celtic water-goddess, Coventina. Even Guinevere's name can be translated as the "White Spirit." There are Welsh sources that call Guinevere the "Three Queens of Camelot," a possible reference to the Celtic "Triple Goddess"—maiden, mother, and crone—that is associated with the land. When the king married this goddess's representative, he symbolically married the land. Interestingly, however, early Welsh and Celtic stories also contain hints of the adulteress role Guinevere is to eventually play; Welsh triads name Gwenhwyfar as the worst offender of the "Three Faithless Wives."

THE PASSING OF MERLIN

Not long after the establishment of the Round Table Arthur was to lose the aid of his greatest helper. Merlin had warned Arthur that he would not be with him forever, and now the time for his departure came. A maiden, Vivien, who had been taught in the practice of magic by Morgan la Fée, came to Camelot to study with Merlin and so enraptured him with her beauty and wiles that he could refuse her nothing. Over time, she learnt all that he knew, until eventually her power rivaled his own. She then took him from Camelot to a wild place where she placed him in a deep sleep and sealed him within a cave.

but she wrought so there for him that he came never out for all the craft he could do

SIR THOMAS MALORY (1408–1471),
LE MORTE D'ARTHUR

This was not the only blow that Morgan la Fée was to strike against Arthur. While he was on a hunting trip she contrived through magic to capture him and pit him in combat to the death against one of his own companions. This battle went badly for Arthur as his half-sister had armed his opponent with Excalibur and its magic sheath. Though badly wounded, Arthur managed to prevail and regained his enchanted blade. While he lay recovering from his wounds, Morgan la Fée visited him. She attempted to steal Excalibur, but was unable to as he slept with the sword in his hand. She took the sheath, however, and threw it far into a lake, so depriving him of its protection.

Despite these setbacks, Arthur succeeded in bringing peace to his kingdom and establishing the rule of good, piety, and chivalry wherever his power extended. The fame of his court and that of the Knights of the Round Table spread far and wide, a shining beacon of noble virtues in an often-troubled world.

THE GREATEST OF KNIGHTS

There are many stories of the heroic deeds, the quests for justice, and the adventures in the name of Arthur's rule that the company of the Round Table embarked upon. It would take a large book to recount them all. They include Culwch and his wonder-filled wooing of Olwen; Tristan and his doomed love for Iseult; Bors the true; gentle Pellias; and many others that made up the court of Camelot.

However, despite the prowess of these knights, the greatest of the knights of the Round Table was Lancelot du Lac, the Knight of the Lake, so called as he was raised and trained by the Lady of the Lake following the death of his father. Lancelot's prowess was such that none could defeat him, and greater than his loyalty to Arthur was only his love of Guinevere: the flaw that would ultimately bring down Camelot and all that it had stood for. The introduction of Lancelot, more than any other character, into the Arthurian mythos highlights the shift over time from the values of the warrior king to those of romance and chivalry. Thus, Lancelot is a great warrior because he is pure.

Below *Merlin and Vivien* by Eleanor F. Brickdale (1872–1945). Merlin's end varies but, in most cases, it is not peaceful. In some tales, the last we hear is of his imprisonment by Vivien and absence from Arthur's final battle. In others, he attends a later battle, but a vision sends him mad and he ends his days as a wild man living in the woods.

SIR GAWAIN AND THE GREEN KNIGHT

A typical Arthurian tale is that of Sir Gawain's encounter with the supernatural Green Knight.

On New's Year's Day, as there was great feasting in Camelot, a massive knight clad all in green rode into the castle hall, seated on an equally imposing and green horse. He challenged the knights: which one will take the large axe he carries and strike him with it. Whoever does so will have to come, exactly one year to the day, and allow the Green Knight to return the blow.

Only the brave Sir Gawain offers to champion the honor of King Arthur. He strikes the Green Knight, cutting off his head. Unconcerned, the knight leaves the hall carrying the head, and reminding Gawain to meet him at the Green Chapel in a year's time.

Gawain later sets off on his faithful horse, Gryngolet, eventually arriving at a castle at Christmas. He is told the Green Chapel is nearby, and he stays as a guest at the castle.

The host strikes a bargain with Gawain: he will give him whatever he kills while hunting each day, if Gawain gives him whatever he receives during the day. The next morning, after the hunt has begun, the mistress of the castle comes to Gawain's room. She flirts with him and demands a kiss. Gawain does not want to offend the lady. Equally, he cannot dishonor his knightly vows, Camelot, or his host, but he offers a kiss. That night, the knight brings home a hart and Gawain passes on the kiss, without revealing its origin.

The next day the same thing happens and Gawain receives two kisses, which he duly passes on to the knight, who has killed a boar. On the third day, he accepts the lady's green belt, after she tells him it will protect the wearer from harm. That evening Gawain gives the knight three kisses but not the green belt.

On New Year's Day Gawain sets off for the Green Chapel, as agreed. The Green Knight is waiting for him and Gawain kneels to take the blows. The knight raises his axe twice without striking Gawain. The third time, he strikes Gawain on the neck, but cuts him only slightly. The Green Knight then admits that he is the knight from the castle, and that he had asked his wife to tempt Gawain as a test. If Gawain had given him the belt, he would not have cut him at all. He also says Morgan la Fée was behind the trick.

Gawain is mortified that he showed cowardice and disloyalty in accepting the green belt. He decides to wear it always to remind him of his failure and to keep him humble. After this, all the knights agree to wear green belts in his honor and to remember to keep their knightly vows.

THE SEARCH FOR THE GRAIL

Before the sad event of the demise of Camelot, there lay the greatest adventure yet to face the Knights of the Round Table: the search for the Holy Grail. The beginnings of this story were long before, in the early years of Arthur's reign. A rash and impetuous knight wounded the keeper of the Grail with a holy spear kept with the Grail. This wound would not heal, and because of it the lands around the Grail Castle were turned into a wasteland.

The only person capable of curing this evil wound was Galahad, the purest knight that ever lived. He

was conceived when the daughter of the wounded Grail King came to Lancelot disguised as Guinevere. Some years later the stage was set by two marvels: first, a stone floating in the river with a sword thrust into it bearing the words, "No man shall draw me save the best knight in the world." Then, Galahad's arrival at Camelot to claim the sword and take the final seat at the Round Table.

The story tells how, one evening not long after Galahad came to Camelot, while Arthur and his knights sat at the Round Table, a great light entered the hall. Floating over them was the Grail, draped in white cloth. It was there for a moment and then gone, leaving them full of wonder.

Sir Gawain was the first to swear that he would seek the meaning of this vision but the others were not long in following suit. The next day Arthur watched as the men who had made his dreams of chivalry a reality begin the quest for the Holy Grail.

THE GRAIL

The Grail is a complex object and its origins go far back. According to ancient tradition, the Dagda, Irish father god, possessed a cauldron of inexhaustible bounty accessible only to the brave. Several Irish stories feature goblet-bearing maidens, like the Grail Maiden, who dispense sovereignty to worthy candidates with a drink. In one Irish tale the sea god, Manannán, gives King Cormac a magical chalice that is shattered by falsehood and reunited by truth. The story's symbolism suggests that the chalice represents the vessel of self. The conception of the Grail as container of self is reinforced by the Welsh version of Perceval, "Peredur." In this version, Peredur sees the Grail not as a cup, but a human head. Some traditions speak of the ancient Celts using skulls as drinking vessels, and in later alchemical symbolism the *vas*, the crucible used by the alchemist, is sometimes identified as a skull. Thus, the Grail quest is, on one symbolic level, a transformative process carried out within the mind.

There is some evidence that the Grail is also connected with pagan fertility rites—the idea of a sickly land finding restoration only through the Grail, as well as the Celtic idea of a cauldron of plenty. Later, the Grail came to be associated with Christian ideas of the Holy Spirit: the Grail as a metaphor for the body containing the Holy Spirit.

Above *Temple of the Holy Grail* by **Wilhelm Hauschild (born 1827)**. This painting is inspired by the opera *Lohengrin*, by Richard Wagner (1813–1883), in which the Grail has come to represent the Holy Spirit.

Above *Sir Bedevere Returns the Sword Excalibur to the Lake,* from a French manuscript (1300–1325). The image of an arm emerging from the lake to grasp Excalibur has captivated the popular imagination for centuries. Sir Bedevere was one of the first knights to join Arthur, and the only one to be left standing at the end of the fateful last battle, the Battle of Camlan.

Right *Sir Lancelot sneaking out of Queen Guinevere's room,* from Le Roman du Roi Arthur by Chrétien de Troyes (died c. 1183). The love of Lancelot and Guinevere was to prove the undoing of the Knights of the Round Table. Some sources say that Lancelot ended his days as a hermit, in penitence for his sins.

ENCOUNTERS WITH THE GRAIL

After many adventures Lancelot and Gawain came together to the Castle of the Grail. Gawain was allowed to enter the Grail chapel but Lancelot, a sinner through loving Guinevere, was denied entry. Gawain's actions removed the curse on the wasteland around the Grail Castle, which began to grow again.

After these two had left, Bors, Perceval, and Galahad arrived at the castle. All three were admitted to the Grail chapel, but only Galahad was given the Grail to drink from. Using the same spear that the young knight had used to wound the Grail King, Galahad cured the wound of his grandfather, and having fulfilled the divine role he had been born for, died. Perceval remained at the castle, married the Handmaiden of the Grail and became the new Grail King. Only Bors was left to return and tell Arthur of the success of the quest.

Perceval was the Grail King's nephew and he had been raised by his mother in the woods. He thought that knights were angels when he first saw them. When he discovered their true nature, he knew that he could not rest until he became as they were, and set off in a ragged outfit with just a small spear. Fortunately, his prowess matched his simplicity. In Camelot he became a great fighter and received a veneer of civilization. Unfortunately, his new manners worked against him in the Grail quest. On an earlier journey, he encounters the Grail at the castle, in the Grail Procession, but remained politely silent, not uttering the question—what is the grail and whom does it serve—that would begin healing the wasteland. When he finally found his way back to the Grail, he was older and wiser. He was then able to take his destined place as the new Grail King.

Many knights never returned from the Grail quest, and times were changing. Arthur was getting older, his knights were elsewhere, and Camelot was no longer as happy a place. As well, certain knights were envious of Lancelot and determined to expose him and Guinevere as lovers. Chief among these plotters was Mordred, son of Morgan la Fée, and some say Arthur's bastard son born of incest.

The lovers were becoming careless and one night the conspirators caught Lancelot in the Queen's chamber. Seizing a sword, Lancelot fought his way free and escaped. Mordred demanded that Guinevere be burnt for her infidelity and, as sworn upholder of the law, Arthur had no choice. Sadly, he agreed.

On the day of the execution Lancelot and his followers appeared. Fighting their way to the stake, they released Guinevere and rode off with her. In the melee Lancelot unwittingly killed Agravain, Gareth, and Gaheris, brothers of Sir Gawain and Knights of the Round Table. They had been unarmed as a sign of grief at Guinevere's impending death.

THE LAST DAYS OF CAMELOT

Gawain, although always a friend of
Lancelot and no supporter of Mordred,
was incensed and swore to take revenge.
Arthur's forces, led by Gawain, besieged
Lancelot's castle. The castle could not be
taken and Arthur was persuaded to take
Guinevere back and allow Lancelot to
go into exile.

For a while a troubled peace lasted,
but the unity of the Round Table had
been broken. Mordred and his followers
continued to agitate against Lancelot,
and Gawain brooded on the deaths of
his brothers. Finally, arguing that Arthur
must avenge his injured honor, Gawain
persuaded the king to once again lead
his forces against Lancelot, leaving
Mordred behind at Camelot as regent.

The siege of Lancelot's castle went on
for many months, Gawain all the time
challenging Lancelot to single combat
and taunting him as a coward. Unhappily,
Lancelot finally accepted the challenge.
He won but would not kill his former
friend. As soon as he recovered, however,
Gawain challenged Lancelot again, and
again Lancelot defeated him. Then a
message arrived from Guinevere asking
for urgent assistance.

In Arthur's absence Mordred had set
about consolidating his power. He spread
the rumor that Arthur had been killed
and, claiming the throne for himself,
tried to force Guinevere to marry him.
Arthur was furious and left for Britain
with all his men, swearing vengeance.
In the first battle Gawain's recent wounds
re-opened; as he lay dying he wrote asking Lancelot
to come to Arthur's aid. Sadly this message was too
late. Arthur pursued Mordred until their two armies
met. The slaughter was terrible. Surrounded by
the dead knights of both sides, Arthur
finally confronted Mordred face to
face. They fought savagely and
Arthur killed Mordred on his
spear but not before he himself
was fatally wounded.

In his dying moments, Arthur called his
remaining knight, Bedevere, to him. Handing him
the great sword Excalibur, Arthur ordered that it be
cast into the nearby lake. Bedevere did as he was
commanded, and as the sword flew out over the

water a hand broke the surface and caught its hilt.
Flourishing the blade, the hand sank beneath the
waves, returning Excalibur to the otherworld where
it had been made. Bedevere returned to the
dying king and helped him to the
water's edge. There they waited
as a black boat drifted toward
them. On the boat were several
women including the Lady of
the Lake and Morgan la Fée.

Gently they picked up Arthur and placed
him on board. Pushing off from the shore they took
Arthur to the Isle of Avalon where he lies to this day,
waiting to be roused from his slumber to once again
assist Britain in its hour of need.

*The sequel of today
unsolders all the goodliest
fellowship of famous knights*
LORD TENNYSON (1809–1892),
MORTE D'ARTHUR

Above *The Knights' March
by Dore Gustave (1823–
1883).* As important as
any character in the tales
is the land itself. While
Arthur and the knights
existed in peace, the land
prospered. When this unity
ended, so too did the
fertility of the land. Today,
much energy is spent
trying to determine
exactly where Camelot,
Avalon, and Arthur's final
burial place may be.

Egyptian and African Mythology

EGYPTIAN MYTHOLOGY

The ancient Egyptian civilization was essentially conservative. Although it spanned more than 3,000 years, once a solution was found to a problem it seldom changed. As a result, most aspects such as art and technology can be studied as a unity. The only exception to this was their religious beliefs system. This developed slowly and changed, sometimes subtly, at other times radically. Consequently, it is one of the most complex areas of Egyptology, and the one that is most open to misinterpretation and debate by scholars and enthusiasts alike.

The reason for this misunderstanding is often a lack of objectivity in Egyptology itself. The scientific field of Egyptology is barely 200 years old; for the first century at least it was inspired by equal desires to prove the authenticity of the Bible and a lust for ancient Egyptian gold and precious treasures. The only sources early academics had were Classical—

Below **Ramesses III makes an offering to the god Re, tomb of Khaemweset (c. 1193–1162 B.C.).** Ever since ancient Egypt was "discovered" by the ancient Greeks, it has fascinated. Its art, architecture, and the Nile itself, hint of treasures yet to be unearthed. Their religious beliefs, shrouded in ritual and mystery even then, retain much of that unique quality today, and perhaps always will.

including Herodotus, Alexander the Great, Ptolemy, and the Bible— and they agreed that the Egyptians were simply "cruel taskmasters." This view has tended to color popular thinking to this day. However, modern scholarship has revealed a very different story.

Archaeology has shown that early settlers along the Nile valley came from a variety of places. We have very little evidence of a native indigenous stock; most immigrants arrived from Africa, the Hamitic region of North Africa, and the Semitic lands of the northeast. They formed isolated communities, developing their own languages, customs, and beliefs. These groups were unified into a single nation in a long series of conquests starting as early as 3400 B.C. and ending around 700 years later. Only around 2700 B.C. did a kingdom we can call Ancient Egypt finally emerge, with a single language under a single king. For the first 1,000 years afterward, their world was dominated by a king regarded as a demigod, feared by all. Myths were passed by word of mouth. Only with the demise of this form of monarchy, around 1780 B.C., was there seen a need to record the myths.

These myths created and supported the world the Egyptians occupied. Perhaps about 0.1 percent of the population could read and write; the others worked on the land and depended on storytellers for their entertainment. For those boys who attended school, writing down the traditional myths was a basic part of their education; and many myths thus survive to us only in schoolboy copies.

Earliest archaeological record shows that before and during the Unification, beliefs were dominated by a cattle cult. These cattle, huge and with great wide horns (similar to Ankole cattle today) were revered and the kings always remained identified with them. We can also see a firm belief in a life after death, as bodies, buried in a crouching position, lay with the head pointing south and facing west, in the direction of the setting sun, and accompanied by food, drink, and personal belongings.

Egyptian myths sought to explain to ordinary people how the world began and what may happen to them when they died. They were peopled with

long-dead heroes whose examples might both inspire them and terrify them. As one writer recently stated, national religion affected few outside the close royal circle; for most, religion was a mixture of magic and superstition. Tales explained to them how the world was created (the Creation myths); how man could overcome death (the murder and resurrection of Osiris); of the power and wisdom of women over villains (Isis); and of how right always triumphed over evil (the battles of Horus and Seth). There were also tales of sheer terror (the destruction of man).

BALANCE AND CHAOS

The Egyptians understood their cosmos as being two identical lands. This earth was created as a mound out of the waters of primordial Chaos. Beyond the western horizon lay the Other World, a parallel land occupied by spirits or the resurrected Dead. Every night, the sun left our world to shine in the Other World. As it sank, the newly dead would have to face the terrors of entry into that realm, and judgment beyond, before they could enter into a land that was a perfect replica of Egypt, without its problems. These two worlds were duplicates. It was absolutely vital to maintain these two worlds in balance, or Maat; if this balance were disturbed, even slightly, then primordial Chaos, or Isfet, was ready to return instantly. The king was the only bridge between the worlds. Daily, secretly, in the heart of the temple, he would reenact Creation. The Egyptians occupied a precarious world, trembling on the brink of disorder. The king's word had to be followed exactly to avoid chaos and devastation.

The myths, told popularly as folktales or as songs, undoubtedly gave comfort to ordinary people, assuring them that those who understood were in control and that their world was secure. They needed this comfort, for according to inscriptions, demons and evil spirits were waiting around every corner. Magic, in the form of amulets and special words of protection, was real to them and they used it to keep their fears of the darkness away.

The Judgment of the Dead

According to Egyptian belief and law, no man could judge another in life or death. Under this unique system, they believed that after death the body, heart intact, was resurrected by the Opening of the Mouth ceremony, and thence passed westward into the hall of Osiris. The deceased there had to recite the deeds of his life. While his tongue may lie, his heart would know the truth. After he had finished speaking, he had to produce his heart for weighing (an amulet, a heart scarab, was placed in his tomb to enable him to do this). It was weighed against Maat, Cosmic Balance. If it was found heavy—full of guilt, because the tongue had lied—then the deceased suffered a second death by the Gobbler. The unfortunate individual then became a malevolent spirit, which could bring sickness and death to humans, and was driven away by physicians using words of power and amulets.

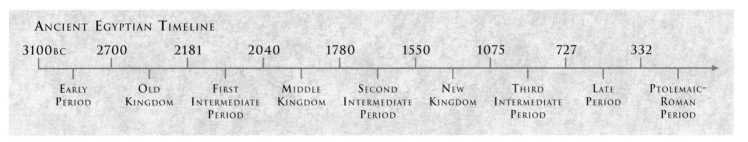

ANCIENT EGYPTIAN TIMELINE

3100BC	2700	2181	2040	1780	1550	1075	727	332
EARLY PERIOD	OLD KINGDOM	FIRST INTERMEDIATE PERIOD	MIDDLE KINGDOM	SECOND INTERMEDIATE PERIOD	NEW KINGDOM	THIRD INTERMEDIATE PERIOD	LATE PERIOD	PTOLEMAIC-ROMAN PERIOD

Amulets

These talismans protected Egyptians in every aspect of their life and were believed to be very powerful. Images of the Wadjat Eye of Horus protected babies; images of Taweret, a pregnant hippo, helped women become pregnant; while a tiny frog assisted against miscarriage. The dwarf god Bes is linked with many kinds of misbehavior but he and his female counterpart, Beset, gave protection to the woman in labor and delivery. Flat or curved pieces of ivory, inscribed with words of magic and legendary figures of griffins and serpents, were laid over the belly of the woman in delivery to hasten the birth and drive away any evil spirits. After death, amulets were provided in great numbers to protect the dead. Kings and wealthy men had them included within their own bandages, from a tiny headrest to protect the neck, to a magical scarab placed directly over the heart, inscribed with words to enable the resurrected body to produce the heart for judgment. Lists were made prescribing the exact shape and type of material needed for the amulet to be effective.

THE CULT

No one knows for certain exactly what went on within the temple sanctuary, as it was a closely guarded secret. In several rural temples (such as Abydos and Esna) pictures show the Servitor entering the sanctuary alone, closing the doors, and serving the cult statue exactly as a servant would treat a living lord: assisting with cleansing, dressing, and feeding. Food and drink, offered before the statue, would afterward revert to the temple staff. In the great national temples like Karnak, at Luxor, where the king himself officiated, the ceremony was very different. Inscriptions make it clear that every day the act of Creation was replayed according to the local myth of Creation. This was vital if the Cosmos was to be kept in balance and Chaos, or Isfet, kept at bay.

the purchase, the buyer would kill and then mummify the animal so that its spirit would then be able to fly to the local god to ask questions and to demand assistance. Millions of these animals were killed and stored in catacombs, where they lie to this day.

Animal Cults

The Egyptians did not, as it is popularly believed, worship animals. In every town, they adopted an animal in predynastic times that represented aspects of local strengths. This might have been an animal such as a wild falcon, which was known for its predatory nature, swooping unexpectedly. Or it could have been a lion or crocodile, animals revered not only for their great strength but also for their tremendous power. In many cases, towns might adopt the natural enemy of their neighbour: if one town adopted a cobra, then the neighbouring town might adopt the ichneumon, Egyptian mongoose, that terrorized and killed snakes. In later times, the local god and the animal that represented it became inextricably linked together. Ordinary Egyptians could not enter the temple or participate in formal religion. However, each temple raised the local animals, which could then be exchanged for goods. After

THE CREATION MYTHS

Several versions exist explaining how the Egyptian world came into being, and these myths are popularly regarded today as having existed concurrently. This suggests that the ancient Egyptians either had a choice of what they might believe or that their beliefs varied across regions—a truly polytheistic basis for religion.

In fact, archaeology shows quite clearly that these myths did not exist side by side, but on the contrary developed one from another, each encompassing the previous myths and adding to them, to the advantage of the following god. This took the form of true "oneupmanship" where later gods literally added on sections to their own advantage. How did these myths come about? They centered, as did almost everything in Egypt, on the king himself. The king, once crowned, served his local temple of the town in which he was born. Here he made daily offerings to some ancient spirit, or *ka,* of a long-dead local hero. If he could persuade this *ka* to return to earth, even briefly, he could negotiate Maat. While a local chief might encourage this in his own temple with simple food and drink, a king could offer instead gold and gifts beyond their wildest dreams. These gifts were then handed over permanently to the temple staff to be stored in their treasuries or used to enhance the temple. So long as this family of kings remained in the ascendant, his temple would remain the richest in the empire. But when a new family took over the throne, then the riches of the previous temple would slowly be removed and a new temple and god would take its place. The cosmologies, or creation myths, exactly reflect the rise and fall of the ruling houses.

Temples and the Servants

The earliest layouts have been discovered as patterns in the ground at Nekhen (modern El Kab) and texts state that the layout of all subsequent temples faithfully copied this first one.

Essentially the temple was a large house, built of stone to last an eternity. Temples had an outer courtyard, accessed only by privileged staff; an inner hall of columns, open to the principal Servitor only; and an inner sanctuary, which held a shrine with the cult image of the god or goddess.

Temples were labor intensive, needing the sweat of thousands of men over many years. The majority of these worked in fields or workshops, though many were specialists, especially the scribes.

The principal temple staff were called Servants of the God, and only the foremost of these could enter the sanctuary. In theory, this would be the king, but others were appointed in his place, since he could not be everywhere. Around 1200 B.C., this post became hereditary in many places, and thus a few families eventually became political threats to the king.

Below **Bull God Apis, the incarnation of Osiris, with Isis and Hathor, bronze votive figurine, Ptolemaic era.** As the embodiment of power and strength, the Bull God Apis has long been worshipped in Egypt. In Memphis, Egypt, a tomb was found that had been carefully prepared for the burial of real bulls that had been specially reared as Apis-bulls. An avenue to the tomb was lined with stone lions, and recesses inside held the carefully entombed remains of the Apis-bulls.

Above **The pyramid of Cheops at Giza.** People have sought the scrolls of Thoth since the time of Cheops. From the Arabian tales of Scheherezade in the eleventh century to the European alchemists who tried to "rediscover" the lost wisdom through experiments, the legend of Thoth has tantalized with its potential for unlimited knowledge—and also the secret to making gold.

CREATION ACCORDING TO THOTH

Thoth was revered in Middle Egypt, in the location today known as Ashmunein. Archaeology may yet have to verify the true age of this site, it is so large and the remains are so deep, but it is agreed that the myths that originate from the city are much older than the unification of Egypt.

Although Creation was believed to take place within his city in a time too ancient to remember, Thoth played only a minor part in it himself. According to the myth, in the time before Existence, there was nothing but a deep, formless, and water-filled void. In this primeval "soup" there existed female and male demi-urges—primeval spirits that could combine together to create physical forms.

Atum, Lord of Completeness and supreme god outside time and space, summoned males and females together. There was Nun, and his counterpart Nunet, symbolizing Nothingness; Kek and Keket, Darkness;

Amun and Amunet, Secrecy; and Huh and Huhet, representing Silence. The males took the form of frogs, the females of reptiles; and from their reproduction, the seed of Creation was sown. Then Atum, in a supreme act of power, created a surface over the Deep and, within it, a mound of land. The centre of this mound was Egypt, and the Nile itself spouted directly from the primordial waters.

At the epicenter of this mound was Ashmunein, and here Thoth, created by his master Atum, set up effective administration, laid down all knowledge and science, and recorded it in 42 volumes of knowledge. These rolls were then hidden away in deepest secrecy until mankind was ready to discover them.

The interplay of the eight demi-urges brought forth Creation on the mound of Ashmunein. Plants, animals, and then mankind, came into existence. Much later, the Greeks identified Thoth with their god Hermes, the Greek messenger of the gods, and Thoth's city became known as Hermopolis. As for the texts themselves, do they exist? Who can say. They were recorded in legend as the Hermetic texts, and wise men and alchemists from the medieval periods to the present day, seeking "the wisdom of the universe," have longed to discover the originals.

Egyptian kings through the centuries longed more than anything else to acquire this original wisdom of Thoth. They looked back to his reign as a time of perfection, before mankind came along and ignored Thoth's rules—an age they called the First Occurrence. The Westcar Papyrus, in Berlin, Germany, tells how Cheops, a king from the Fourth Dynasty and builder of the Great Pyramid at Giza, is introduced by one of his sons to a great magician. The king asks him if he knows the whereabouts of the lost wisdom. The magician, Djedi, tells him that the rolls lie in a series of seven boxes, watched over by an immortal serpent curled around the outer box. This in turn lies in the deepest part of the river near Coptos. Cheops orders him to go and get it, but the magician has to refuse. Destiny, undeniable to all ancient Egyptians, had fated that it would not be found by him and his family but by the next family of kings, the Fifth Dynasty.

Did the kings of this fated dynasty find the lost texts? History does not record it, but at their center in Heliopolis, the seers became the inheritors of wisdom. They passed this knowledge from one generation of kings to the next, including the secrets of how to communicate with the land of the gods, and how to maintain Maat.

THE CREATION BY PTAH

The Unification saw the building of Egypt's capital city at Memphis (around 3000 B.C.), where the local god Ptah was identified with craftsmen. As the kings built and then served in the great temple there, the ancient story of the creation according to Thoth eventually succumbed to a new myth.

The Shabaka Stone, now in the British Museum, relates how the Libyan King Shabaka, about 850 B.C., found a "worm-eaten leather roll" in the library of the temple of Ptah and ordered it copied onto stone for posterity. The language in it is truly ancient, and could not have been written easily in the time of Shabaka— suggesting that the story was true.

The new tale maintains the previous Creation myth of the god Thoth almost completely, although the eight demi-urges were not part of the mythology any more. Instead, it tells how, on the mound of Atum, the god Ptah was brought into existence. His myth is interesting as he conceived ideas in his heart, considered them with his reason, and then spoke the words from his mouth. As the words dropped from his tongue, they turned into physical entities. This is the earliest account of Creation through logic, literally *logos*, the spoken word.

Later sources that have since been considered by many researchers to be far more orthodox and less pagan recorded this same tale with only very minor differences. "In the beginning was the Word; and the Word was with God; and the Word was God." Very few people today realize just how similar the opening sentence of the gospel of St. John is to the ancient Egyptian myth of Ptah.

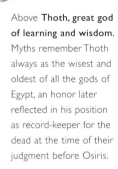

Above **Thoth, great god of learning and wisdom.** Myths remember Thoth always as the wisest and oldest of all the gods of Egypt, an honor later reflected in his position as record-keeper for the dead at the time of their judgment before Osiris.

Left *Ptah in his shrine,* from *Monumental History of Egypt* by W. Osburn (1854). The god Ptah is always shown in profile, wearing a tight-fitting skull-cap, false beard, and standing on a low plinth. He is a tall, slender figure wrapped as a mummy but holding a staff or scepter, which represents stability, life, and longevity. He is the creator god, builder of the boats to be used by the souls of the dead.

THE CREATION ACCORDING TO RE

The cult of the sun as creator of life flowered at the end of the Fourth Dynasty (around 2600 B.C.) and lasted only briefly. It was centered on Heliopolis, under the Kings of the late Fourth and early Fifth Dynasty (c. 2350 B.C.), and was a turn toward solar worship for the first time.

At Heliopolis the religious celebrants were called the Seers. Their job was to interpret signs, to read dreams (included as the Wise Men and Magicians of Genesis), and also to instruct the crown prince in his future duties as king.

Re, or Ra, was the sun in all its varied aspects. We have no idea how the name was spoken—the nearest hint, from Egyptian Foreign Office archives of the later Eighteenth Dynasty, suggest it should have been "Ria." In Egypt, the sun has many faces, as it always had; the first faint light widening above the hazy eastern hills; then the tongues of light that bring day, but no heat; later comes the striking of power as mists dissipate and scorching power burns the earth; the kinder sun of mid-afternoon, when the intensity of the sun's rays starts to soften; and finally, the fabled scarlet sunset and the sun's disappearance into the Other World. In mythological terms, Re was brought up into the physical world by Khepri, a cosmic scarab beetle pushing the ball of the sun upward into the mortal realm. The first light was Re-Hor-em-akhet, or Har-machis as the Greeks called it, "Re who is Horus of the horizon," where Horus is depicted as a falcon, wings outstretched, its pinion feathers mirroring the rays of the sun. As the sun grows stronger, the god Re himself was believed to steer the sun's boat into the mid-heavens where, at its zenith, it became Aten. As it set toward the western horizon, he took the form of Re-Hor-akhetwy, or Horakhte, the "Falcon of the second horizon." As the sun set, Re entered into the night barque and sailed into the parallel world of the spirits of the dead, becoming one with Atum, great lord of Creation and Completeness.

On the first mound of existence, the myth recounts, there grew a lotus flower. As the bud opened into sweet heady fullness, Re, the sun, emerged from the heart of the flower, bringing first light into the world. The bennu bird then emerged, the legendary phoenix of later Greek legend. Created in the image of a heron, the bennu was the first life to appear on this original

mound of existence and its cries broke the first silence. Re, the sun and greatest god of them all, brought into existence first Shu, air, and then Tefnut, moisture, to be brother and sister. In time, they married and soon bore two children: a son, Geb, and a daughter, Nut. Geb and Nut grew to love one another and wished to marry, but Shu, their father, opposed the match. One day he found them in a passionate embrace; angry, he separated them, forcing Geb to remain lying down while he held up Nut away from the body of her beloved brother. Geb became the earth; while Nut, with only the tips of her feet and fingers allowed to touch Geb, became the arch of the heavens above, her dress sparkling with the stars. So there she has remained, forever driven apart from her brother-lover by the power of air, her father.

Finally, Re, sorrowing because he needed to be banished from the earth every night, commanded that Thoth be the moon, a colder light than his own but maintaining a little of the old myth of Thoth.

In time Nut would give birth to four children, Osiris, Isis, Seth, and Nephthys. Isis later gave birth to Horus. These became the Nine gods of Heliopolis, and were known as the Great Ennead: Shu, Tefnut, Geb, Nut, Osiris, Isis, Seth, Nephthys, and Horus.

THE REVENGE OF RE

A favorite recurring myth relates how Re created a partner for himself, Sekhmet. This word in ancient Egyptian means "power, might" and the word became reality in the form of a wild lioness.

Re became angered with mankind, believing that they plotted against him continually. He is persuaded by the Great Ennead to send his Eye, seat of his power, in the form of the lioness Sekhmet, down to earth. Sekhmet kills humans relentlessly until all the land is filled with their moans of terror. Re, now calmer and ashamed of his anger, summons Sekhmet back to him. But she is now filled with blood-lust and will not come to his call. Re therefore tricks her. He changes the river Nile into the color of blood, which attracts her, but turns the water into beer. The lioness drinks deeply until, sated, she falls into a drunken slumber. When she awakens, she forgets why she has been sent and returns quietly to Re.

This myth reflects many aspects of Egypt itself. Every year, the Nile did indeed run the color of blood, as the first water of the Inundation arrived colored with the rich red topsoil from the southern mountains of Ethiopia (a potent image that was to be repeated in the stories of the plagues in the time of Moses). Sekhmet is a metaphor for plague of some kind or another, which occurred regularly before the coming of the new waters, and would have terrified the Egyptians. In Egypt during the summer months the temperature often soars, and in the past the river at this time would have been little more than a bare trickle, fetid and infected. Food and water would have been running out, with disease and famine ravaging the land until the coming of the fresh water banished disease.

Despite its great status, the sun was never popular as a single focus for worship, probably because it was open to view; the secrecy associated with ceremonies in darkened rooms brought power to those inside and mystery to those outside. Instead, Re was syncretized with other gods: Sobek (local god of the village Kom Ombo and the lake Fayum), Amun ("the hidden"), and others.

Left **Line fishing in the reeds, bas-relief, tomb of Kagemni, Sixth Dynasty.** The Nile teemed with life, in and out of the water, but no more so than after the annual inundation. This bounty was considered to be a gift from Hapy, the God of Inundation. He is normally shown as a man with a round belly and a headdress of reeds and lotus blossoms.

Left **Sandstone statue of Akhenaten, from Tell El Amarna.** In the mid-Eighteenth Dynasty (c.1350 B.C.) the sun-cult reappeared in a new guise in Middle Egypt under a king born as Amenhotep but renamed later on as Akhenaten. The Aten was not the disk of the sun, as some say, but the power of the sun at its zenith at midday. It was believed that you could no more look upon the face of the god than look upon the sun at noon, and that the god gave life to the earth just as the sun's rays touched everything on earth. The cult aroused political antagonism and fierce opposition from the army, who, after the death of Akhenaten, tried to eradicate all traces of it.

THE STORY OF AMUN

Although Amun was once one of the eight demi-urges of Ashmunein, he seems to have been a local god also, in Tod, south of Luxor. The Kings of the Twelfth Dynasty (approximately 1780 B.C.) were born here, but took the city of Luxor, a wide and fertile area on both banks of the Nile, as their place of rule. Here they overlaid the attributes of their Amun over those of the local god. The local god had been represented by a goose; their Amun was represented by a curly-horned ram.

The foundations of the great temple complex of Amun, today called Karnak, most probably began before the Twelfth Dynasty; but it was only now that real greatness first came to Luxor.

Amun wholeheartedly adopted the earlier myths of Thoth, Ptah, and Re. He united with Re, to become the supreme god Amen-Re, uniting Creation and Wisdom into a single force for the first time. He appeared upon the mound formed by Atum and created mankind himself, either by spitting—the Egyptian word "to spit," *remetch,* was the same as the word for mankind—or, as is more frequently believed, by masturbation. His seed then formed the very essence of all Creation.

Within the temple of Karnak, the rite celebrated daily by the king had this act of Creation at its center. Images show Amen-Re with an engorged phallus, while a succession of kings kneels before it and venerates it. In this version of the story, however, Amen-Re becomes head of the Nine Gods, supplanting and removing Horus, son of Isis, from the story as told earlier in the myths of Heliopolis, the cult-center of Re. During the Eighteenth Dynasty (around 1550–1075 B.C.), the period of Egyptian imperial expansion, warrior kings came to Karnak to beg victory from the hands of Amen-Re. Later, in thanks for their success, they poured booty plundered from foreign lands into the coffers at the Karnak temple.

Successive kings added to the temple building complex for more than 500 years, until eventually Karnak became so rich that it challenged the wealth and therefore the very authority of the king himself. As a result, in the Late Period, kings living in the

Above **A young Ramesses II supports a staff that bears the ram's head of Amun, granite statue, Karnak.** It was believed that Amun could assume any form that he wished, including other gods. At the height of his powers, in the Eighteenth Dynasty, he did subsume many of the lesser gods. Apart from the ram, Amun is often represented as a bearded man wearing a cap from which two plumes emerge.

> *He created "five days that were not days, and five nights that were not nights."*
>
> PLUTARCH (C. A.D. 45–120), *DE ISIDE ET OSIRIDE*

north managed to dominate the temple and control its enormous wealth by "marrying" their daughters to Amen-Re. These god's wives lived as virgins and assisted the king or his appointed deputy in the temple in the daily enactment of the first act of Creation. They became known as the "God's hand." As wife of Amen-Re, they controlled the wealth of the home, as did every Egyptian woman. The wealth of Karnak became theirs, which they were then able to divert into the coffers of their fathers in the north.

THE OSIRIS LEGEND

Amen-Re, ruler of Egypt, grew old and weary. Thoth, oldest and wisest of the gods, attempted to persuade him to retire to his solar duties in the heavens, but Amen-Re adamantly refused.

Thoth challenged him, predicting that Nut, the sky, would give birth to four children, and that the first-born would rule Egypt in his place. Amen-Re remained stubborn and swore that Nut would never give birth, not in any day or night of the month.

Thoth's prediction seemed doomed. But he had a plan. Khons, son of Amun and his divine consort Mut, now occupied the Moon, where he resided alone, playing *senet,* a favorite and most ancient board game in Egypt that is almost identical to modern backgammon. Thoth challenged Khons to a game, but demanded a parcel of moonlight if he won. They played and, of course, Thoth won. With the moonlight, he created "five days that were not days, and five nights that were not nights." The five days and nights, not part of any month, were then added between the end of one year and before the next, bringing the days of the year from 360 to 365, righting the calendar. The moon, weakened by the loss of some of its moonlight, has waned a bit every month ever since.

Finally Thoth could fulfil his prophecy. On the first day, Nut bore Osiris; on the second, a daughter Isis; on the third, a son Seth; on the fourth, a daughter Nephthys; and on the fifth day, she rested to recover from the strange multiple births. It is said that when Osiris was born a voice cried out from the heavens proclaiming his birth.

A New Ruler

Osiris and Isis grew in beauty and wisdom. Isis, known as Great of Magic, was both beautiful and very strong, and was the loyal protector of her handsome and fit husband Osiris. For his part, Osiris brought agriculture and wealth to Egypt. But still Amen-Re refused to retire, despite the pleas of Thoth and Isis.

ISIS

Isis, sister-wife of Osiris, was revered as the perfect wife and mother. At the same time she was called Great of Magic for her part in the drama of her husband's life and death. In the Late Period (727 B.C. onward) her cult grew and temples to her were built all over Egypt. The Romans (30 B.C. onward) found her cult appealing, and Iseums (Isis temples) were built throughout the Roman Empire, as far as the northern reaches of Britain.

Above **The golden Isis, sarcophagus of Ramesses III (c. 1184–1153 B.C.).** Isis was, and still is, worshipped across Egypt. She is the protector of the dead, and her winged form often graces sarcophagi.

At last, Isis tricked him. In his old age, as Amen-Re walked, he drooled. Isis gathered his spittle, mixed it with dust and created a snake, which bit him on his heel. Amen-Re seemed in danger of dying. He called for help from Isis, Great of Magic. Isis, however, could only heal him if he told her his secret name.

According to Egyptian mythology, everyone has a secret name; if this is passed to anyone else, they can assume total control over you. Amen-Re knew this and therefore resisted. At length, weakened, he had no choice. He spoke the name; Isis pronounced it and was thus able to banish him to his barque to rule the heavens and guide the sun. She handed the throne to her husband Osiris.

Above *Anubis ministers to Osiris, Attended by Isis and Nephthys,* from *Gods of the Egyptians* by E. Budge (1857–1934). The legend of Osiris is one of the most enduring of Egyptian myths; the classic good versus evil. Though murdered, Osiris would rise again. Anubis, as the patron of embalming, provided rare herbs and ointments for the preparation of the body. He also supplied linen, specially prepared so that it would never decay.

Right **Anubis as a jackal, terracotta pectoral pendant (c. 664–525 B.C.).** The cult of Anubis is very old and probably precedes that of Osiris. His role has always been connected with the dead, and in the Osiris legend it became more directly linked with guarding the dead in the Other World. Nephthys is always given as his mother, though the father varies— usually Seth or Re.

THE MURDER OF OSIRIS

Osiris, now King of Egypt, was beloved by all, while Isis, shining in gowns and crowns of brilliant gold, was always at his side, always the loyal and devoted sister-wife. She became the role-model for all women of Egypt. Seth, however, grew ugly, contorted with anger and jealousy at his successful brother Osiris and resentful that, as second son, he was entitled to nothing. His life filled with hate, which he focused on Osiris. He was united reluctantly with his sister Nephthys, although she, like most people, adored Osiris and Isis.

Osiris went away from Egypt into battle while Isis remained and ruled on his behalf, much to Seth's fury. As Osiris returned victorious, Seth with 72 loyal friends came to greet him and welcomed him to a grand banquet that they had organized in his honor. At the end of the banquet, doors opened and a coffin of solid gold was wheeled in. As everyone gasped in awe at its beauty and great weight, Seth called, "It shall belong to he who fits it best." The coffin had been made deliberately to fit the exact size of Osiris, bigger, broader, and stronger than all other men.

Each man tried, but none of them fitted it. At last it was Osiris's turn. As he stepped into it, Seth and his cronies slammed the lid shut, bolted it down, and fled with it to the Nile. They threw it in the river, so the coffin containing the body of the dead Osiris was swept north by the current and was lost.

Eventually, the coffin was washed by the currents of the river onto the shore of Byblos, where a great tree grew around it, enclosing it within the trunk.

The King of Byblos came and marveled at its great size and straightness and ordered it cut down to form a central column within his palace. The column-trunk emitted lights and sounds, and everyone who came near it was mysteriously healed.

In Egypt, Seth now ruled the land with terrible cruelty, while Isis, desolate, wept and mourned in a secret invisible island in the Nile delta called Chemmis. She heard of stories of the miracles of Byblos and knew at once what had happened. She sailed north at once, but on the way transformed herself by magic into an ugly old crone. When she arrived, she went straight to the palace and offered her services to the King and Queen as nursemaid to their son. They, impressed by her age and apparent wisdom, accepted happily. Isis stipulated one condition, however; they must give her full charge of the child and never question or observe what she did. The couple reluctantly agreed.

Every night, strange cries and lights came from the child's room. At last, unable to control herself a moment longer, the Queen made a tiny hole in the door to watch what was happening. As she watched, Isis spoke words of power, and was transformed from an ugly woman into her beautiful self, clad in gold clothes with a cloak of feathers that formed great wings like a bird. She then flew up like a kite over the child, swooping and crying. At last, she picked up the child gently in her wings and placed it straight on a brazier of burning coals.

The Queen, in terror, burst open the door and confronted Isis in her power. Isis, dismayed, rebuked the Queen, saying that she had been burning away the child's humanity, making him an immortal, but that the Queen's entrance had destroyed her work. The Queen, desolate, offered Isis anything in the palace as recompense. Immediately, Isis asked for the giant pillar in which her husband was encased.

Isis freed the coffin containing the body of her husband and took it back with her to Chemmis. That night, she transformed herself once again into the golden kite, but with her wings breathed life into the phallus of Osiris, and conceived a child of his spirit. Later, under the cover of darkness, Seth crept in, seized the body and tore it into 14 pieces, which he flung into the Nile.

From that day, Isis, pregnant and loyal to the last, sought out the torn pieces of her husband's body. At Philae, she found his head, at Abydos, she found his spine, and wherever she found a piece, a temple was erected. But the phallus was eaten by a fish, forever

OSIRIS AND ABYDOS

It was believed that the dead became *akh*, or transfigured spirits, and took the form of stars. According to inscriptions, in earliest times Osiris was associated with the constellation of Orion, seen by the Egyptians merely as the "belt" of the hunter we see today.

Long before Egypt was unified, the site of Abydos became holy to Osiris. The first Kings of Egypt, who originated further south in Nekhen and who also built Memphis, the capital in the north, chose to be buried here because of the sacredness of the site. At Abydos, probably at around the time of the

building of the pyramids—the Old Kingdom (2700–2181 B.C.)—a shrine was built for Osiris. The site later fell into disuse.

Around 1500 years later, Seti I, the second King of the Nineteenth Dynasty, decided to renew it. Workmen uncovered the old shrine, now underground, and carved the ancient walls with his name. Every year, in a special secret series of rooms, the resurrection of Osiris was reenacted, giving hope to every Egyptian that they too would have life after death. Thus Abydos became the first true pilgrimage site.

lost. Isis now bandaged the pieces together, forming the first mummy, and placed it in a tomb at Abydos. She said words of magic over the body, the words of the Opening of the Mouth, thus freeing it as an *akh*, a resurrected body. Thus was the resurrected Osiris, the first to travel over the western horizon where he settled at the entrance to the land of the dead, giving the promise of an eternal life to all mortals afterward. The care lavished on the dead in ancient Egypt is the same care that was first bestowed on Osiris.

Nearby towns to Abydos yielded their own local gods, which became part of the legend. From Assiut, the local god Wepwawet, the Opener of the Ways, became Anubis, the guardian dog that crouched at the western horizon, ensuring that no living person could accidentally travel across to the land of spirits. He had to inspect the body, check it was dead and was properly prepared for resurrection. Paintings show a priest wearing a mask of Anubis carrying out the inspection. Thoth of Ashmunein now became the Recorder of the Verdict.

Below *Anubis Weighs the Heart of the Deceased Hunefer* from *Book of the Dead,* known as *Papyrus of Hunefer* (1294–1279 B.C.). On the left, Horus guides the deceased to the Great Scales, which are weighing his heart against Maat, to determine if he has told the truth. On the right, Horus leads the deceased to his father Osiris, who sits in a shrine protected by Isis and Nephthys.

THE BATTLES OF HORUS AND SETH

Below **Personified Wadjat Eye of Horus holding the sacred flame, fresco, tomb of Pashed, Thebes, Ramesside period.** The Wadjat Eye, or healed eye, is shown here offering incense, as it emerges from the hills of the west bank of Luxor. As an amulet, the Wadjat Eye was usually placed over the embalming incision of a dead body, ensuring evil spirits could not enter it.

With Osiris removed into the land of the dead, Seth continued to rule Egypt, though this inheritance rightfully belonged to Horus, the son of Osiris. Isis had raised her son in secret on Chemmis, an island near Bhutto. As soon as her son became old enough, Isis, his mother and protector, made him swear he would avenge his father's murder.

Horus thus declared war on Seth. Bloody battles were fought, lasting many years. Every time, Horus triumphed and then demanded of the Great Ennead (of which he was not part, according to this myth) the return of his father's land and title. The Ennead always prevaricated.

Seth appeared in a variety of different guises—sometimes a pig, or a hippopotamus, sometimes a crocodile. Always Horus sought him out and killed him, but to no avail. On one occasion, Seth put out the left eye of Horus. His mother replaced it with the healed eye, or Wadjat Eye. This had power and magic of its own, and could be sent out against those who opposed him, always returning to its master. It was said that the eye Horus lost represented the moon, and that the time it took to heal equaled one full revolution of the moon.

The Creation of Hathor

Horus went to his mother and demanded that she represent him before the tribunal of the Ennead and help him win his inheritance. She once more wavered and urged him to yet more fights. Horus became enraged. Later that day, Isis fell asleep on the hills of the west bank of Luxor. Horus came to her, cut off her head and buried it in the sand. From one eye grew the white lotus, from the other, the blue lotus.

When she awoke, she sought her head, in vain, and, at last, in desperation, took the head of the only animal she could find, a cow that emerged from the hillside. Isis was thus transformed into Hathor and became the consort of Horus. As a result, Horus now took the title Kamutef, or "bull of his mother."

One explanation for this unusual story is that every member of the Ennead, except Horus, had a partner. To rectify this, Hathor was created, and was therefore a later addition to the myth-cycle.

The Victory of Horus

After 40 years of fighting, Horus was finally vindicated by the tribunal of the Ennead. Seth and all evil was banished and Horus was granted kingship over the entire land of Egypt, with Isis-Hathor at his side as Queen. From this time onward all kings were identified with Horus. The double crown, symbol of political unity in Egypt, even took the form of the Wadjat Eye. This became the basis of the evil eye of later legend.

Origins in History

The story of the battles between Horus and Seth is told on a later papyrus to that of the legend of Osiris and does not fit entirely with the older myth of Osiris and Isis. In the original story, Horus was the son of Isis, conceived with the spirit of her husband, thus making Seth his uncle. In the account of the Battles of Horus and Seth, the two are brothers, Horus fighting for his rightful place as Elder Brother. The Greeks sought to separate the two, calling Horus the Child, Hor-pa-khered or Harpocrates. In the story where he and Seth are brothers, he is called Horus the Elder, Hor-wer, or, in Greek, Haroeris.

The myth of the battles is a folk-memory of the war between two cities, Nekhen and Naqada, fought to unify the Nile valley in ancient times before the first unification. Horus was the local god of Nekhen, and Seth of Naqada. The military supremacy of Nekhen, whose leader became the first King of Egypt, over the defeated Naqada was thus remembered in this myth where Horus finally manages to vanquish the evil Seth.

In Edfu, home of Horus, every year festivals were held to celebrate the victory. Reliefs show an actor playing Horus who, publicly and no doubt to great acclaim, hunted down the creatures associated with Seth in the streets of the town. As well, images of kings show them as Horus, hunting Seth the evil one. In the Roman era, a statue now in the British Museum shows Horus dressed as a Roman Centurion, riding horseback and spearing Seth, the crocodile, beneath him. In time, this first became the story of St. Menas, and later St. George and the Dragon. The Egyptian name for Seth, *Sutekh*, may have evolved into the word Satan.

Horus, Fighter of all Evil

As a triumphant figure it is not surprising that the might of Horus was turned toward earthly illness. It was believed that nature destined everything to be perfect, according to the First Occasion, but demons existed that would bring illness and much chaos to humans and to the world. These had to be driven out. Papyri listed symptoms of the sick, a diagnosis, and a prognosis, this being either "something against which I can struggle" or "something against which I can do nothing." Lists then gave external or internal remedies, amulets, and words of power. Horus-cippus figures—small, rounded, upright stela carved with reliefs of Horus—were used in the treatment of illness. They show the child of Isis with a serpent in each hand, often standing upon two crocodiles, the whole covered with magical texts. Most of them were nonsense: the word "abracadabra" came from one of these. Water was poured over the cippus figure, absorbing the power of the words, and collected in a dish at the base. The water could then be used as a powerful remedy to drive out evil. Egyptians believed in the figures and would position them at the front of the house or in the garden as protection.

Left **The god Horus in the form of a falcon, wearing the double crown, temple of Horus, Edfu, Ptolemaic era.** Ancient Djeba, today's Edfu, was believed to be the location of the battle between Horus and Seth. The temple complex was begun around 237 B.C., and two huge granite statues of Horus as a falcon stand at its entrance. A number of Horus gods exist; the oldest was believed to be a creator god, represented by the falcon who flew at the beginning of time.

Below **Sarcophagus with eye of Horus, Anubis, and mourners, c.1450 B.C.** This sarcophagus of Lady Madja, Eighteenth Dynasty, is from the western necropolis of Gurnet Murrai, Egypt. The eye of Horus has, and still does have, great potency. Of the many Horus gods, subsumed into this one, all were connected with the sun. The Wadjat Eye has been linked by some with the "eye in the sky," seen at eclipses of the sun.

AFRICAN MYTHOLOGY

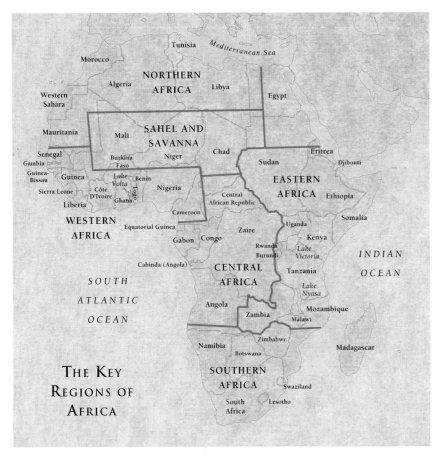

THE KEY REGIONS OF AFRICA

Africa is a vast continent comprising a diverse range of landscapes and economies, and a history of mankind traced, archaeologically, through more than a million years. There may be no connections between those distant days and the present, but there is certainty about the long histories of some of the people who currently inhabit the continent. While northern Africa, the Mediterranean, and the Red Sea shorelines were in trading contact with southern Europe and western Asia 4,000 years ago, the southern part of Africa was remote, and isolated from the Western world, until European exploration brought seafarers and traders to the country in the fifteenth century, and settlers thereafter.

The Khoi-San people of southern Africa and the Pygmy people of the great forests of central Africa represent ancient lines of humankind who may once have been more widely spread across the continent. Later migrations of Negroid people, taller in stature and more varied in physical type, moved south and east at different times in the last two millennia, taking up empty land and infringing on lands of the earlier inhabitants.

ORAL TRADITION

There was no written language in Africa until Islam spread westward across the Mediterranean plains in the eighth and ninth centuries A.D., and southward in the twelfth century across the Sahara Desert, into the interior of Western Africa, and through the Sahel. Europeans brought their own written scripts, along with the Christian missionaries, shipping agents, and trading companies in the fifteenth and sixteenth centuries, to the coasts of Western Africa, then around to the southern and eastern shores, and eventually into the interior. Writing impinged only slightly on the mass of the population, for whom an oral tradition had long existed. Written language and knowledge of the Koran (Qu'ran) and the Bible had a social impact, associated as they were with external influences, power, and the rise of elite individuals or groups, but a resilient oral culture survived into the twentieth century, albeit with lessening prominence in a technologically-advanced world.

Right **Yoruba twins.** In African mythology the theme of twins is common. The original placenta of Amma, the supreme being of the Dogon people, was a double one to attach the pair of twin Nommo, her offspring. This doubling up or twinning represents the formation of the earth and the sky, the creative act of Amma.

The stories that are examined here cover a range of African societies from north to south, and east to west, from coastal and island people to those of the interior, the vast savanna lands, forests, and mountains. They come from differing economies, many containing symbolic references to pastoralism, agriculture, fishing, metalworking, and other livelihoods. Some are sacred, and others secular. Invariably the stories have significance to the tellers and the listeners in terms of the history, or the origins of the people themselves, or their beliefs in the creation, or the origin of their worlds.

African creation stories have some similarities with understandings of creation in Western preliterate cultures. Knowledge of a supreme being is common to most African traditions. There is an array of lesser gods, goddesses, and spirits that bridge the gap between the supreme being and men and women in their daily lives. Embedded in some of these stories is the history of specific ethnicities—ancestors form a central part of the mythology, forming a link between the present day and the origins of both the people and their world.

Christianity and Islam have been newcomers in the history of African religions, and although they have made quite a powerful impact on African people, there has been a very strong resilience toward these influences in some of the older traditions and mythologies.

THE IMPORTANCE OF MYTH

The stories included here are categorized under a series of headings, but these are artificial categories, and there is a crossover between types of stories. The mythology of the African peoples has evolved over very long periods of time, and has retained some consistency within the changing worlds. Creation myths and stories of the origin of a people tap into historic, even ancient understandings of where people came from, and how they perceived their world in earlier times. Myths that involve animals are often about people, their faults, weaknesses,

Left **Obas (kings) of Benin performing for the supreme god.** This war ritual was done to honor the god of creation. The acrobatic dance, Amufi, recalls a legendary war of the gods against the sky.

Below *North Africa and the Sahara* **by Alberto Cantino (b.1502).** This map shows the populations of the north of the African continent, and traces the movement of the cultures. Strong storytelling traditions were resistant to outside influences.

strengths and foibles. Heroic stories, likewise, tell of people who capture the imagination and provide an empowering model for ordinary mortals. Trickster myths can have close relevance for people in today's world of the misuse of power, and in their dealings with authority in various forms. Some myths are relevant to people of all times.

Today, as in earlier times, the mythology of the African peoples has significance in the socialization and education of children and young adults. In addition, it provides entertainment, a function that was of more importance in times when there was no mass media, but which continues to be significant, in some areas more than others. In parts of Africa the telling of creation myths and stories of origin is under pressure where schooling in Western methods puts emphasis on rational thought. The telling of stories in the homestead or village used to be performed by the elderly, which gave them important roles in educating the younger generation. In a changing world, this tradition is not always maintained.

SIGNS, KNOWLEDGE, AND CREATION

The history of an extensive region of Western Africa is known through the oral traditions of the Bambara, Malinke, Diala, and Kassonke language groups and through the stories of populations that now inhabit the lands that lie between the Atlantic coast of Senegal and the deserts of northern Nigeria and the countries that border the Gulf of Guinea.

Providing a common thread, the mythology tells of an original homeland in the Mande, the upper reaches of the Niger River, and of 30 related families that dispersed from the Mande in the twelfth century to found the Mali Empire. Subsequently, they returned to their land of origin at intervals, recording their genealogies and performing certain rituals. The Dogon were, and are still, settled in the rugged mountains of Bandiagara, and maintain much of the traditional religion and mythology. Remote from the influences of modernity in their mountain homes, the Dogon practice a sign system of communication that links back to their earliest history, bringing together an understanding of creation, and with it, knowledge.

The Creation of Day and Night, The Bat Myth

There are many stories that tell of the creation of night. One, from the Kono people of Sierra Leone, relates how the creator provided light from the Sun by day, and twilight from the Moon, so that it was never dark, nor was it ever cold. The deity asked the Bat to take a basket of darkness to the Moon, but the Bat became tired, put down his load to rest, and to feed. Meanwhile, some animals discovered the basket, and opened it, causing the darkness to escape. Since that time, the Bat has slept through the day and woken at twilight to start his eternal journey in search of the darkness that had escaped, and to try to resume his futile attempt to put it back in the basket, and continue his errand to the Moon.

Among the Yoruba pantheon of gods, it is the supreme deity Olorun, creator of the universe, who is responsible for the creation of day and night. The supreme being also features in the separation of day from night among the Abaluyia people of Kenya, where Wele, the creator god, put the Sun and the Moon in the sky. But the Sun fought the Moon, and thrust him from his position, then the Moon knocked the Sun down. Finally, Wele decreed that the Sun

Right **God of the sun.** There are a number of myths that credit a supreme being with the creation of night and day. According to some legends, it can be the messenger of the god, who misreads the god's instructions, that throws the sun's motion into chaos.

MARKING SIGNS

For the Dogon, signs are inscribed on rocks, on the ground, in caves, and on gourds. The first signs that were created were those of a placenta on which were marked signs denoting seeds and beings—two pairs of twins, the antecedents of man and woman. Inscriptions on the landscape are reminders of the power and meaning of features of the land to ancient people, and to the dependence of all people on the land.

A symbol of significance in Dogon understandings of creation is the placenta; they believe every human placenta to be a replica of the placenta of the womb of Amma, the supreme being, who conceived the universe.

According to various stories, the egg within which primordial events occurred was divided into a double placenta, each part of the placenta containing a pair of twin Nommo—the offspring of Amma. Each twin was made up of both male and female principles, with one principle more dominant than the other. The male Nommo, Ogo, forced his way out of the egg. He hurtled through space clutching a torn fragment of placenta that became the Earth with a predominantly male soul, creating an imbalance and an impurity. Ogo realized he couldn't rule without his twin, and tried to find her, but could not. According to legend, he still searches for her.

should be out in the day, and the Moon would shine
at night. An ancient Twa story also gives responsibility
to the supreme being, Khonvum, for the ordering of
creation of the earth and the sky, the
forests and the animals. At night,
it is the task of Khonvum to
ensure the regular renewal of
the Sun in the morning. Twa
storytellers say that he collects
together broken fragments of the stars, and
hurls them at the Sun to ensure that it will rise again.

In another range of stories, night and death come
together. A Maasai myth tells of the ancestral figure
Le-eyo, who was responsible for proclaiming on
the death of a child that the child should go away,
and then come back; and also had the job of telling
the Moon that it should go, and stay
away. Poor Le-eyo became extremely confused when his
own child died. In his confusion, he incorrectly told the
child to go away, and stay away,
and told the Moon to go, and then return.
Because of this error, say the Maasai, the moon has
continued in its cycle of continually rising and
setting, waxing and waning.

> *There is always
> something new out of Africa.*
> PLINY THE ELDER (A.D. 23—79)

Opposite page **Upright Nommo (an offspring of Amma).** A Nommo figure with raised arms symbolizes the close connection of the land, river, and sky. It also represents the male Nommo twin, Ogo, who falls from the heavens to earth.

Below Mask of Gu. Ogun, the god of war, is recognized by different culture groups, such as the Yoruba. He is the protective god of blacksmiths and hunters. "Gu" refers to the metal used for making tools or swords.

The Myth of the Sky God

Across the length and breadth of Africa, people of widely different origins and cultures have a mythology which gives the founding ancestors divine status. They are honored in terms of social relationships, and provide a harmony that holds societies together. The converging of social organization and mythology are well demonstrated by the pastoral Nilotic people inhabiting the floodplains of the upper Nile basin in Sudan, western Ethiopia, and northern Uganda, among whom are the Dinka, Shilluk, Nuer, and Anuak. Social organization is dependent on close-knit ties with land, river, and sky. The changing annual pattern of seasons, alternating between rain that floods the river and the drying out of the land, are essential to the survival of their cattle herds and themselves. As in all flat lands, the horizon is close, and the arch of the sky is more extensive than in landscapes of hills or mountains. A common thread of belief in a powerful sky god is found throughout these groups. Offerings and sacrifices are made in simple shrines throughout the land, which are situated on forked branches, small mud-constructed altars, rocks, man-made stools, and pots. A narrative mythology gives praise, through songs and poems, to the god-kings who are also the ancestors. Central to this is the organization of clans, and lines of descent that link the present-day people with their ancestors.

At the core of the mythology is the world of earth and sky, which were believed to have joined so that the first humans could move between earth and sky, and have access to the sky god. The sky and the earth were linked with a rope, just in reach of a man with outstretched arms. In one myth, the first humans, Garang and Abuk, had to be careful not to lift their hoes or pestles in case they touched the sky god. The founder of the Shilluk royal dynasty, Nyikang (or Nyikango), is, in one story, descended from a man who came from the sky.

Each new king is immortalized as Nyikango, and becomes both king and priest. In another telling, Nyikango was created as a cow, and married a female crocodile, or a womanlike crocodile.

THE STORY OF GU

The Fon stories of Mawu and Lisa vary. In one, the use of metal as a source for making tools is told. Mawu sent his "child" Lisa to the earth with a metal sword to show the people how to clear the forests, plow the cleared land, and cultivate crops. A metal sword is called "gu", a word that is associated also with the Yoruba god, Ogun. Gu is the name of the god of metal to this day among the Fon people. He protects warriors, blacksmiths, and hunters; today he is also the protector of trucks, bicycles, and cars.

Mawu-Lisa Myth

Among the Fon people who inhabit a region that used to be called Dahomey (now Benin), is a story of Mawu and Lisa, the Moon and her twin brother, the Sun. They combine to form the androgynous creator figure, Mawu-Lisa, who oversees a range of gods of the weather, the earth, metal, and the forests, and has a daughter called Gbadu. Mawu-Lisa created the world, and then delegated different duties to the other gods. This story of creation is like those in other traditions, invoking an evolving order of creation over a period of days leading to the creation of man on the final day.

The Fon are a warlike ethnic group with a complex history of fighting. Some scholars believe that the Fon may have appropriated the gods of their vanquished foes, which may be a partial explanation for their composite pantheon of gods. In war, the gods of the vanquished had to be appeased, so they were assimilated into the Fon pantheon. Mawu-Lisa was from the Aja people in western Dahomey.

In another myth, Mawu and Lisa are said to have been born to a primordial mother, Nana Buluka, who was creator of the world. In this telling, the division of night and day is narrated, since Mawu lived in the west and was the Moon, and Lisa lived in the east and was the Sun. The division of male and female is also implied, for the female Moon came together with the male Sun in an eclipse. The Sun is fierce and fatherly; the Moon is gentle and motherly. The Fon associate eclipses with Mawu and Lisa coming together and making love, which in the past resulted in the birth of a hierarchy of gods, all of them twins.

Above **A Dogon cosmology stool.** The three parts of the stool reflect the concept of the cosmos. The seat (sky disc) is connected to the base (earth), by a central tree. The figures represent ancestral twins.

Left **The heavenly blacksmith.** This Dogon cultural hero, also known as the thief of fire, was the bringer of the art of metal work to the people.

Above **Benin butchers.** In the palace of the Benin Obas (kings), cows were the most prestigious of animal sacrifices. Special butchers were used to prepare the offerings.

Right **San rock paintings.** San cultures of Zimbabwe died out many centuries ago, but the stories of people's spirits going up to the sky, to become "star" ancestors, after their death are recorded in rock art.

THE KHOI-SAN PEOPLE

Like the Pygmies, the San, or Bushmen, are descended from an ancient line, and used to be spread more widely across southern, central, and eastern Africa. The San, like Pygmies, are small of stature, and come from a late Stone Age culture that are hunter-gatherers in their traditional lifestyle. Evidence of their former habitations is found not only in collections of stone tools distributed widely across the southern half of the continent, but also in rock paintings, which are also abundant. Later, southward migrations of Negroid people, with a different language and culture, established contact with these people. It was customary to believe that the new arrivals destroyed the existing communities. Recent research suggests that the San

established trading contact with the new arrivals, taking on new practices and a modified culture. Over time many of their communities merged.

One such modification was pastoralism. The Khoi people, with languages of a similar type to the San, became herders of cattle and sheep. Groups of the Khoi and San people were encountered behind the coastal lands of the Cape of Good Hope and in the high plateaus of the veldt when Dutch settlers arrived after A.D. 1650. Competition over land drove the San and the Khoi to the margins of good land, the San more able to survive in the dry semidesert of the Namib and the Kalahari. In these remote areas, their distinctive culture—including their mythologies—endured, though under pressure from external influences, at least into the twentieth century.

One story tells of a man or a woman's spirit, on death, going up to the sky and becoming a star. Stars are seen by some as the ancestors of the San. There is, however, as with the Pygmies, a wide range of stories about death, rather than a single myth. Death is also associated with water holes, and the belief that people's spirits go to a huge hole in the ground after death which they find by going along a "Bushman's path." In this version, it is the heart that goes to the sky. In the wide, open spaces of veldt and semidesert, the sky is expansive, and it is unsurprising that a cosmology of sun, moon, and stars is very prominent.

The supreme being, called Nladima by some San groups, is the creator. The word Nladima also means "sky." Nladima and his wife are believed to live in the sky, and humans and animals are their children. Another figure, with more evil characteristics, is Great G'mama, who shoots arrows of evil at humans.

MYTHS OF ORIGIN

The following myth is just one example of many myths that have a similar central figure, a crucial link between the sky god and ancestral origins. Variations on this myth would be dependent on the particular oral traditions and culture groups.

Efé, the First Man

Among the Pygmies, there is a story told of the first man, Efé. The story combines elements of a sky god with ancestors, and the forest environment in which the Pygmies live. The creator god placed Efé on the earth, but recalled him to heaven to hunt, drawing him out of the forest on a liane (vine) that festoons the tall trees of the forest. Efé went across the heavens

until he found, and killed, an elephant whose tusks were the size of trees. Everyone was happy, especially the women, and they feasted to satisfaction. Efé was eventually sent back to his forest home where nobody recognized him, but there was some fear because of the spears he carried. After some time, Efé's brother recognized him, and asked him why he had been away so long. Efé told him of their father in heaven, and of the gifts, including spears, their father had sent. At this discovery, there was much joy and wild celebration. Pygmy myths are manifold, and vary across a large geographical area. Like the San and Khoi people, much of their mythology centers on the universe—

Above **Pygmy mask.** Although little is known about the Pygmies, they are believed to be an ancient race of African peoples. These hunter-gatherers probably used this mask as part of an initiation ceremony.

Left **Ceremonial cow head from Nigeria.** Cattle have great symbolic significance in many African cultures, and have a special place in the language of the Shilluk, Nuer, Dinka, and Auak people. In traditional African economy, cattle were the sole measure of wealth and status.

Above **The chameleon bringing death.** The chameleon is a wayward messenger of the supreme being. One legend sees the animal forgetting to deliver his message of immortality to human beings. Another sees him being tricked into handing over new skins, intended for humans, to a snake.

stars, the sun, and the moon over which the supreme being reigns, and from which man gains his spiritual essence. Spiritual fire is part of this, coming from the heavens at birth, and returning with death. Fire is sacred, and Pygmies maintain fire in fireboxes, and carry it with them on their journeys.

Pe, the Moon, is associated with fecundity, and feasts of the Moon are women's celebrations, while those of the Sun belong to men. Many myths incorporate the founding ancestral figure, Efé, and can be seemingly read with an historical meaning concerning the origins and movement of the people. Some tell of Efé crossing a vast stretch of water in a boat, others tell of frozen lands far away. Some have associations with the creation stories of Koranic (Qu'ranic) and Biblical origins, such as those telling of the coming of a great flood.

In one story, Efé escaped from the chaos of war by climbing into a tree through a hole in the trunk, staying there while the battles raged throughout the area. A chameleon man came along with his axe, and cut into the trunk of the tree. From this hole, water flowed, forming a river. Efé emerged completely dry from this watery hole.

MYTHS OF DEATH

Myths concerning death and the origin of death come in different forms. The eminent anthropologist J.G. Frazer, in a study of African myths, divided them into four types: those that described "the two messengers," those concerned with the waxing and waning of the moon, those about the serpent and the casting of its skin, and those about the banana plant. Over and above these are individual stories that are specific to a people or an area.

The story of the two messengers and the origin of death is widely told throughout Africa. The creator god sent the chameleon to earth to tell humans that they would live eternally, and he sent the lizard with a contrary message that humans would die. The chameleon dawdled on the way, but the lizard scurried to deliver its message, arriving before the chameleon. Thereafter, death became the destiny of all humans.

A variation of this myth is found in Liberia. The creator, Sno-Nyosa, sent four sons to visit the Earth. When he wanted them to return, they declined as they wanted to stay. The Earth also wanted them to stay. One by one they were recalled by Sno-Nyosa's magic power of death. It is said that before the creator quarreled with the Earth about the return of his sons, there was no death.

A different story of death comes from the Kabyles, a Berber people from Northern Africa. Here, in an ancient myth believed to predate Islamic influences introduced in the seventh and eighth centuries A.D., there is a woman described as the First Mother of the World. A woman known in many regions, she is responsible for bringing bad omens, misfortune, and ultimately death.

In an interesting analogy with Greek mythology, the Mende of Sierra Leone have an understanding that, after the rites of death have been performed, the soul crosses the water to reach the country of the departed. In this journey the soul is assisted by the ancestors who inhabit the territory in between, and by the burial goods that accompany the body in the grave. Among the Mende, as is found among the Baganda in Eastern Africa, the ancestors are part of the spirit world, mediating between the supreme being and humans, sometimes meeting with humans in their dreams, when the Baganda believe that the human soul leaves the body temporarily.

A PANTHEON OF GODS

In Western Africa around the Gulf of Guinea, an extensive mythology has evolved around a supreme being and a pantheon of minor deities. Among the Yoruba of southwestern Nigeria there are cults of minor deities, the Orisha, who stand as intermediaries between Olorun, the supreme deity, and human beings. Olorun is also "Lord of Heaven" and he is Olodumare, "Almighty." In the creation myth, the Yoruba describe Olorun inhabiting the sky while the earth was still too wet for human habitation. With Olorun in his heavenly realm were other minor divinities that sometimes descended to the Earth to play. Olorun decided to create dry land, and gave this task to Orisha Nla, the chief of the Orisha, who descended to the wet Earth with a snail shell that held some dry soil, a pigeon, and a hen. He emptied the soil on a flat, marshy area, and soon the hen and the pigeon scattered it around

Left **Celebrations of death.** Death rituals are seen by some African groups as an affirmation of life. Colorful funeral fabrics are often used to reflect the vibrant approach to death and mourning.

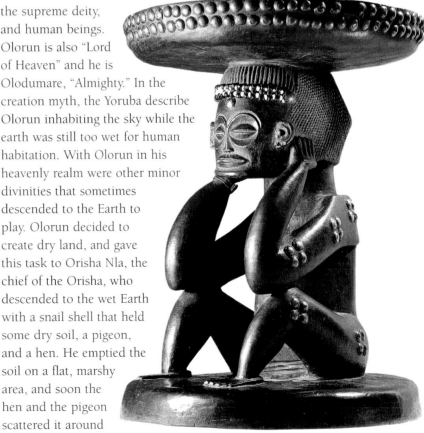

Below **A matriarchial ancestor, Chokwe people.** The seated posture of this figure, with its hands behind its ears, indicates the ritual of mourning. Carvings like these remind the living of the necessity of sacrifices to the dead, to appease the spirits.

Far right **Shango, god of thunder.** Olorun, supreme deity of the Yoruba people, sent Shango to Earth as a baby. When the people on Earth started to steal from each other, Olorun commanded that Shango create thunder to punish them.

Right **Eshu, the Yoruba messenger of the gods.** It is agile and quick-witted Eshu who delivers the sacrifices prescribed by Ifa, the divination god. Eshu's long hairstyle is a symbol of his close bond with Ifa.

earth were brought to life by Olorun. The first men and women were then sent to occupy the dry land, to till the soil, and produce crops.

The realm of Olorun is a remote place, beyond the human world, where he reigns supreme, and is too far away for mortals to access him, or present their supplications. But like the Orisha, Olorun is served by priests who enjoy high social status, and are consulted about the happenings of everyday life. The Orisha are the intermediary divinities, appealed to with offerings and sacrifices.

The creation stories link with those of the origins of mankind, the Orisha regarded as ancestral figures to the Yoruba, each with a special connection with natural forces, such as thunder, rain, and disease. This pantheon of gods is still central to the ceremonial and celebratory life of the Yoruba today.

Spear Master Myths

A myth from the Dinka people of southern Sudan includes a range of stories of the origins of a priestly lineage, stories that tell of relationships between religious or cosmological concepts, and the political histories of traditional people. The Dinka, like the Shilluk, live on the floodplains of the Upper Nile, an environment dependent on the annual flooding of the river and prone to extreme drought, which dries out of lands, including the grazing areas for the all-important cattle. The spear master myth has many variations. One tells of a woman, who, being without a child, caused her husband's lineage to have no line of succession. Bemoaning her barrenness by the river, the woman was told by the spirit of the river to go into the water, and to allow the water to ripple into her. The river deity gave her a spear, symbolic of giving birth to a boy. The woman became pregnant, and produced a son named Aiwel. Born with a full set of teeth, a sign of spiritual power, Aiwel performed feats, even as a baby.

One story tells of him rising from where he was lying on the floor, picking up a gourd of milk, and then drinking from it. Amazed at this achievement, his mother is sworn to secrecy on pain of death by Aiwel. But she cannot contain her secret, and dies. In this, the ability of the spear masters is preempted, for

Left **Yoruba Orisha.** Representations of these lesser gods are carried in rituals. It is believed that the deity will enter and live in the figure, bringing protection to the fortunate owner of the carving.

Below **Yoruba Orisha shrine.** Orisha, or minor deities, are seen as intermediate figures who mix with gods and mortals. This shrine figure displays the attributes of wealth (the horse), fertility (mother and child), and power expressed by the number of followers at the base of this statue.

to create a patch of dry land. A chameleon was then sent to test the dry land, and he returned to say that the land was not completely dry. After his second visit, the chameleon declared that the land was dry.

This creation, like that of other creation stories, was measured in days, and on the fifth day, Orisha Nla was worshipped, as has happened ever since in the Yoruba calendar. Then, Olorun sent Orisha Nla to create forests and land suitable to grow food while, in heaven, people molded from handfuls of they are known for their amazing powers to foretell the future of others in their early childhood.

Aiwel's powers stay with him as he grows. During a drought, Aiwel makes water pour from a stump of a tree. In another telling, he takes the cattle out to the dried-up pastures beyond the village, pulls up tufts of grass, and from beneath them the water gushes. After a severe drought, Aiwel offers to lead the people and their cattle to better pastures. The elders of the village do not want Aiwel to lead them, and they move off alone. As they cross a river a fence made of reeds—the sort used by the Dinka to trap fish—blocks their way. As they attempt to cross over it, Aiwel appears on the riverbank, spears each of them with his fish spear, and kills them all.

Spear master Aiwel was the founder of Dinka clan groups related through male lineage descent. These stories combine notions of the supernatural with the origins of the people.

ANCESTRAL ORIGINS, MOUNT KENYA

The people who live in the foothills around Mount Kenya all believe that they are descended from Gikuyu. Gikuyu was called to Mogai (the supreme being), and given a large stretch of land that included rivers and valleys, forests, and all the animals and plants that lived there. Mogai had also created the mountain, called Kere-Nyaga (Mount Kenya), which became the resting place for Mogai when he traveled around the world. Mogai took Gikuyu to the mountain top, and showed him all the land that had been given to him, and pointed to a place where wild figs were growing near the center of the country. it was here that Gikuyu created his home. Every Gikuyu child knows this story of the origin of the Gikuyu people. They also know the next chapter, in which Mogai gave to Gikuyu and his wife, Mumbi, the promise that their sons and daughters would roam

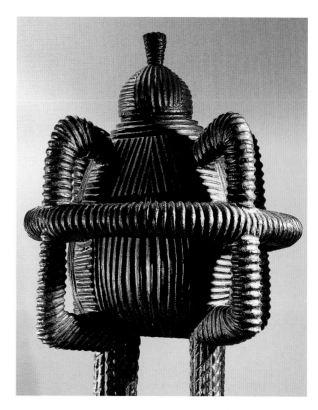

and multiply. Nine daughters were born to Gikuyu and Mumbi, but how were they to multiply in the absence of husbands?

Again Mogai brought deliverance, telling Gikuyu to sacrifice a fat ram, which would bring nine handsome young men into being. There was a great celebration when Gikuyu brought the young men home. The daughters accepted the men as husbands, on the one condition that they allow the women to be head of the household, and all live together in the same village. All Gikuyu, to this day, believe that they are descended from one of the nine clans named after Wacheera, Wanjiko, Wairimo, Wamboi, Wangari, Wanjiro, Wangoi, Waithera, and Warigia.

It is told by the Gikuyu, that for a number of generations all the women served as the rulers in their particular households. However, the men's telling of the story suggests that the women were harsh rulers, and eventually the original agreement was broken, the status quo was shifted, and the men were given the role as the head of their household.

THE KING AS GOD

The African king is the active representative of the supreme god, incorporating mystery and remoteness among his characteristics, and these are expressed within a context of rites, symbols, and a complex formula by which the royal person is identified with the nation. The king is the medium for supernatural elements that are a common feature of Bantu conceptualization. Whatever happens to the king affects the nation as a whole. If he is wounded, the entire country is affected. If he dies, everything comes to a standstill.

SACRED KINGSHIP

Stories of sky gods introduced the idea of divine kingship to many African cultures. Viewed through filters of rationality, kingship with divine attributes can give stability to social structures.

Kingship stories are widespread among the Bantu-speaking populations of central and southern Africa. Among the Zulus of South Africa, myths concerning the origins of the kings are also those of the origins of the people. One story tells of the son of a deity who was expelled from heaven for stealing his father's favorite white cow. He was lowered through a hole in the sky by an umbilical cord tied round him, and was later sent a wife from his father. These two became the founding couple of the Zulu people.

In the Great Lakes region of central-eastern Africa, several kingdoms, each with its own distinct language and culture, have their own myths concerning the foundation of their dynasties. In Ankole, a district of southwestern Uganda, an oral tradition traces the Bahinda dynasty of the Banyankole back through

We carry with us the wonders we seek without us: there is all Africa.

SIR THOMAS BROWNE (1605–1682)

several centuries. The founding myth describes the supreme being, Ruhanga, descending from heaven to rule the land. He bore three sons: Kakama, Kahima, and Kairu. To test them, Ruhanga gave them each a pot of milk to be left untouched through the night. Kakama spilt some of his, but the other brothers re-filled his pot from theirs. Kairu later fell asleep, and knocked his pot over, losing all his milk. In the morning, Ruhanga called the brothers together to determine the results of their testing.

Ruhanga then decreed that Kairu should be the servant to his brothers, Kahima should be the herdsman of Kakama, and Kakama should be Ruhanga's heir. This was how the main divisions of the people of the Ankole region were created, the lineages of which were fixed when British explorers and colonial administrators came in contact with the Banyankole at the end of the nineteenth century, and continue to be relevant in the social structure.

Even today, the stories and rituals surrounding the milk pots and the protection of these sacred rituals are an important element of the Banyankole culture in this primarily pastoral society.

Above **Oba (Benin king), flanked by two attendants.** The Oba is considered to be the descendant of a god, and is therefore divine. He is said to have amazing mystical powers, and is an object of great reverence, awe, and fear.

111

STORIES OF THE RAINBOW

As in the mythologies of other parts of the world, the rainbow features widely in African myths. Associated with rain, the colorful rainbow sometimes has good meanings, though it can also be regarded as strange and ominous.

Among the Luba people of the Democratic Republic of the Congo, another society in which kingship is connected with divine origins, the founder of the kingdom was Kalala Ilunga. Kalala Ilunga was born in the court of the Rainbow King, Nkongolo. His mother was Nkongolo's sister, and Nkongolo brought up Kalala Ilunga as his own child, after sending the father away. Kalala Ilunga became a good runner and dancer, and was so popular that Nkongolo became jealous, and planned to kill him. Kalala Ilunga heard about this, escaped the kingdom by crossing the Lualaba River, and found his real father, who gave him an army to destroy Nkongolo. Nkongolo's spirit is the serpent, which is often intertwined with the rainbow. This story has much that resonates with the significance of the mother's brother in the stories of many Bantu-speaking people.

Among the Fon people in Benin, the rainbow is again linked with the serpent, and may be seen as a portent of danger. In this legend, the serpent is intertwined with the rainbow, the red part being the male part of the serpent and the blue part, the female. Among the Pygmies there is also an association between serpent and rainbow. Khonvum, the supreme being, is, in some stories, cast as

Above **Kalala Ilunga, a legendary Lubahero.** Nkongolo, the Rainbow King, invited his nephew, Kalala, to perform a dance over a concealed pit full of upright spears. Kalala avoided being impaled by uncovering the pit with his own spear.

the great hunter carrying a bow made of two serpents, and this appears to those living on earth as a rainbow.

In Kenya, the Luyia have many stories about rain, and the control of rain by rainmakers. They believe that the rainbow is magical. The supreme being's creation of the rainbow is in two parts, a narrow male part, and a wider female one. If the male part occurs first, then the rain will stop.

The San people, found mainly in the dry lands of southern Africa, have a story that rain was once a beautiful woman who girdled her narrow waist with a brightly colored rainbow.

WATER SPIRITS, GODS, AND GODDESSES

Across Africa, people living close to major watercourses, lakes, and the sea believe them to be the dwelling place of water spirits. The Songhay, of the upper reaches of the Niger River, have many stories of water spirits known as Zin. One tells of a snake that inhabited a lake, and wanted to marry a woman. Her parents agreed, and for the bride-price payment, they asked for ownership of the lake. The snake agreed to this, and left the lake in the care of his wife's parents, returning from time to time to control the fish, the crocodiles, and the hippopotami. The guardianship of the creatures of the lake passed down from the snake to his son, and then on through the generations to this day.

The stories of the birth of Aiwel, founder and spear master of the Dinka, are associated with barrenness, and in this myth the river god plays a part in bringing fertility to Aiwel's mother. Among the Baganda people, the god Mukasa is associated with the waters around the shores of Lake Victoria,

and Mukasa is said to inhabit an island. The rivers, too, are believed to have sprung from spirits, or from humans. One river began when a young woman, after being deserted by her lover, gave birth to their child. On either side of the river, offerings are made by those wanting to cross the river safely.

Water spirits and gods or goddesses of water are often linked with birth, fertility, or infertility. In Nigeria, the Yoruba and the Ibo people have a tradition of water goddesses. In the Yoruba pantheon, the mother god, Yemaja, married her brother, Aganju, and gave birth to a son, Orungan, who later fell in love with his mother and, in the absence of his father, raped her. In a continuing struggle, Yemaja fell to the ground, swelled up, and poured two streams of water from her body to create a lagoon. From her abdomen, a number of minor deities emerged. The place where this happened has remained a sacred place for the Yoruba. The novels of the Ibo writer,

Flora Nwapa, describe the lives of Ibo women within traditional contexts. The cult that focuses on a river goddess, and the honor given to her chosen worshippers, is an aspect of Nwapa's novel, *Efuru*.

MYTHOLOGY OF MOTHERHOOD

The bearing and rearing of children, as in many other parts of the world, is celebrated in a wealth of stories told throughout Africa. Marriage and childbearing are essential to the realization of identity for women in all regions. When a woman is childless in marriage, her condition of "barrenness" is a problem for her. Rituals and myths surround these stages and states throughout women's lives.

Traditionally, initiation rites at puberty had an educational purpose. Stories were used to convey the meanings of womanhood to young girls, or, in some cases, the meanings of manhood to young boys.

Above **Olokun, god of the sea.** Seashells and animals were often used as offerings and sacrifices to this god. He rules from the depths of the ocean, and has similarities to the Greek god, Poseidon.

Opposite page **Mythical python.** Snakes symbolize the power of Osun, the god of nature. The python is also a symbol of Olokun, the god of the sea. It is said that pythons are sent from Olokun to punish wrongdoing.

In Western Africa, there is a widespread tradition of life coming from water, and of women's fertility associated with water. In the oral traditions of the Ibo people of eastern Nigeria, the mythical figure of Ogbuide is a mother to all. As a goddess of lakes, Ogbuide is associated with women, who come to the river to collect drinking water, and to bathe. Ogbuide is known as a goddess of great beauty, and is believed to leave her watery home and wander through the marketplaces, mingling with women. She calls on women to serve her as priestesses, and through these special few, women bring their fertility problems to Ogbuide, and seek advice or consolation from the goddess. The divine women of African mythology, or goddesses of rivers, lakes, and the sea, are often beautiful women. They live beneath the water, and are very rarely seen.

The idea of water as a source of life is also a part of the belief system of the Oromo of Ethiopia. The

Below **Yoruba mother and child.** African mythology places importance on the stages of a woman's life cycle. Various fertility Orishas are given offerings to ensure that the lineage of a family continues.

dead are spoken of as having become dry, and a barren woman is also described as a dry woman. A barren woman will beseech the supreme being, Waqa, to make her womb wet so that she might sprout children. More important than Waqa to women is the goddess Maram, who is called on in all the rituals of childbirth, and is seen to look after women during their pregnancy and labor.

As mothers, women became involved in issues of heirship and inheritance. The mother of a king, or an elder, was often highly honored. In the history of the Bafokeng people of Lesotho, there is a story of a chief, Tshukudu, who, practicing polygamy, as was customary, would visit his three favorite wives and tell each of them that her son would be the chief after he died. Such an honor was thrilling to each of the women, but woeful after the old chief's death. The warring factions, named after the mothers of the three contenders, fought each other, leading to the splitting of the people into the three groups, who settled on different tracts of land. This story is also part of the mythology of the Sotho people.

HEROES AND MYTH

The stories that tell of heroes often merge myth with history. This is true of many heroic tales of southern African people, for whom the last 200 years has witnessed a turbulent struggle for land and resources, not only between various African people, but also between Africans and Europeans.

This is a complex and fascinating history, involving the movement of Bantu-speaking people into southeastern Africa, their dispersal into a range of scattered chiefdoms, then the merging of chiefdoms under the power of a paramount ruler.

From the late eighteenth to the second half of the nineteenth century, there were momentous happenings, battles, and epic migrations over extensive tracts of country, the essence of stories that have

come down to the present day as part of the mythology. History has been interwoven with and reflects the traditional stories of the past.

Zwide, Soshangane, and Zwangendaba of the Ndwande people, and Dingiswayo of the Mthethwa people are heroic figures competing to extend their kingdoms in the area of what is now southern Mozambique. The Ndwande under Zwide were defeated by Shaka in the area close to what is today the heartland of the Zulu people. Their defeated force split into two groups, one under Soshangane that moved into and settled in what later became southern Mozambique. The other force led by Zwangendaba spread north and west, fighting local populations, suffering defeats and gaining victories, resting awhile, and marching on, eventually covering more than 1,000 miles. This group, in their original homeland described as Jere, became known as the Ngoni, and used the military skills they had

acquired in their fighting further south, and also developed political inclusion of the people they conquered. Thus the Ngoni increased their power. They moved through the territory of the Shona in modern Zimbabwe, then crossed the Zambezi River, moving north toward Lake Nyasa. Where they might have gone after reaching the southern area of modern Tanzania is anyone's guess, but it is told that Zwangendaba was tired, ageing, and ill, and his people had become weary. Zwangendaba died before any further moves could be accomplished by his people. This was only 20 years after the great migration had begun so far to the south, ending in the defeat, and dispersal of the Ndwande.

Stories of the heroic leader Zwangendaba have been told from the mid-nineteenth century to the present; he was a figure of history who became enveloped by myth. But it is the hero, Shaka who has captured the imagination of, and is familiar to, many Western observers and history readers. Shaka was the younger son of

Above *Battle of Isandhlwana, 1879.* The British invaded Zululand in 1879, which was at that time ruled by Cetewayo. The six companies of the 24th Regiment and a force of Natal volunteers were overwhelmed and massacred by the Zulus, who were inspired by the legend of the heroic figure, Shaka.

Left **Ashante fertility symbol.** Legend tells of a young woman, Akua, who was unable to become pregnant. On the advice of a wise man, she carried a wooden carving of a child around with her, and very soon she conceived.

115

Right **Ivory leopards.**
In Benin cosmology, the leopard is a symbol of royal power. At one time, leopards were sacrificed to ensure the well-being of the kingdom.

Below **A leopard plaque.**
The Obas (kings) of Benin surrounded themselves with images and statues of leopards. The power and strength these animals represented were qualities passed onto the Obas and their offspring.

the chief of the small kingdom of the Zulus. Shaka's prowess as a military leader was widely known during the Zulu–British war of 1879, although he was no longer alive. Shaka established an enlarged Zulu kingdom by incorporating all the neighboring chiefdoms into Zululand, and eventually worked on overthrowing the Ndwande chiefdom, to great success.

ANIMAL MYTHS

In African mythology the natural world is close to the social. In the same way that the landscape, the sky, the mountains, and the forests feature in stories, so too do animals, birds, and reptiles. Some creatures are more prominent than others. The chameleon and the serpent have eminence over wide areas of Africa. Others, such as the leopard, the hare, the rabbit, and the tortoise, are featured over more limited areas, perhaps determined by the environment. There are stories about hares and tortoises that tell how their cunning can, at times, be used to get the better of larger, more powerful animals. Often these tales are actually about the features of human beings, but are often told to entertain and serve as moral tales.

A small child asks his father why a little snake comes to visit him, the one that the child's mother forbids the family to kill. The father answers that the snake is the guiding spirit of their race, and explains how the snake came to make itself known to the family. First, the snake appeared in several of the father's dreams. Then, one night in a dream, the snake tells the father that he would appear in reality, giving the time and place for the meeting. However, the father sees the snake, and is filled with fear as the snake looks like any other snake. The father fights hard to stop himself from killing the snake. Seeing the father's reaction, the snake turned and disappeared the way he had come. The following night, the snake appeared again in the father's dreams, and asked why the father didn't receive him kindly, telling him that he, the snake, was the guiding spirit of the race, and if he was accepted, he would bring good fortune. The second time the father saw the snake, he received him without fear, and accepted him with kindness. From that day on, the kindly snake has brought the family nothing but good fortune.

Relations between human beings and animals may be expressed in other ways, such as in the stories from Malagasy (Madagascar). Certain clans in Malagasy call their menfolk "Sons of crocodiles," explained by a tale about a crocodile that lived in a river, whose wife was a human female. She became entangled in a fish trap, then was removed from the river and taken away by a man with whom she lived for a period of time. After bearing him two sons, she returned to the river.

A story about Gina tells how the crocodile came to have a humpy, ridged back. Gina, who was a man, was sleeping under a tree when a fire overtook him, and badly burned his back. Gina jumped into the river to put out the flames, and turned into a crocodile. This is a common story of animal origins that explains the characteristic features of a species. Another story tells of how the crocodile moved through the hills, and when as became tired, he turned himself into a rocky ridge to rest.

TRICKSTER MYTHS

There is a type of story found throughout the continent that is more secular than those with sacred connotations of creation and origins. Such stories contain circumstances in which the guileful, seemingly weak or innocent character is pitted against one with more power. In Western Africa, these stories reach a high level of importance, sometimes transferring from the traditional into a situation of modernity and current political significance. When ordinary men or women get the better of officialdom, there is entertainment, even though a more complex situation of deception or suffering may be involved.

A genre of tales about Ananse, the spider trickster, concerns the most popular characters in the mythology of the Akan and Ashante of Ghana, which are told more widely through Western Africa. One story tells of Ananse promising to cure the mother of Nyame, the supreme being, of her illness. She dies, and Nyame, holding Ananse to his vow that he would forfeit his own life in the event of failure, sentences him to death. Ananse performs his trickery, using his son, who burrows under the place where Ananse is held captive. The son cries out, as Ananse has instructed, that the Ashante will not survive if Ananse is killed, but will thrive if he is given a reprieve. Through these means, Ananse survives to perform further acts of a dubious nature. Many Ananse stories are coarse, even crude, with sexual misadventures, and they often demonstrate human foibles and weaknesses.

Another trickster, associated with the Fon people of Benin, is Legba, who is both a god and a mediator between the gods and humans, and between humans themselves. Legba, a linguist, knows the languages of all the gods in the pantheon, as well as the language of Mawu-Lisa, the supreme being of the Fon. As each god knows only his own language, as does Mawu-Lisa, this attribute enables Legba to move between the deities and, in effect, to manipulate situations to his own ends. Legba's nickname is Aflakete, which means "I have tricked you."

Left **The elephant as a wise chief.** Ashante legend says that this enormous animal can only be defeated with magic. The elephant is also believed to be a human chief from the past. When a dead elephant is found, it is given a proper burial.

WHAT IS A TRICKSTER?

The trickster is portrayed as a character that anyone can identify with: humorous, lawless, and something of a "jack-the-lad." Trickster figures appear in the myths and stories of many traditional societies in Africa. He sometimes appears as a god, sometimes as an animal. Trickster figures are well loved for their unconventional behavior.

Right **Trickster shrine figure.** While the trickster is playful, there is often a tragic side to some stories, with people being hurt. Tricksters appear in many forms, such as Ananse, the spider in Ghana; and Ajapa, the dog, of the Yoruba people.

MIDDLE EAST AND
ASIAN MYTHOLOGY

MESOPOTAMIAN MYTHOLOGY

Above **Banquet of King Ashurbanipal, the Palace at Nineveh, relief, 650 B.C.** The ruler of ancient Assyria, King Ashurbanipal lived around 668–627 B.C. A famed military leader, he was also a learned man who established one of the greatest libraries of the ancient world, with over 20,000 cuneiform tablets.

Right **Accounting tablet, Sumerian, c. 2350 B.C.** This remarkable early form of record-keeping was widely used, as it allowed for all sorts of knowledge to be stored and accessed. This tablet gives an account of sheep and goat numbers.

Mesopotamia is Greek for "the land between the rivers," referring to the Bronze Age world of the ancient Middle East circa 3500 to 330 B.C. Mesopotamians lived in mud-brick houses behind protective city walls, and built palaces and temples of stone that towered into the sky. They were an industrious people in a difficult landscape, and they struggled together there to create magnificent empires and armies, noted for their opulence, gold, and monumental grandeur. Theirs was the era of epic heroes and fabulous beasts, of kings and divine powers.

The Mesopotamian region stretched from the Mediterranean Sea in the west to the Iranian plateau in the east, bordered on the north by the Caucasus mountain range, and on the south by the Arabian Desert and the Persian Gulf. Permanent cities had begun to appear as early as 3500 B.C. in the area referred to as the Fertile Crescent, known as "the land between the rivers," the Tigris and the Euphrates. These emerging cities expanded into powerful city-states, such as

Uruk, Ur, Eridu, Kish, Babylon, Lagash, Susa, Nimrud, Kadesh, Assur, and Nineveh. The Assyrians and the Mittanis were the principal northern tribes. The main southern tribes were the Sumerians and the Akkadians. Over the centuries, these city-states rose and fell—at times coexisting—and created the ruling nations of Sumeria, Akkadia, Amorite, Assyria, and, later, Babylonia. By the end of the third millennium B.C., for example, the Sumerian city of Ur (in the area of present-day Iraq) was politically dominant, and a great many of the recorded Sumerian texts date to that golden era. The Akkadians followed, under Sargon the Great (c. 2334–2279 B.C.). Various minor states followed, but by the eighteenth century B.C., the Semitic tribes of the Amorites and their related clans had swept through the region on the thunderous wheels of horse-drawn chariots. King Hammurabi made the city of Babylon their capital and their god Marduk king of the gods. The Sumerian language was exiled to temple texts and religious ceremonies, surviving there in written form for another 1,000 years.

CRAFTSMEN AND SCHOLARS

From the earliest times, the people of Mesopotamia have proved themselves to be superior metalworkers and tool-makers. They were responsible for major improvements in agricultural technology, inventing plows and hardware that made it possible for peasant-farmers to harvest enough for their own families, as well as support vast armies of soldiers and builders.

Mesopotamia is sometimes hailed as the birthplace of the written word and the cradle of Western civilization. Cuneiform script, which is the earliest known writing system, evolved here, and recorded, for more than 3,000 years, many of the details of life of the various Mesopotamian cultures. As a tool for organizing trade, business, and bureaucracy, the use of permanent standardized record-keeping reached its first zenith in the Mesopotamian empires. Weights, measures, and values made it possible to trade even in unstable regions, and meticulous inscriptions on clay tablets and stone walls controlled and maintained extensive temple complexes and populations of workers.

Around 1800 B.C., King Hammurabi of Babylon ordered that a list of laws, known as The Code of Hammurabi, be carved in stone in order to erect a permanent system that applied to all, from king to commoner. In this way, the Code established the enduring concept of written law as a formal guide for society, and is considered to be a prototype for the Ten Commandments.

This sense of permanency extends to their myths. Many Mesopotamian mythological themes can be seen in the later Homeric epics and in the stories of the Old Testament. The Tower of Babel, the slayer of Leviathan, the sieges of walled cities, tales of heroes that are part-god and part-man, quarrels among the gods, and a flood that cleansed the world at divine command can be found in their earliest forms in Mesopotamian myths and epic tales.

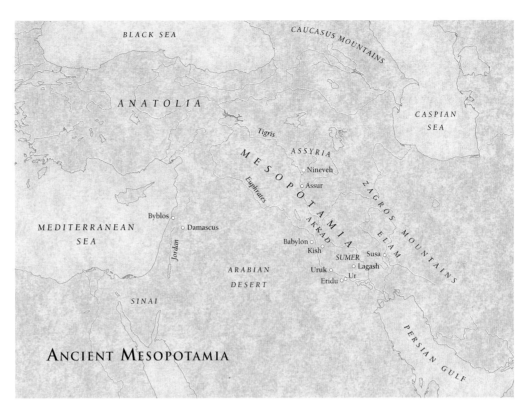

ANCIENT MESOPOTAMIA

Above **Mesopotamia, the land between the rivers.** The Sumerian empire was centered in the city of Ur, and included Akkad and Elam. Under Ur-Nammu (ruled 2112–2095 B.C.), it saw the construction of the first ziggurats. After the fall of the Sumerians, the Amorites, Assyrians, and Babylonians rose to power. By 1757 B.C. all of Mesopotamia came under the rule of King Hammurabi, with Babylon its center.

THE ZIGGURAT, STAIRWAY TO HEAVEN

The great stepped stone terraces of the Mesopotamian temple, the "ziggurat," are as immediately connected with Mesopotamia as the Great Pyramids or the Sphinx are with ancient Egypt. These massive buildings dominated the view, rising tier upon tier over the city. The architectural form dates back to the earliest days of the city-states: whenever the walls of a temple collapsed because of age, earthquake, flood, or fire, the rubble was not cleared, but instead faced with stone, and used as the base for a new temple to sit on top. Thus, generation upon generation, the temples stood taller, lifting the priests and the aristocracy to ever more remote heights above the common people in their mud-brick houses below.

Ziggurats were covered in fine stone and magnificently painted and decorated inside, reflecting the wealth of the temples and royal courts. Wide staircases on the outside were platforms for seasonal processions and religious ceremonies. Divine beings stepped down from the sky to the tip of the ziggurat. The royal marriage bed of the king and his goddess was up there in a splendid temple room. Their nuptials linked earth to heaven and heaven to earth, and established the divine right of the king.

Left *The Ziggurat of Marduk, at Babylon,* from P. Spamer's *Illustrirte Weltgeschichte* **(1880).** This wondrous seven-staged tower probably inspired the biblical Tower of Babel.

Above **Babylonians bringing a humpbacked cow as tribute to Darius I, King of Persia, relief, fifth century B.C.** Just as the gods demanded propitiatory tributes so, too, did the human rulers. Darius I (550–486 B.C.), "King of Kings," founded the Achaemenid dynasty in Persia, which is present-day Iran.

Right **Limestone statuette of a bearded god, third millennium B.C., Sumerian.** The staring eyes of this statue evoke the belief that the gods are all-seeing deities. It was believed that the statue of a god provided a direct physical link to the god's awareness.

122

APSU, THE WATERY ABYSS

Different city-states, empires, and language groups in Mesopotamia shared many of the same gods, though they used a bewildering variety of names for them. Indeed, the fundamental elements of religious belief were very consistent throughout the entire ancient Middle East. This created a continuity, a recognizable "Mesopotamian" culture that existed over three and a half millennia and across a vast territory, even in times of conflict. Marduk of Babylon replaced earlier gods, such as Assur in Assyria and Ninurta in Sumer, yet he fought the same battle, defeated the same cosmic enemies, and was responsible for the creation of the living universe of god and man.

The cosmos itself, Mesopotamians believed, floated upon Apsu, the watery abyss, which existed before creation. The divine power of gods and monsters was drawn forth from these primeval waters by magical recitations and heroic acts.

The Mesopotamians, particularly the early Sumerians, were among the earliest and best sailors. They had an intense relationship with the borders between land and water, and the stories of their gods are rich with the power and potential of water in a dry land. In the cycles of Gilgamesh, one of the most ancient and enduring of their stories, the hero conquers the might of mountain, desert, dark forest, and wild beast, yet the magic of immortality in the waters of the world remains forever beyond his grasp.

Golden Gods and Human Clay

Mesopotamian origin myths show a belief in human servitude to divine powers. Even with the passage of time, this theme remained central to their myths. Humankind was created to be the slave of the gods, toiling in the fields and gardens of the gods, building their temples, and digging their irrigation ditches. In order to create these human servants, the gods had to kill one of their own and mix his divine blood with clay and ashes.

Mesopotamians envisioned reality as ascending hierarchies of order built out of chaos by the labors, loves, betrayals, and heroics of gods and humans. Generation was piled upon generation, struggling for the limited resources of a dramatic environment: a land of fertile soils and flooding rivers, searing deserts, muddy shores, and inhospitable mountain heights. They patterned their gods on the caprice and majesty of that environment. Their heroes, both human and divine, were inspired by the strength of the wild beasts around them: powerful bulls with massive horns, lions, eagles, serpents, and scorpions.

The primary gods and goddesses were the supreme deities of the spheres of heaven, air, earth, and water. There were more than 3,000 in all: a god for every aspect of human interaction with nature, with the gods, and with each other. Every kind of tool, product, or activity had a god, even if only a minor one. The gods watched carefully over everything their human servants did, ever ready to provide divine guidance or to deliver divine punishment. Statues of their gods had wide-open staring eyes to emphasize this supernatural surveillance.

As well as gods, demons and angels also influenced the human world. The supernatural forces of demonic chaos, seething in the underworld depths and in the watery abyss of Apsu, were balanced by the equally supernatural forces of divine light. The tales tell of the struggle of humans to keep their backs safe from the one and their faces turned to the other. Their safeguards: ritual, prayer, hard work, and sacrifice.

CREATION STORIES

The Mesopotamian story of creation is best known today from several Babylonian editions of the *Enuma Elish,* the Poem of Creation, recorded in temple archives from the twelfth to the seventh centuries B.C. These versions are themselves based on translations, expansions, and adaptations of even older Sumerian, Akkadian, and Assyrian texts. The basic elements, no doubt, had been part of the cultural and oral tradition throughout the region long before they were written down. The imagery in the stories comes from the time when the first city-states of the Fertile Crescent were being established. The tales reflect the conflicts that grew with the rise in power of the towns and cities as they grappled for land and water, and the demand for the most vital resource of all: human laborers. In these early tales, the primordial world had a dark and savage nature to it. Generations of gods and demons were tossed together in a swirling darkness, living on each other's spilled blood and torn flesh, child gods devouring parent gods in order to acquire their divine powers.

The early myths provide various scenarios for the separation of earth, sky, and heaven, as well as for the creation of man. The supreme Sumerian deities were the heaven god, An, ruling the sky; Enlil, ruler of the air and earth; and the mother goddess Ninhursag. The fourth god Enki, ruler of the meeting-place between water and land, had different roles in different myths. The Babylonians altered their names but not their primary roles. An, for example, became Anu; Enlil became Ellil; and Enki became Ea.

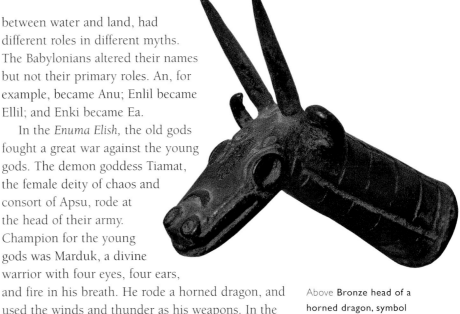

In the *Enuma Elish,* the old gods fought a great war against the young gods. The demon goddess Tiamat, the female deity of chaos and consort of Apsu, rode at the head of their army. Champion for the young gods was Marduk, a divine warrior with four eyes, four ears, and fire in his breath. He rode a horned dragon, and used the winds and thunder as his weapons. In the terrible battle that ensued, Marduk trapped Tiamat in a net. Each time she screamed in rage, he forced one of the seven winds down her throat, until she was distended and helpless.

Marduk split Tiamat, and formed the sky, stars, and planets from her upper body, and the earth from her lower body. Her many breasts were piled up as the mountains. The Tigris and Euphrates Rivers flowed from her eyes. Marduk then organized the landscape revealed by this creation, and set the sun, Shamash, on its course. Marduk was made leader of the gods in return for these labors.

Above **Bronze head of a horned dragon, symbol of the god Marduk, sixth century** B.C. The name Marduk means "bull calf of the son," that is, the son of the god Ea. After defeating Tiamat, Marduk took the tablets of destiny and fixed them to his own breast. He created the earth, and at the center of this new world was Babylon, the capital of the Babylonians, who championed Marduk as their supreme god.

Left *The Hero Marduk Defeats Tiamat, the Fearful Goddess of the Deep,* from *Gilgamesh* by Zabelle Boyajian. Tiamat is an intriguing figure: though represented as a female dragon and the bringer of evil and chaos, she is also the source of all that exists in this world.

Right Terracotta relief of Inanna-Ishtar, around 2000 B.C., Larsa period. Inanna-Ishtar is shown as the winged goddess of heaven, earth, and the underworld. She wears a crown of lunar horns, which is also present in Egyptian and African cultures, and a rainbow necklace. Owls and lions sit calmly at her feet.

Below Bull's head design on a harp, c. 2400 B.C., Sumerian. The lunar bull, consort of the mother goddess, was sometimes depicted as a bull-shaped harp of gold. This harp was found in the tomb of Queen Shub-Ad in the Sumerian city of Ur, along with the skeletons of the Queen, her guards, hand-maidens, and a harpist.

THE CREATION OF MAN

The younger gods celebrated the defeat of Tiamat and the design of heaven and earth. However, their elation faded once they discovered that their various duties involved hard work, and they did not like to work. Gods of earth and air bore the brunt of the work, digging riverbeds and irrigation ditches, planting, and harvesting crops to feed the gods. They complained bitterly about these burdens to the sky head god, Anu (An), and to the large pantheon of major gods. The hierarchy of divine workers needed a broader base.

Ea (Enki), god of magical spells, with the help of a mother-goddess, made little clay figures that would do the work for them. As punishment for his role in the great war between the gods, Tiamat's general, Kingu, had to be sacrificed to provide the vital force for the slave race that would serve the gods. So Marduk killed him and Kingu's blood was used to animate the clay figures.

The various versions of the creation of humankind reflected the demanding lifestyle imposed by the climate and landscape, and behavior in heaven to some extent reflected the social structure on earth. It was not enough that these human slaves must do the gods' work; they must also endure the gods' whims and caprices. In the oldest stories from Sumerian times, the gods played cruel and careless games with the clay figures, creating them just for the drunken entertainment of lazy overlords. Perhaps evident in these tales is an attempt by the ancient Mesopotamians to explain the difficult nature of their lives, to find some sort of rationalization for the unpredictable violence of the weather and the random violence of men. Some clay figures were deliberately deformed so that the gods could bet on the resulting creature's behavior in life. In another early story, a herder and a farmer were tricked into a ruthless competition so that the gods could bet on who was the more valuable to them.

As Mesopotamian civilization expanded and became more successful, the officials recording these stories modified them, putting greater emphasis on loyalty to the gods and on the ruthless power of their revenge if offended or betrayed by their mortal slaves, than on cruel games. Even so, humans remained the mortal playthings of the immortal gods, seemingly valuable only for the hard work they could do—tools to be discarded once they wore out.

ISHTAR AND THE SEVEN VEILS

Arabian women around the world today honor this ancient story in the "Dance of the Seven Veils," even though the cosmic power involved is no longer of religious significance.

In the oldest, Sumerian, versions of the myth, the goddess Inanna was tricked into the underworld by the gods. Her story was later transformed into a tale of divine romance: the tragedy of an immortal goddess in love with a mortal, Dumuzi. He is the supreme farmer, the superlative herder, fairest of all humans, and ruled by his complete devotion to his goddess wife. Yet other versions recount that Dumuzi was banished to the underworld by Inanna for some months of every year for his lack of feeling for her. During this time, the earth became barren, only returning to fertility when they were reunited.

In the later Akkadian version, these same roles were played by the goddess Ishtar and her beloved Tammuz. In this version of the tale, when Tammuz died, Ishtar followed his corpse into the underworld, the realm of her rival Ereshkigal, a gloomy place where the dead fed on dust, wore feathers, and stood about as servants in the hall.

Massive walls protected this multilayered underworld, one within the other, with locked gates and monstrous guards. Ishtar not only had to name each part of the gate and the staff who maintained it, she also had to pay to cross its dimensional threshold. One by one, she took off her jewels and garments as payment.

When Ishtar finally passed through the seven gates and reached the throne of Ereshkigal, she was naked and defenseless, and had only a glimpse of her beloved husband before she was slain. Her death left

The goddess—with her there is counsel. The fate of everything, she holds in her hand.

HYMN OF ISHTAR

the earth in turmoil: the soil would not yield, and no womb could conceive. Ishtar, however foolish in love, was no fool. She had left her faithful lieutenants prepared. A comely transvestite priest was trained and equipped, and sent as messenger of the gods to beg for Ishtar's corpse. Through flattery and eloquence, the priest reached Ereshkigal and won her heart. He carried in secret a vial of the water of life, provided by Ea (Enki), and with this he revived Ishtar.

In the complex bargain that was ultimately struck, Tammuz agreed to take Ishtar's place in the underworld for half of every year, during which time Ishtar's great grief brought on winter. Tammuz' sister took his place for the other half, and then Ishtar's happiness and sexual activity made the earth flourish.

At each gate on the return, Ishtar recovered another piece of her wardrobe. In the same way, the world of nature redressed itself as the seasons went through their cycles.

Above **Alabaster statuette of a lady, 2500–2400 B.C., from the Temple of Ishtar, Syria.** The goddess Ishtar appears in many guises and across many cultures. In Syria, she is connected with their goddess Astarte, and in Egyptian mythology the goddess Isis and her beloved husband, the god Osiris, similarly represent the cycles of fertility.

Left **Soldiers, from the Stele of the Vultures, circa 2450 B.C., Sumerian.** This famous stone relief is dedicated by Eannatum of Lagash, celebrating his victory over the city-state of Umma. These soldiers, so uniform in appearance, are similar to the little clay figures of men made for the gods' pleasure.

Above **Gilgamesh supports the sun, flanked by two demi-gods, ninth-century Hittite stele.**
The tale of Gilgamesh is one of the oldest recorded stories in the world—and even older in oral history. The hero-king may have, in fact, existed: the Sumerian King List records a King of Uruk called Gilgamesh. He was the builder of the wall of Uruk and supposedly reigned for 125 years.

GILGAMESH, THE ORIGINAL SUPERHERO

Gilgamesh is thought to have been an early king of Uruk, and with mythical additions, he was a legend throughout Mesopotamia for millennia. The story of his exploits was told and retold in every household and inn, by those working in the ports and harbors of the Mediterranean, and by the herdsmen in the hard lands of the Caucasus Mountains. His adventures were parables of heroics and hubris, and many of the themes in the Homeric epics (c. 800 B.C.) and in the Old Testament are rooted in these tales. The standardized version of this oral epic was recorded in the Akkadian era, around the third millenium B.C.

The cornerstones of Mesopotamian faith are to be found at the heart of this story: the separation of human and divine; the absolute nature of human mortality and of human servitude to the gods; the assignment of roles to gods and to men for the maintenance of order against chaos; and the need to be obedient to one's divinely assigned role. Gilgamesh challenged these for the sake of human loyalty to the life of his beloved other self, the forest man, Enkidu.

Gilgamesh was unique because he was two parts god and one part man. The beauty of the sun god, Shamash, shone in his face, and the courage of the storm god, Adad, was in his blood. He was a man born of woman, yet endowed with divine attributes and supernatural powers; thus he represented a living link between gods and men.

In his youth, however, he abused these powers. He made stormy assaults on the lands and peoples around Uruk. There was a divine irony in his search for battle and adventure: he was created to be the greatest warrior of the world, yet that very fact denied him the fulfilment of that position because no one could stand up to him. There were no challenges worthy of his nature and, in frustration, Gilgamesh turned to excess and indulgence. He celebrated his victories with too much debauched partying, disturbing the folk in the city and the gods in the temples. He wasted food supplies with his revelry. He demanded the royal right to be first in every virgin's marriage bed, and he led men to their deaths in useless wars. The gods began to worry that someday Gilgamesh would ask for a greater part of his divine heritage. He could challenge the gods and rock the pillars of heaven if he wasn't controlled.

Enkidu, the Equal of Gilgamesh

The gods devised a plan. They believed that, if he was provided with an equal, Gilgamesh would divert his dangerous energies toward that rival and cease challenging heaven. The sky god, Anu (An), and the mother goddess, Ninlil (Ninhursag), created a mirror image of Gilgamesh from clay and gave it life. They sent a dream to Gilgamesh in which the stones of heaven fell at his feet, announcing the arrival of his new companion, Enkidu.

Dreams play a major role in the story. At crucial moments Gilgamesh performs elaborate rituals to evoke dreams to advise and guide him; indeed, he follows this internal guide over every other counsel. In a world dominated by the command of the gods, kings, and priests, this represented a dangerous course of individual willpower and self-determination.

The gods dropped Enkidu into the wilderness, where he lived and ate like an animal. He became beastmaster there at once, as dangerous in the sphere of nature as Gilgamesh was in the sphere of men. Herdsmen and farmers felt threatened by Enkidu's presence, and asked Gilgamesh for help.

Gilgamesh sent a wily temple courtesan to tame Enkidu, since the wild man retained his powers only so long as he remained innocent. Six days and seven nights passed with this educated lady, who changed Enkidu into a civilized man. She cleaned him up and brought him to Uruk, where the people were greatly excited by his likeness to Gilgamesh. They threw a great party for him, and Enkidu became boastful the more he drank. He announced himself as the man born in the hills, come to change the old order, and the people begged for his protection.

Enkidu intercepted Gilgamesh as the king set out to invade yet another bride's marriage bed. Enkidu issued his challenge to the king who was part god. Their fight is glorious, full of awe-inspiring deeds and destruction, but neither could prevail against the other. Finally, Gilgamesh succeeded in tossing his rival Enkidu to the ground.

The gods had not considered that, by creating Enkidu from a mirror image of Gilgamesh but without the divine portion, they had emphasized in him the humanity of Gilgamesh. That which inspired arrogance in Gilgamesh sparked humility in his alter ego. Enkidu did not become the rival, as the gods had planned him to be; instead he became Gilgamesh's trusted and loved companion.

An Inseparable Team

With Enkidu beside him, Gilgamesh prepared for his greatest adventure yet. He prayed and wept, begging Shamash, the sun god, for support. Shamash relented, and ordered that weapons be forged that had never been forged before. This part of the epic is told in loving detail, a warrior's adventure told by people who were proud of their skills and of their weapons. Together, Gilgamesh and Enkidu set off, entering new territory and accomplishing what no one else could.

Left **Statuette of the god Baal,** 1400–1200 B.C. The power of this storm god was matched by that of Gilgamesh. The god Baal was worshipped by many ancient cultures, in particular the Canaanites, and was held responsible for disasters such as droughts and plagues.

Below **King Ashurbanipal hunting,** Assyrian relief, c. 645 B.C. The power and skill of Gilgamesh inspired all. Young boys played at being him in their games, and great kings wished to be like him. In the famous library of Ashurbanipal at Nineveh, the story of Gilgamesh was found, recorded in clay tablets for posterity.

Guided by powerful dreams about gods, falling mountains, and showers of glory, Gilgamesh and Enkidu set out for the divine mountain. This place was covered in a magnificent forest of cedar trees, and guarded by an ancient, primordial being, Humbaba, who radiated seven kinds of savage glory. Like Ishtar, Humbaba loses these one by one and, in an echo of the battle with Tiamat, Shamash sends the winds to immobilize Humbaba. Gilgamesh strips Humbaba of his magic weapons, and beheads him despite his pleas for mercy. Humbaba's wild radiance is absorbed by the lion, the hot dry lands, and by Erishkigal's dark and gloomy underworld.

The magnificence of Gilgamesh's victorious return inflamed Ishtar's passion, and she tries to seduce him. Gilgamesh scorns her, naming the many men she has ruined and the gods she has scorned in the past.

Ishtar is furious. Worse, she is humiliated and she demands revenge. The gods create the Bull of Heaven, but Gilgamesh and Enkidu were not to be defeated. They throw the bull's bloody thigh at Ishtar in her temple, and take its head home in triumph.

The rage in heaven could not be contained. Someone had to die. The great gods argued over which of the two should be punished, but they finally decided that Enkidu had to die for the sins of Gilgamesh.

Enkidu's dream of the underworld and the fate of the dead that reside there is one of the most moving passages of literature in the ancient world, and expresses the underlying angst that drove the entire culture. Cursed by the gods, Enkidu had to die, not as a warrior, but as he lay trembling and weak with fever. Disease in that era was powerful beyond the strength of even the greatest of warriors. Gilgamesh, overwhelmed by grief, sings a long beautiful lament for Enkidu, and gives him a hero's funeral. Gilgamesh has learned, at last, to fear death.

The Search for Immortality

The mightiest warrior in the world, who had challenged heaven and the gods with the might of his arm and the power of his will, could not bear sorrow. Gilgamesh set off alone on his final adventure. Like Ishtar, he could rule the world but not his heart, and was fated to travel through hell in the hope that he might revive his dead friend, his mortal half.

Grieving Gilgamesh wanders the world, seeking Utnapishtim, "The Faraway." Only this man and his wife, of all humanity, were graced by the gods with eternal life. Gilgamesh travels through the Mountain of the Rising Sun, somewhat like the Egyptian god Re's underworld journey, arriving at the garden of the gods. There he persuades Ursanabi, ferryman of the dead, to take him to Utnapishtim.

Left *Ishtar Tries to Seduce Gilgamesh*, from *Gilgamesh* by Zabelle Boyajian. Despite her efforts, Gilgamesh rejects the goddess, knowing the evil fate that befell her previous lovers. In an eloquently bitter passage from the story, Gilgamesh decries the faithlessness of woman to man.

Gilgamesh begs to learn how to acquire immortal life. Utnapishtim answers first with a stark answer that nothing is permanent, that everything living must die. Gilgamesh rejects this, demanding to know how Utnapishtim had achieved immortality. The wise old man responds with the story of the great flood—startling in its similarity to the later biblical story of Noah and the flood, complete with ark.

The story goes thus: the constant noise of human multitudes annoyed the gods, and Enlil decided to flood the earth entirely and silence them. Ea (Enki), secretly warns one human, Utnapishtim, instructing him to build an ark, to fill it with livestock, goods, family, and craftsmen, then to seal it up and ride out the flood inside it. Six days and six nights of storm raged, but the seventh dawned clear. Utnapishtim then sent out a dove, but it found no land and so returned. At last a raven flew off without returning, and the people, plants, and animals in the ark went forth to rebuild. The gods were angry until the god Ea reminded them how much they needed their human slaves. Utnapishtim and his wife were made immortal, and allowed to dwell in the Garden of the Sun with the promise that the gods would never again attempt to destroy the human race.

Utnapishtim did not give Gilgamesh the secret of immortality, since that could only be given by the gods. Instead, he gave Gilgamesh a plant to revive Enkidu but, as Gilgamesh slept, a serpent stole it.

Gilgamesh had failed, and he spent his last days upon the walls of his city, brooding on the tragedy of life and death. After his death, he is mourned by all.

Scholars of Mesopotamia have often commented on the unusually pessimistic nature of the themes and conclusions found in the mythological and epic material, referring to Gilgamesh as "the first tragic hero." Some say that Egypt gave the world a vision of heaven and Mesopotamia gave the world a vision of hell. At the very least, the Mesopotamian view of the afterlife was starkly different from that of nearly all the other cultures of the time. Such a grim ending to a life of hard work—an eternity without light or hope—must have been a difficult future to anticipate.

Opposite page **Gilgamesh, or the Lion Spirit.** stone relief, eighth century B.C., Assyrian. The ancient tales of Gilgamesh say that he was able to kill lions with his bare hands and destroy whole armies with his skill in war. Despite his abilities, however, he was a poor ruler and an ill-fated hero.

Left *Gilgamesh, in Search of Immortality, Reaches the Palace of the Goddess Siduri, with its Beautiful Gardens*, from *Gilgamesh* by Zabelle Boyajian. Siduri is sometimes known as the goddess of wine; she vainly urges Gilgamesh to put aside his quest and enjoy life instead.

MIDDLE EASTERN MYTHOLOGY

Right **Persian Empire, 600–500 B.C.** At its peak, the expansive Persian Empire stretched from Egypt to Afghanistan and central Asia. This diverse range of cultures contributed to a rich tradition of storytelling, and fueled ideas that still influence the region today.

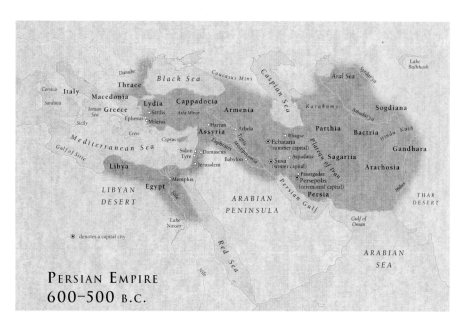

PERSIAN EMPIRE
600–500 B.C.

Most readers would not be surprised to find that the biblical stories of Creation and Eden are often considered mythological. What would surprise quite a number of readers would be to find a collection of biblical stories of patriachs, kings, and prophets included in a section on Middle Eastern mythology. These stories, found in what Christians call the Old Testament, play a fundamental role in the Jewish, Christian, and Muslim religions. However, there is no archaeological or historical evidence for most of the events and characters found in these stories. Furthermore, we still do not know when, where, or by whom these stories were composed and collated to form the books of the Bible. Most scholarly opinion would see this process taking place in the periods of the ancient Persian or Hellenistic Empires in the Middle East, that preceded and succeeded the era of Alexander the Great (356–323 B.C.).

Seen from this perspective, the biblical stories can be located as part of major religious movements that were then occurring in the ancient world. The millennium preceding the time of Christ was marked by the rise and fall of empires and the resulting intermingling of cultures and religions. Questions of universalism and diversity, the One and the Many, arise, together with the questions of justice, good and evil, suffering, and death. It is this dynamic inter action of Babylonian, Palestinian, Assyrian, Egyptian, Syrian, Persian, and Greek religious ideas that resulted in the biblical narratives.

THE INFLUENCE OF THE PERSIAN EMPIRE

The Persian Empire was the first to bring together, under one rule, these diverse cultures. Established under Cyrus the Great in 559 B.C., at its peak the empire would stretch from Egypt and the Balkans in the west to Afghanistan and to central Asia in the east. The importance of Persia for the biblical writers is attested not only by Cyrus being credited with the release of the Judeans from Babylonian captivity and authorizing the restoration of the Jerusalem Temple, but also by his being declared, in Isaiah, as the divine shepherd and the Lord's anointed or the messiah. What then were the religious beliefs of this messiah and of his successors?

The evidence is unclear for Cyrus, but it seems certain that his successors practiced a form of the Zoroastrian faith, a religion which continues today in small communities in Iran, among the Parsis of India, and elsewhere. Zoroaster was the great Iranian prophet who probably lived around 1000 B.C. He did not so much start a new religion as transform existing Iranian religion. Central to the Prophet

Left **Alexander the Great and the Talking Tree.** An illumination from *The Book of Kings,* an epic poem by Firdowsi (A.D. 941–1020). According to legend, Alexander came across this tree as he searched for the Fount of Life.

Middle Eastern rhyme, the *Shahnameh* (*The Book of Kings*), completed by the poet Firdowsi in A.D. 1010.

TELLING THE STORIES

The Islamic triumph shows how the biblical narratives, originally shaped by ancient religious processes, came to shape those same processes themselves. While the biblical texts were authoritative for ancient Judaism, there was not the rigid, literalist approach to reading sacred texts that is found in Christian and Islamic fundamentalist groups today. Ancient Judaism was diverse and complex, and had an active folkloric relationship with these stories. The biblical narratives are often full of gaps, and the Jewish tradition, from the very earliest times, has not been afraid to fill those gaps, and to expand and develop the biblical stories. By the practice of *midrash*, the Jewish people have retold and expanded on these stories and continue to do so. Consequently, these expansions have become part of authoritative scripture. The Sages say that everything one finds in scripture, and every interpretation, was originally revealed to Moses on Mount Sinai. The meanings of the scriptures are infinite—it is through reading, interpretation, and *midrash* that these meanings are uncovered.

By the time of the Prophet Mohammed, there was a rich Jewish story world derived from the biblical narratives. Much of this material was then incorporated into the Islamic scriptures, the Koran (also known as the Qur'an), which is itself a *midrash*, or retelling of the Jewish and Christian biblical narratives. This retelling process continues today within Islam. Despite the Islamic suppression of Zoroastrianism, the encounter of the two religions sparked a new creativity in the retelling of the biblical narratives, and in the weaving of new stories such as those found in the epic tale *One Thousand and One Nights*.

Left **Death of Firhoud.**
A story from *The Book of Kings* tells of the death of the great king Firhoud. Surrounded by his family and loyal subjects, with his last breath he asks them to follow him in death. They did, and were saved from the brutality of the invading Iranian army.

Below **Zoroaster dying in the flames of a temple fire.** Zoroaster was an Iranian prophet, whose teachings were recorded in the scriptures called the *Zend Avesta.* Zoroaster's death is often portrayed in a spectacular manner, surrounded by flames and worshippers. It is believed that he was murdered, at the age of 77.

Zoroaster's teaching was the struggle between good and evil, a struggle in which everyone had a part to play, and would ultimately see the triumph of good. The Zoroastrian religion was the main religion of Persia up to the Arab Islamic conquest of A.D. 642.

Following the conquest, Islamic supremacy led to the decline of Zoroastrianism, which was regarded as an infidel religion. It was only then that some of the ancient Zoroastrian traditions were compiled in the scriptures known as the *Zend Avesta*. Other traditions were translated from the ancient Avestan language and compiled in the Middle Persian texts, *Bundashihn* and *Denkard*. Many other mythical tales of kings and heroes were written down in the epic

PERSIAN MYTHOLOGY

It was the Persian Empire and the bringing together of a diverse range of cultures that began a rich tradition and the development of mythological stories. Ideas of good versus evil, life versus death, and explanations of how the natural world was created remain as constant themes throughout these narratives.

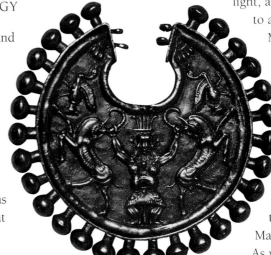

The Divine and the Demonic

The Wise Lord, Ahura Mazda, is the god of gods, the supreme goodness, wisdom, and light. He is the Creator of all that is good: sun, stars, humans, animals, light, and dark, and he is opposed to all suffering. However, Ahura Mazda is not all-powerful but is locked in a cosmic struggle with Angra Mainyu or Ahriman, who is the archdemon or Evil Spirit and the god of darkness. This Evil Spirit, this personification of evil, constantly tries to harm all living things and aims to destroy the world. At the end of time, the great Ahura Mazda will defeat him.

As well as Ahura Mazda, there are a number of divine figures that form his heavenly court. Most prominent are the Amshaspends, the Sons and Daughters of God, who are seven aspects of the divine, directly willed into being. These are Spenta Mainyu (Bounteous Spirit), Vohu Manah (Good Mind), Asha (Truth), Kshathra Vairya (Desired Kingdom), Armaiti (Devotion), Haurvatat (Integrity), and Ameretat (Immortality).

Below them are the Yazatas, the Worshipful Ones, who are the older gods and goddesses of the Iranians. Most important are Anahita, goddess of all the waters, and Mithra, the god responsible for controlling all of the cosmic order.

Similarly, the Evil Spirit is assisted by a variety of demonic beings whose diabolical nature consists of their devotion to trickery and falsehood. Their vocation is to "thwart" all efforts to achieve good. Demons or *div* included Aeshma, demon of fury, and the *Druj*, who were creatures of deceit, often female, always monstrous. The most vicious of these beings was Azhi Dahaka, who evolved into a serpent with three heads. Pairaka, a class of female evils, disguised their malevolence under beauty and charm and became most active in the darkness of night, seducing and harming men.

The Created World

At first creation was good. Ahura Mazda began with the sky, followed by the water and the earth. He created the Primal Tree without bark and thorn, the white ox, and then the archetypal human, Gayomart. However, the forces of evil attacked heaven and earth, devastating all that was created. Drawing from the victory of evil, the forces of life and of good used these lessons as a way of defeating the Evil Spirit. From the body of the ox came corn and medicinal plants, and from the purified seed of the ox came the different animal species. Gayomart was killed in the first battle between good and evil, but from his

SATAN

In the Hebrew Scriptures, Satan is not the name but the title of a functionary of the heavenly council, the Satan. This title may come from an ancient Semitic word meaning, "to obstruct." The main role of the Satan seems to be that of an accuser. Possibly due to Persian influence, by the time of Christ the Satan was transformed into an arch-demonic figure, also known as Beelze-bub. In Judaism, the chief demonic figure is known as Sammael, the angel of death, who led his angels in rebellion against the creation of humanity. A similar account is found in the Koran (Qur'an) where Satan, also known as Iblis and the mightiest of the angels, refused to prostrate himself before Adam, and was expelled from heaven. He was given the power to roam the earth to lead astray those who are not true servants of God.

preserved seed grew the first human couple, Mashye and Mashyane. Undeterred, Angra Mainyu infected their thoughts, forced them to cleave unto him, and tricked them into uttering the first lie—that the world was created by an evil being. This was the first human sin, and from that point on humans lost their orientation in life.

Humans were created as God's helpers in the struggle against evil. Humans and God need each other. The Prophet Zoroaster was crucial for bringing the Good Religion to humanity, restoring them to the path of their true purpose. Zoroaster's divine conception and birth signaled the beginning of the era when evil would be defeated. His conception and birth were miraculous works of the divine, and throughout his life the forces of evil struggled to thwart his acts of kindness. During his childhood, many demonic attempts were made to destroy him. According to the *Zend Avesta* (Zoroastrian scriptures), the final days before the defeat of evil will see the coming of three successive, savior figures or Saoshyants, each of whom are descended from the Prophet, whose seed has been preserved in a lake. The first two figures, Aushedar and Ashedar-mah, will bring

about the destruction of some of the evil in the world. With the third, Astva-terata, all disease, death, and suffering will be overcome, the dead will be raised, and the original Good Creation restored. The overthrow of evil will see the last judgment of humanity. The wicked will be consigned to hell, but not for eternity as this would contradict the divine goodness.

Above **Iblis (Satan).** Some myths say that Iblis was actually a Jinn (a nature spirit). After he was captured by angels, he became one of the mightiest of their kind.

JEWISH AND ISLAMIC MYTHOLOGY

Powerful religious influences filtered into the Arabian peninsula from Syria and Palestine, as well as from Christian Abyssinia (known as modern-day Ethiopia) just across the Red Sea. It is from these extensive sources that tales from the Jews and the Christians merged with ancient Islamic stories.

In the Beginning

The Hebrew Bible contains two creation stories in the opening chapters of Genesis. The first in chapter one is a beautiful, poetic account of creation out of a watery chaos over six days. These days are structured in matching pairs. The first day God creates light and separates the light from the darkness, to form day and night. On the fourth day, God creates the sun, moon, and stars, giving rulership of the day to the sun, and of the night to the moon. Similarly, on the second day, God creates the hard vault of the sky to separate the upper waters from those below, while on the fifth day God creates the creatures of the sea and the birds of the air. On the third day, God separates the dry land from the lower waters, and causes all manner of plants and trees to grow. This act is balanced, on the sixth day, by the creation of all the creatures that live on the land including, of course, humans who are created male and female in the likeness of God. Echoing Ahura Mazda in Persian mythology, God declared he brought humanity into being to be good and blessed it. On the seventh day, God decided to rest, instituting the tradition of Sabbath.

Sex and Death

The second account in Genesis is really about the origins of sex and death. It begins as a dry land creation with God creating a human being (in Hebrew *adamah* or groundling) from the ground. God plants a garden

Below *The Creation* by Miguel Gonzales. On the sixth day God surveys all he has created. He then rests on the seventh day. The animals are led to Adam so that he may name them, and choose from them a companion. None are suitable, so God creates woman from Adam's side.

LILITH

Lilith is a female winged night demon, who preys on men, endangers women in childbirth, and strangles children. She seems to be derived from ancient Babylonian demonology and a class of female evil spirits called *lilitu*. In Jewish tradition, it is said that when Adam and Eve separated, he fathered demons from the spirits that were attached to him. At this time, Lilith bore him many male and female demons. Most famous is the story that Lilith was Adam's first wife and created before Eve. Lilith refused to submit to him and, pronouncing the divine name, she flew away from him. Later she became the permanent partner of Sammael. Another story says that for a time she became a consort of God.

She eats, and convinces Adam to follow her example. The fruit causes Adam and Eve to gain knowledge of good and evil. They become aware of their nakedness, and they hide from God, who realizes that they have eaten the forbidden fruit. God curses the serpent, and as punishment condemns Adam and Eve to a life of struggle and pain. They are expelled from Eden, and are then unable to eat from the Tree of Life which grows in the Garden of Eden. The fruit of this tree provides immortality to all that eat from it. From this point, death becomes a part of human life. Eden is placed under the watchful guard of the Cherubim. In Jewish tradition, Sammael took possession of the serpent, in order to deceive Eve and to gain supremacy over humanity. Sammael is said to have slept with Eve, and Cain was the child of this union. After the birth of Cain and Abel, Adam and Eve separated for 150 years before they came together to conceive Seth, who was born in his father's image, unlike his earlier brothers. In Arab tradition, Iblis tempted Eve. To gain access to Paradise he asked the peacock to smuggle him in but it refused. The peacock told the serpent of Iblis' promise to give the animal that helped him to get entry into the garden, the knowledge of the three sacred words for immortality. Hearing this, the serpent hid Iblis in his mouth and carried him into Paradise. From his hiding spot, Iblis spoke to Eve, who mistakenly believed it was the seemingly magical serpent speaking to her.

Left Expulsion of Adam and Eve from Paradise. This Turkish miniature illustrates the Arab tradition of this tale. In the background stands a peacock, whose haunting cry is said to be a warning or a bad omen. It was the peacock who refused to help Iblis, but inadvertently gave Satan an opportunity to find another creature to take him into Eden.

Below Adam and Eve forbidden to eat from the Tree of Life. This twelfth-century bronze portal shows the couple being escorted out of the garden by an angel. As a result of eating forbidden fruit, immortality is now lost to humanity.

in Eden, places the male human being in the garden, and tells the human being that it may eat of any tree in the garden, except for the Tree of the Knowledge of Good and Evil. God warns that the fruit of this tree will bring death.

God creates all the animals from the ground as potential companions for the human being. Each of the animals is brought to the male human being to be named, but none of them are suitable companions. Finally, God puts the human to sleep, takes one of the human's sides to shape into a woman (the original Hebrew is better translated as side instead of rib). God brings this woman to the male human, who rejoices for he now has a true companion. He names the woman Eve, from the Hebrew word for being, for she is the mother of all the living. In Jewish tradition, Adam and Eve were originally two sides, or two faces, of the one being, which God finally separated to form woman and man.

The story goes on to describe how death entered the world. Firstly, the serpent tempts Eve to taste the fruit of the Tree of the Knowledge of Good and Evil.

Above **Scenes from the life of Abraham.** At the top of this illustration, Abraham proves his loyalty to God by preparing to sacrifice his son Isaac. Abraham is also pictured burning in the furnace—his punishment for refusing to recant his belief in God to King Nimrod.

CHERUBIM AND JINN

The biblical Cherubim are huge, supernatural, eagle-winged beings with lion-shaped bodies and humanlike faces. They guard the gates of Paradise, protect the Ark of the Covenant, and support the Divine throne with their wings. It is believed that they are the beings who enable the Divine throne to fly. God is also said to ride on a Cherub.

The Jinn are invisible nature spirits of Arabian tradition. Before Mohammed, they were revered almost as gods. While angels are made from light and humans from clay, the Koran (Qur'an) says that the Jinn are made from smokeless fire. Mohammed proclaimed a message that both humans and Jinn, can be either Muslim or non-Muslim.

Abraham, Primal Father of Arabs and Jews

Jewish and Islamic accounts agree that Abraham was a prophet of God who attained the highest degree of prophecy. He vigorously preached monotheism. When Abraham was born he was hidden in a cave because the king of the time, Nimrod, was warned that a child born in that year would dethrone him. Nimrod decreed the killing of all newborn male children. Abraham was nursed in the cave by the angel Gabriel. At the age of 13, he emerged from the cave committed to the worship of God. His constant struggle against idolatry brought him into conflict with his father and with the authorities, causing him to smash the idols of his father. In the Islamic account these are the idols of the city. Jewish and Islamic traditions agree that Nimrod eventually ordered the building of a great fiery furnace, threatening Abraham to recant or be cast into the fire. Abraham refused and was thrown into the furnace, but was saved by the intervention of God.

At God's command Abraham and his household move to the land of Canaan. Abraham finds he is without an heir because his wife, Sarah, is barren. To remedy this she sends him her handmaiden, Hagar, and from this union Ishmael, father of the Arab people, is born. God once again intervenes and Sarah miraculously conceives, giving birth to Isaac, father of the Hebrew people. However, Sarah becomes fearful of the enmity from Hagar and Ishmael toward her, so she asks Abraham to take them both into the wilderness. Almost dead from thirst, Hagar and Ishmael are saved by an angel who leads them to a well. According to Islamic tradition, this is the well of Zamzam found at Mecca.

As a test of faith, God demands that Abraham offer up Isaac in sacrifice. Abraham takes the boy to Mount Moriah, and just as he is about to kill him an angel saves Isaac and offers a ram in his place.

According to Jewish tradition, Sammael instigated this angelic intervention, accusing Abraham of selfish piety to God. It is God who decides to test Abraham by asking him to offer up his beloved son. Sammael persuades Abraham not to sacrifice Isaac, and to get Isaac to rebel against this trial. When he saw that Abraham would not disobey God, Sammael revenged himself by telling Sarah that Isaac had been brutally slain, causing her to die of grief and terror. After Sarah's death, Abraham marries Hagar.

Solomon and the Queen of Sheba

In both Jewish and Islamic traditions, Solomon is the great wise king and ruler of a mighty empire. He could speak all the languages, including those of the animals and birds, many of which submitted to his

judgment. He is believed to have built the first temple in Jerusalem with the help of angels and demons. In the Islamic tradition, Solomon ruled over all the Jinns, as well as humans, animals, and birds. It is the hoopoe bird that tells Solomon of a land to the south that does not know of him, and is ruled by the beautiful Queen of Sheba. Solomon asks the bird to deliver to the queen an invitation to come and honor him. Before her arrival, treasures and 6,000 beautiful boys and girls are sent ahead. After a journey that takes three years, the queen arrives in Jerusalem. On meeting Solomon she tests him with many riddles, all of which he answers and proves his wisdom. Solomon then tests the queen by receiving her in a hall with a floor made of crystal. Believing the hallway floor to be a waterway, she raises her skirts, exposing hairy legs and feet, proving to Solomon that she is not a demon. Islamic tradition says that Sheba was Queen of Yemen, where she is commonly known as Bilqis. It is also said that on her arrival at court, she found that a Jinn had set up her throne beside Solomon's. The Ethiopians claim she ruled their city of Axum, and her name was Makeda. After marrying Solomon, she gave birth to a son, Menelik, who became the founder of the Ethiopian royal lineage. Jewish tradition says that Nebuchadnezzar was descended from Solomon and Sheba.

Above **Detail from a nineteenth-century Ethiopian painting.** Solomon meets the elusive Queen of Sheba. According to Ethiopian legend, the son of this union was the founder of the Ethiopian royal family.

Left **Bilqis, the Queen of Sheba, showing her hairy legs to King Solomon.** The Queen of Sheba was tricked into revealing what her legs looked like. Hairy legs and feet were viewed as an aspect of womanly beauty and purity.

One Thousand and One Nights

Also known in English as the *Arabian Nights*, this epic brings together a wide variety of tales from Persian, Arabian, and other backgrounds that draw on biblical, Iranian, and other Middle Eastern mythological elements. The collection is framed in a story about a king, Shahriyar, who discovers that his wife is unfaithful to him and orders his grand-vizier to execute her. Fearing the repeat of infidelity and declaring that all women are as wicked as his first wife, he seeks his revenge by marrying young virgins, and then executing them the morning after the wedding night. Every day the grand-vizier is asked to find a new wife for the king, each day a girl is married, and a wife is dead. The city is filled with the pitiful cries and lamentations of the doomed young women and their grief-stricken families.

One day, Shahrazad, daughter of the grand-vizier, volunteers to marry the king in attempt to stop his barbarous practices and to change the fate of the young girls in the city. On her wedding night Shahrazad wins a promise from the king that he will not kill her until she has told him a story. She begins to tell a story that Shahriyar has never heard before, but the sun rises before Shahrazad can finish this spellbinding story. The king is captivated and halts the executioner's hand so that he might hear the rest of the story. This continues for a thousand and one nights and many different stories are told over this time. After the many nights of storytelling, the king asks Shahrazad what she would wish for and she asks that her life be spared for the sake of the three children she has borne him. He grants her this wish and they live happily ever after. The tales she tells are stories of magic, fantasy, love, and heroism, including the stories of Sinbad, Ali Baba and the Forty Thieves, and Aladdin.

The Fisherman, the Jinn, and the Enchanted Prince

One such tale is the Fisherman, the Jinn, and the Enchanted Prince. An old fisherman hauls in a bronze jar that bears the seal of King Solomon. The poverty-stricken fisherman decides to sell the jar at the bazaar to make a small amount of money to cover his lack of fish. On finding that the jar is quite heavy he breaks the seal and releases a Jinn who has been imprisoned for rebelling against Solomon. Once freed, the Jinn threatens to kill the fisherman, but the wily fisherman uses his wits and tricks it back into the jar, threatening to throw it back into the sea. Finally, the Jinn swears by the divine name not to

harm the fisherman if he frees him and promises to show him how to become a prosperous man. The Jinn leads the fisherman to a lake containing the most remarkable fish that have ever been seen—they are brightly colored red, white, blue, and yellow.

The Jinn tells the fisherman to sell his fish to the king of the land. As the king's maid cooks the fish, apparitions of a young woman and a slave appear and call out to the maid. Seeing these strange things happening, the curious king is determined to find out why these fish are enchanted.

He sets off for the lake and walks until he finds a palace whose only occupant is a melancholy prince whose lower body is made of stone. The prince tells how he found his wife to be unfaithful, and in a jealous rage he maimed her lover without his wife's knowledge. For three years she mourned, building a tomb where she hides her sick and mute lover.

Discovering that her husband, the prince, has injured her love she enchants the prince to become half stone, half man, as well as turning the city into a lake, and its people into fish. Every day she tortures the prince by whipping him brutally 100 times.

Outraged by the injustice, the king kills the sick lover, then tricks the wife into freeing the prince and the city from her spell. The king then kills the wife, and makes the prince his son and heir. The fisherman is rewarded handsomely, for being the first person to alert the king to the dreadful enchantment.

> *Vistas of fairy-land, where beauty reigns ... Of life in tents and palaces and fanes.*
> ISABEL BURTON (1831–1896)

Above **Mohammed and Fatima.** In this eighteenth-century Turkish painting, Mohammed is pledging his daughter Fatima to her cousin Ali. Mohammed and Fatima's faces are covered with divine light. Fatima is said to be one of the most important women in Islamic mythology.

Opposite page **Saif ul-Muluk, an Egyptian prince, and Badi'al-Jamal, a Jinn princess.** According to *One Thousand and One Nights*, the lovers are brought together by the Jinn, and carried off in a golden carriage.

INDIAN MYTHOLOGY

Right Writings from the Sri Bhagavata (ancient text). A story from the *Bhagavata Puranas* is written in Sanskrit on a roll of silk paper. *Puranas* are legendary texts and the most extensive sources of Hindu mythology.

The Indian subcontinent is a vast, highly populated region with a rich and colorful mix of cultures. Many different ethnic groups exist side by side. Throughout India's long and tumultuous history, it has been invaded and colonized on numerous occasions, initially by the Aryans from the north, and later in the fourth century B.C. by Alexander the Great. Invasions by the Muslims followed, and later the Mongols from central Asia, and then colonization by the British also helped to shape the face of modern India. All these different influences have been incorporated into the fabric of Indian culture.

India's earliest religious scripture, the *Rg Veda*, appeared some time in the second millennium B.C. This consisted chiefly of hymns to a host of deities—the war god; the fire god; and animistic spirits of the sky, sun, and moon, of rivers and storms, of animals and trees. Some of the Vedic hymns, however, expressed a spirit of philosophical inquiry. After the composition of the *Rg Veda* came a significant portion of literature, a collection of philosophical speculations. This collection of writings, begun about 700 B.C. and called the *Upanishads*, contained many of the themes that inspired the originators of Jainism and Buddhism,

and provided the religious foundation for Hinduism.

Throughout the centuries, Hinduism, with its pantheon of gods and goddesses, has remained the most widespread of Indian religions, and its exciting mythical dramas seem like a mirror for the eventful history of this region. In practice, different gods and goddesses from this mythology have become the focus of the many different cults and traditions found within Hinduism.

The body of Hindu mythology is gigantic, and is found in numerous religious and literary texts from as far back as 1200 B.C. until the present day. Much of this mythology was told by the storytellers in villages and towns, and became very widely known by the majority of the Indian population.

In its variety lay Hinduism's strength. By accommodating all classes, all intellects, and all personalities, it became more than a religion; it established the framework for the uniquely Indian society, in which people of widely varying backgrounds, beliefs, social standing, and education go their own separate ways—together.

A full pantheon of gods can be identified in the earliest (Vedic) literature, and is added to via the great epics, the *Mahabharata* and the *Ramayana,* and the texts of legendary stories called the *Puranas.* Of the millions of deities in the pantheon, five stand out—Brahmā, Vishnu, Shiva, Ganesha, and Pārvāti, also known as Umā or the Mother Goddess. Myths associated with the Hindu gods are, at once, heroic tales and moral lessons. These gods are often just symbols of the interplay of larger themes—focused on the creation, preservation, and destruction of the world; tensions within families; and on the nature of the devotional relationship between god and devotee—explored in the narratives, in the same manner that problems in contemporary societies are often explored today across many soap operas.

Below The wedding procession of Rama. The epic Sanskrit poem the *Ramayana* narrates the adventures of Rama, a mythical hero. In this scene, the celebrations for his wedding spill on to the village street.

Left **A mythological universe.** This diagram shows the great Mount Meru at the center of the universe. The writing outside of the circle tells of the importance and beauty of the mountain, which is also a meeting place for the gods.

India is the birthplace of several religious traditions. These new religions often adopted the creation myths from Hinduism, but sought social change through new religious expression, just as it happened with the development of Christianity. Buddhism has become a great world religion; Jainism has remained largely confined to India, probably because of its extreme asceticism; and Sikhism initially strove to overcome the conflict between Hinduism and Islam. All of these religions developed on Indian soil through the activity of spiritual teachers or gurus. Numerous myths are associated with these teachers; many are recorded in sacred texts, but many more myths are told within the practice of the various Indian religions.

Pilgrimage is an important part of the religious practice in India. Pilgrims enjoy hearing accounts of the trials and tribulations of their gods, sages, and gurus—events from the mythical or historical past that took place at the holy pilgrimage sites. There are many sacred sites throughout India that are shared by peoples of different faiths, and visited by pilgrims from different spiritual traditions. The last three myths included in this chapter are all associated with Rewalsar, in Himachal Pradesh, in the foothills of the Himalaya in northern India.

SOME OF THE HINDU PANTHEON

BRAHMĀ THE CREATOR was once thought to be the greatest of gods because he set the universe in motion. He has faded in importance with the rise of Shiva and Vishnu.

VISHNU THE PRESERVER is also known as the universal god. Whenever mankind needs help, this benevolent god appears on earth as an avatar or reincarnation. He is often represented by the color blue.

SHIVA THE DESTROYER is one of Hindu's two mightiest gods, and represents power, whatever his aspect.

GANESHA is the roly-poly elephant-headed son of Shiva, and is probably the most popular god in the pantheon.

PĀRVĀTI represents the unity of god and goddess. She is the daughter of the Himalaya Mountains, and sister of the River Ganges.

Above **The churning of the sea of milk.** Vishnu plans cosmic order by instructing demons and gods to wrap the cosmic serpent, Vasuki, around Mount Meru. They all pull together to churn the sea to create ambrosia, the source of immortality.

THE CHURNING OF THE OCEAN FOR IMMORTALITY

One creation myth is focused on defining the roles of the gods and demons, and distinguishes them on the basis of who possesses the gift of immortality, and who is stuck with mortal death.

In ancient times, the gods and the demons fought, and when the demons died they were revived with a magical potion provided by the god Shiva. The other gods sought advice from Brahmå. He said, "Make peace with the demons, and churn the ocean for the nectar of immortality, ask Vishnu to help. Use the Meru Mountain as the churning stick, and the serpent Vasuki as the string attached to the churning stick."

All the gods and demons went to the ocean, and different ones took hold of the mountain, and turned

it around for 100 divine years. Animals and plants fell into the ocean, thickening up its waters, and wine was produced. The rubbing of trees on the mountain caused fire, which began driving out the rest of the animals. The ocean turned into milk, and clarified butter came out of it.

Various gods came out of the ocean holding many precious objects, then came fire and snakes. As the churning continued, the dreadful *Kālakuta* poison was created and enveloped the universe. This potent poison threatened to destroy all the gods and demons, so Shiva swallowed the poison, which turned his throat black.

Finally, Dhanvantari appeared with a pot of ambrosia, the nectar of immortality. Both gods and demons cried out "It's mine!" Vishnu assumed the form of a woman named Infatuation, who bewitched

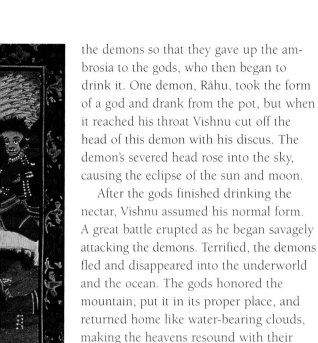

the demons so that they gave up the ambrosia to the gods, who then began to drink it. One demon, Râhu, took the form of a god and drank from the pot, but when it reached his throat Vishnu cut off the head of this demon with his discus. The demon's severed head rose into the sky, causing the eclipse of the sun and moon.

After the gods finished drinking the nectar, Vishnu assumed his normal form. A great battle erupted as he began savagely attacking the demons. Terrified, the demons fled and disappeared into the underworld and the ocean. The gods honored the mountain, put it in its proper place, and returned home like water-bearing clouds, making the heavens resound with their thunderous shouts. The precious nectar of immortality was given to Vishnu to guard and keep safe.

SHIVA'S DESTRUCTION OF DAKSA'S SACRIFICE

Shiva, often called Rudra in Hindu mythology, is associated with destruction, nonconformity, and ascetic practices, all of which are regarded as being, in some way, antagonistic toward the order that creation needs to survive, and it seems that these practices will always appear to be on the outskirts of the ordered world. In this myth, Shiva threatens Daksa's sacrifice. The sacrifice is always identified with the capacity to create, and also functions as a model of the ordered world.

Rudra was born as a result of Brahmâ's anger at being unable to create. Brahmâ then gave Gauri, as a wife, to Rudra, forbidding him to perform ascetic practices, instructing him to create the world instead. Rudra refused, and plunged into the water. Brahmâ took Gauri back, and from his mind created seven sons, including Daksa, so that these offspring would, in turn, create. Brahmâ offered Gauri to Daksa as a daughter, causing Daksa to rejoice, and he enthusiastically performed the supreme sacrifice to the pleasure of Brahmâ.

After 10,000 years Rudra came out of the water, wishing to create the universe and the gods, but saw that the world had already been created, as a result of Daksa's sacrifice. Overcome by anger, Rudra violently destroyed Daksa's sacrifice. Eventually, he restored it at the request of the gods, and went with Gauri to his own dwelling place.

THE CREATION OF DEATH

In Hindu mythology, Death is always represented as a divine figure named Myrtu or Yama. He presides over one of the worlds of the dead, and supervises the enumeration of the good and bad deeds *(karma)* of all of the people who have died. The nature of these deeds directly affects where people are born in subsequent lives.

Sometimes Death disappears or takes a holiday, and the Earth becomes overcrowded and has to ask Brahmâ to do something about the huge number of people on her surface. Brahmâ's response is to either create Death, or to arrange Shiva to create Death, and place it among people as the origin of evil actions and the outcomes of these actions.

The gods in heaven also experience great fear when Death is absent because humans, characterized by their mortality, become immortal—thereby undermining the gods' own unique status.

Below **Vishnu the Preserver.** This god is also known as the solar god. The story of the "Three Steps" illustrates how Vishnu can clear the sky, the earth, and the lower world with three steps. He drives away the darkness as he travels.

Above **Krishna (right) and Balarāma in the forest.** In one story involving Krishna, to protect him from the murderous anger of his uncle, Krishna's parents exchange him for the daughter of a poor cowherd.

KRISHNA AND BALARĀMA

A later body of mythology, not found in the earliest literature, focuses on the important devotional god Krishna, one of the many forms of the god Vishnu. The Krishna myths combine a set of graphic word images containing strong theological and devotional messages for the devotees who read and hear them.

Some of the most devotional stories of this mythology center on the pranks of Krishna as a child, and his capacity to disguise his true form as the most powerful god in the universe.

Balarāma and Krishna used to play in the village, crawling into the fields, and come back to their mothers covered in mud. But their mothers loved their sons, and would hug them and put them to their breasts. When they were boys they used to play tricks on the village animals, and when Krishna was a little older, he became the leader of a group of youths who used to get up to all sorts of pranks. The wives of the cowherds would tell Yashodha, Krishna's mother, that he had been untying calves, stealing curds and milk, and was being a general nuisance.

One day the other boys told Yashodha that Krishna had eaten dirt. He denied this, and told her to look in his mouth. When she looked into his gaping mouth she saw the whole eternal universe, including heaven, the regions of the sky, and the earth with its mountains, islands, and oceans. She saw the whole universe in all its infinite variety, with all the forms of life, and time, nature, action, hopes, her own village, and herself. Then she became afraid and confused, wondering, "Is this a dream or an illusion wrought by a god? Or is it a delusion of my own perception? Or is it some portent of the natural powers of this little boy, my son? I bow down to the feet of the god, whose nature cannot be imagined or grasped by mind, heart, acts, or speech; he in whom all of this universe is inherent, impossible to fathom. The god is my refuge."

When his mother came to understand the true essence, in this way, the Lord Krishna spread his magical illusion in the form of maternal affection. Instantly, his mother lost the memory of what she had just seen, and the fear and confusion she had experienced, and lovingly took her son on her lap.

become a bull pulling a plough. Samudrå cursed the *brahmin* to become a donkey. She was cursed by the beggar to become an outcast woman. The curses became true, and Sulabha, Samudrå, and the poor *brahmin* beggar changed form.

Wandering in the city on the day of a festival of Ganesha, Samudrå saw a Ganesha temple. Suddenly, a violent storm started up, and the terrified Samudrå approached many houses in the city for shelter but was thrown out of every one she came to. Despairing, she made her weary way to the temple.

Samudrå started a fire with some *durva* grass so she could warm herself. Wind moved a blade of grass and, driven by fate, the grass fell on Ganesha's head. At the same time the cold, frightened donkey came into the temple, as did the bull freed from the plough. The animals ate the woman's grass, and then fought near the image of Ganesha. From their mouths two blades of *durva* grass fell onto Ganesha's trunk and foot, which pleased him. To stop this calamity, Samudrå struck the donkey and the bull with her staff, and then began worshipping Ganesha.

Watching the three of them, Ganesha considered that they had worshipped him well enough, and decided to send them to his own special heaven on a remark-able flying vehicle. Worshippers at the temple saw this benevolence, and were astonished, believing this had come about because of good *karma*.

Some of the great *yogins* approached Ganesha's entourage, and asked why the result was such a happy one, despite the depravity and obvious bad *karma* of the three misfits. The *yogins* couldn't understand why their devotion to Ganesha hadn't rewarded them. Incensed, they declared that they would stop their own worship immediately so that they, too, could find out how to reach Ganesha's home.

GANESHA AND SULABHA

Ganesha has been one of the most important Hindu gods for the last 1,000 years, largely because he is the god responsible for creating and removing obstacles. Many myths show devotees worshipping him for the removal of obstacles, whereas other myths show how the unwitting worship of him will also produce positive results.

In the city of Jamba there lived a warrior named Sulabha who constantly sang hymns of praise to the god Ganesha. Sulabha's wife, Samudrå, was virtuous and beautiful.

One day a very poor *brahmin* beggar named Madhusudana appeared. Sulabha bowed, but laughed at the *brahmin*, who then cursed him to

Left **Pãrvãti, Hindu goddess and wife of Shiva.** A feminine divinity who personifies the power of Shiva, this goddess is often portrayed with 10 arms brandishing various weapons, which signify the destructive side of her nature. In this image she gently nurses her baby son, Ganesha.

Below **Ganesha, son of Shiva and Pãrvãti.** This elephant-shaped god is worshipped as the god of wisdom, good luck, and the remover of obstacles. He was born from the dew of Pãrvãti's body, mingled with dust. Shiva, in anger, cut off Ganesha's human head. In remorse, Shiva replaced it with the head of the first animal he came across—an elephant.

Above **Detail of the Hindu trinity or Trimurti.** The absolute god manifests himself in three different aspects: Brahmå the Creator, Vishnu the Preserver, and Shiva the Destroyer. The sound of the mantra "om," comes from these gods' names.

HINDU: HOW MAHA-RISHI LOMAS REALIZED THE EXISTENCE OF GOD

We learn in the *Skanda Purana*, a very ancient text (the earliest known manuscript of the *Skanda Purana* dates from the eighth century A.D.), that the name of a particular mountain lake is Hridalayesh, meaning the "lake abode of the master," indicating its spiritual value. However, no one these days uses that name. This place is now called Rewalsar.

The oldest sage in the universe, great Rishi Lomas (also known as Maha-Rishi Lomas, as Maha means "great"), through the power of his meditation was rewarded with an exceptionally long life,

> *What is found in this epic may be elsewhere; What is not in this epic is nowhere else.*
>
> THE *MAHABHARATA*, THE BOOK OF THE BEGINNING

for only one hair on his body had decayed in each age (*Kalpa*). Rishi Lomas appears in the well-known Indian epic, the *Mahabharata*.

Rishi Lomas went to meditate on the Infinite, in the caves on the mountain Brahmå-Pārvāti, from where he saw this wondrous lake, with magnificent geese, ducks, and other water birds swimming and making beautiful sounds. Lovely young maidens were playfully splashing in the water. In the middle of the lake an exquisite blue lotus was blooming. The lake itself was surrounded by thick groves of trees, and Rishi Lomas recognized that the trees were actually forms of the gods, and the creepers entwined around them were the goddesses.

Rishi wandered down to the lake, and found a place conducive to meditation on the western bank. Controlling all his senses, Rishi dedicated his practice of penance to the Lord Shiva. Rishi Lomas received special teachings from Shiva, so that he really understood the existence of God. Sometimes he saw Lord Shiva and Pārvāti seated on a floating island in the middle of the lake, enjoying divine play. He also witnessed Lord Shiva sailing on the lake on a huge snake called Sheshnag. Lord Shiva gave this lake and seven others nearby to Rishi Lomas. The floating islands on the lake remind pilgrims of Rishi Lomas's realization of the existence of God, and flags are placed on the islands as offerings.

Rishi Lomas's meditation led him to experience the presence of all five gods: Vishnu, Brahmå, Ganesha, Shiva, and Pārvāti, who all reside together at this lake, having met there and enjoyed its great beauty, as told in the *Puranas*. There is a single image of these five gods together in the temple at the lake, as well as various representations of Brahmå-Pārvāti and Rishi Lomas. It is an extremely beneficial place for the pilgrim, particularly if they take a dip in the lake on special days associated with Shiva, as this purifies all sins.

BUDDHIST: HOW MANDARAVA, PRINCESS OF ZAHOR, MEETS HER VAJRA MASTER, PADMASAMBHAVA, AND THE ORIGINS OF THE SACRED LAKE TSO-PEMA

The city of Mandi was the capital of the ancient kingdom of Zahor. The King and Queen had a beautiful young daughter, Mandarava, who developed great faith in the teachings of the Buddha. She refused marriage to the princes of all the neighboring kingdoms, devoting her life to meditation, along with 500 other young women.

One night, Mandarava had a dream where she saw the Buddha, sitting on a lotus in rainbow light, who told her to come to a beautiful grassy hill nearby to receive teachings the next day. Mandarava, accompanied by the other female devotees, went, as instructed in the dream, to the hill that was covered in sweet-smelling flowers. Padmasambhava, whose name means "Lotus

Born," appeared before them in a rainbow light. All in his presence were filled with great devotion on seeing him, and hearing his sacred teachings of the secret-mantra *Vajrayana*. They invited the Master to come to their convent. Each day Padmasambhava instructed them in the esoteric teachings. Princess Mandarava, being a truly spiritual and blessed being, was the foremost disciple, quickly understanding the real meaning of her guru's chosen words.

Sometime later, a no-good, layabout cowherd came across the female devotees and their Master rejoicing in the teachings. He continued on into the city, spreading rumors about the Princess, saying she was keeping company with

Above **Padmasambhava.** An eighth-century mystic whose background has a princely origin, he is believed to be the son of the blind king, Indrabhuti. Padmasambhava imitates the Buddha in his desire to abandon the world.

Left **Buddha Sakyamuni.** The founding Buddha was born on the banks of the Ganges in 563 B.C. He was never portrayed in carvings or statues until A.D. 300, when the first sculptures of the Buddha were created.

some ordinary fellow instead of practicing meditation. The King heard these rumors and was infuriated, not believing that his daughter would behave in this way. However, the rumors persisted, and when the King investigated the situation, he did not believe his ministers who informed him that a great teacher was in his daughter's company. He thought that some ordinary man was courting his daughter, and was outraged because he had refused the advances of the neighboring princes so that his daughter could meditate.

The King ordered that the man be caught and burnt alive on a funeral pyre, and that Mandarava be imprisoned. Padmasambhava was very easily captured, taken to the grassy hill, and set alight on a pyre. The flames burnt high. Padmasambhava was

seen as an eight-year-old boy, sitting on a splendid lotus, surrounded by rainbows. The fire continued to burn for many days. A lake formed around the flames, and the lotus throne of Padmasambhava rose out of the lake.

That lake is Tso-Pema, the Lotus Lake, called Rewalsar by the Indians. The nine floating islands on the lake move contrary to the wind, and were formed from the ashes of the pyre that burnt so fiercely, yet did not harm Padmasambhava. These islands are covered with greenery, and the reeds offer protection to many beautiful birds.

The King's ministers heard about this extraordinary scene and came to investigate. They were totally convinced that this was a great Vajra Master, and reported this back to the King who also came to investigate. He realized he had made a grave error of judgment, and confessed to Padmasambhava, requesting him to take his place as King and spiritual teacher of Zahor. Padmasambhava consented, and wore the fine silk clothes and crown that the King supplied to him. Padmasambhava was, from then on, known as Guru Chimé Pema Jungné—the Immortal Lotus Born Teacher.

Mandarava was freed. She became one of Padmasambhava's closest disciples, and one of his two main consorts, later practicing with the Master at Maratika Cave in Nepal, where they both realized and came to understand the Long-Life Practice.

Now Tso-Pema is a great power-place of pilgrimage, where Buddhists from all over the world come to visit. There are several caves near the lake where *yogins* and *yoginis* meditate. Pilgrims also circle the lake many times, saying their mantras.

SIKH: THE NAMING OF THE REWALSAR, AND THE UNIFICATION OF THE HILL STATES

Rewal, the son of King Reva, ruled over the Kingdom of Mandi. He had a few enemies. The one that caused him the greatest fear was Yaksha, who lived in the dark forest, Naina Dhar. Yaksha caused many problems for Rewal, including engaging him in battles. Unfortunately, because of his fear, Rewal lost his kingdom to Yaksha. He then became a wandering beggar, and through his meditation lived for a very long time, moving from place to place.

Sikh Guru Gobind Singh (1675–1708), the tenth and last Sikh Guru, came to Mandi at the same time that Raja Ajmer Chand from the Kingdom of Bilaspur was being installed, sometime in the seventeenth century. On this occasion all the Rajas from the surrounding 22 Hill States from Garwhal to Chamba

JAINISM

The last of the prophets of the Jains was Mahavira (born 540 B.C.), a contemporary of Buddha Sakyamuni. It is likely that these two men were aware of each other's teachings, although no records of their meeting have been found. Mahavira was important in the development of the Jain community and philosophy, but he was not the founder of Jainism, as is sometimes claimed. The previous prophet, the twenty-third, was Parsva, who ruled in the thirteenth heaven in his previous incarnation as Indra. He was born

to King Avasena and Queen Vama, who saw a great serpent at her side one night during her pregnancy. Her child was called Parsva, meaning "flank." Parsva renounced the world, and through his asceticism overcame his *karma* and achieved omniscience.

Below **Jain wheel of life.** Devotees of Jainism believe that the soul is constantly being reborn on either a higher or lower plane. The circles represent these levels, and outline the worship of the relevant deities.

hiding in the forest, for he could not attend the coronation since the loss of his kingdom. He saw the Guru, and prostrated at his feet, beseeching the Guru to help him. Although he had meditated for a long time he had not obtained any blessings. He knew this was because of his long-standing fear of Yaksha.

Guru Gobind Singh, being a true King, freed Rewal from his fear by killing Yaksha. He also instructed Rewal that if one meditated with a selfish motive, such as that of regaining one's kingdom, one never received blessings. Instead, one should always meditate on God-the-Timeless-Being, without any selfish motives. Only in this particular way can salvation be gained by a person. Subsequently, Rewal overcame all his worldly attachments and fear, and gained true understanding.

The beautiful lake, beyond the dark forest, is now called Rewalsar. This is a special place, and anyone coming here on pilgrimage will purify all sins. At times of great disturbance, when the whole land is flooded, this sacred place of Rewalsar is believed to be a haven for all Sikhs.

had gathered together. Fearing the tyranny of the Muslim Emperor, they decided to meet with Guru Gobind Singh. This great Guru formed the community of the Sikhs, the Khalsa, who were devout warriors prepared to unite together and fight for their Hindu religion against the Muslims. All the Rajas of the Hill States formed a united group, under the guidance of Guru Gobind Singh and the Sikh Khalsa.

While in the area, Guru Gobind Singh went hunting in the dark forest, Naina Dhar. Rewal had returned to the region near his kingdom, and was

Below **Twenty-four *Tir-thankaras.*** This sculpture represents saints who have reached perfection and absolute freedom. *Tirthankara* means "fordmakers," people who have managed to find their way across the swirling current of *samsara* (the eternal cycle of life and death).

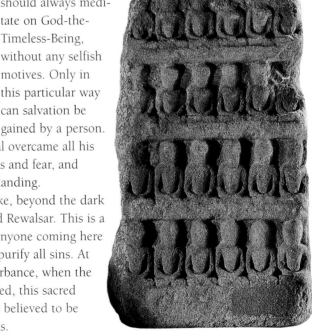

CHINESE MYTHOLOGY

In most civilizations, the earliest traditions and often the earliest literature are mythological, and deal with ultimate origins, or the creation of the world, as well as tales of supernatural beings. China, at first sight, seems an exception. In the *Classics,* the most ancient Chinese books, and the textbooks of the Confucian school, we find stories of men, kings and nobles, soldiers, and peasants, but not gods.

The *Book of History,* although probably partly legendary, has no record of creation stories, and deals mainly with human activities. The famous *Book of Changes* is symbolic, but is not in story form, and was traditionally interpreted as relating to real events. *The Book of Songs* mostly consists of folksongs, but there are traces of mythology in the ritual hymns. The *Classics* are resolutely antimythological, reflecting the ideals of their Confucian editors.

The founders of the early dynasties are claimed to have had miraculous or divine origins, and these were alluded to in the *Classics.* For example, the first emperor of the royal lineage, that became the Shang Dynasty, was conceived when his mother swallowed an egg. Jiang Yuan, the mother of Hou Ji, ancestor of the Zhou rulers, became pregnant when she inadvertently stepped in a toe-print of God. Such stories probably reflect much earlier myths, which can only be glimpsed between the lines of the official literature that is available.

The myths collected from tribal peoples (the so-called national minorities) in modern China, probably represent the traditions of the various peoples out of which developed the Han, or core Chinese group in north China, and these are certainly full of creation stories and prominent heroic mythological figures.

Right **Mystical dragon.** The dragon was long regarded as a god in China. The Dragon Kings rule the seas, and are approached in times of drought and to avert flooding. The clouds around the dragon are symbols of eternal youth.

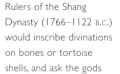

Right **Oracle bones.** Rulers of the Shang Dynasty (1766–1122 B.C.) would inscribe divinations on bones or tortoise shells, and ask the gods for solutions to rain, flood, and famine, or predictions on the outcomes of wars.

MYTHICAL FIGURES

What is clear in the records is that the ancient Chinese seem to have historicized mythical figures. Unlike the ancient Greeks who, according to Euhemerus (*c.* 300 B.C.), turned men into gods, the ancient Chinese turned gods into men. The interest of the Confucian scholars, who were the keepers of the tradition, was in society, government, and morality; and history served these scholars better in these areas rather than the ideas of mythology.

The very earliest writings we have from ancient China are the short inscriptions on the oracle bones from the second millennium B.C., and they reveal a variety of spirit-beings to whom sacrifices were offered. Very little is known about any of them. They must have been regarded as powerful, and their names suggest they arose from nature myths, but their stories are lost forever. As Derk Bodde, an authority on Chinese myth and ritual, says, there were certainly myths in ancient China, but not a systematic mythology.

The earliest writings of the Daoist tradition, the *Daode Jing* and the *Zhuangzi,* contain references to mysterious figures that may come from traditional mythology. Their names suggest they are allegorical or symbolic figures. For example, in *Zhuangzi,* there is a story about Chaos, whose friends try to help him out by boring apertures into his body so that he is able to breathe, see, hear, and eat. He is literally bored to death by his friends. Such stories make their point well, but are really only conscious literary productions rather than the stuff of myths, which come from deeper sources in the unconscious and preliterate Chinese traditions.

FOLK MYTHOLOGY

Among the popular local cults of female deities, one stands out, with variants along the Chinese coast, in Taiwan, and in Southeast Asia. She is known by various names, with Mazu and the Queen of Heaven (Tian Hou) being the most popular. The associated mythology varies widely, but the basic details are similar. A woman mysteriously appears to still a storm, and saves the lives of sailors; in one popular version, the sailors she saves are her brothers. Her festival on the twenty-third day of the third lunar month is the major festival of boat people throughout China. The name of Macao is derived from a famous old temple dedicated to her on the peninsula's harbor.

There is one popular god everyone will have seen in Chinese restaurants and businesses—Guan Di. He was an historical figure, Guan Yu, a general of the Three Kingdoms period (third century A.D.). Logically enough, he became God of War, but because he was so powerful he was worshipped by students wanting to pass examinations, and then worshipped by shopkeepers wanting to increase their profits. This is what Chinese mythology is about: a projection of human desires, especially for success, wealth, and children.

INFLUENCES ON CHINESE MYTHOLOGY

The arrival in China, in about the first century A.D., of the Indian religion, Buddhism, transformed Chinese mythology. The stories of the life and previous lives of the Buddha, of Indian gods, and miraculous events found in the Buddhist sutras were translated into Chinese, and became the stock in trade of the marketplace storytellers. They influenced popular literature, folk religious practices, and organized Daoist religion which systematized and developed old Chinese traditions. They also brought a new interest in ultimate origins, in cosmogony (where the world as we know it came from), and in cosmology (what the world is like).

In Chinese popular religion it is impossible to disentangle sources deriving from the great traditions of Confucianism, Daoism, and Buddhism from those that come from local and very ancient sources. Every village or area has its own God of the Place (Tudi Gong), and their shrines can be seen in streets and in temples throughout the Chinese diaspora, and now in the People's Republic. These all have their stories and their myths. But, once again, especially in the case of City Gods, they are often found to be deified humans, upright officials, generals, and heroes from the past. The Chinese gods even have birthdays, wives, and children, and a bureaucracy to serve them. As in all societies, Chinese myths are closely related to the involvement of rituals and festivals.

There are myths and practices associated with the New Year; the coming of spring (Qing Ming); harvest time; the birthdays of the Jade Emperor (the Daoist high God), Confucius, Buddha, and Laozi; the lantern festival; the dragon boat festival; and the "Hungry Ghosts" festival.

CONFUCIAN MYTHOLOGY

In Song 245 of the classic *Book of Songs*, there is a hymn that probably accompanied a sacrificial ritual of the kings of the Zhou Dynasty (traditional date from 1122–221 B.C.). It celebrates the origins of the

Above **Laozi, Confucius, and baby Buddha.** Laozi wrote the text which forms the basis of Daoism. He is said to have been a contemporary of Confucius, the scholar and a teacher of Buddha. Daoism, Confucianism, and Buddhism all have contributed to Chinese mythology.

151

Opposite page **Emperor Ming Huang on his journey to Shu.** Legend has it that while on a journey to another province, Emperor Ming Huang (A.D. 713–756) dreamed that a small demon stole his belongings. A larger demon appeared, grabbed the smaller demon by the throat, and gouged out its eyes.

Right **Confucius, an influential scholar (551–479 B.C.).** Renowned as a philosopher and an advisor to the Zhou Dynasty, Confucius's teachings impacted on Chinese mythology by creating culture heroes, that is, men that were worshipped as gods.

Below **Emperor Xuanzong and his horses.** Legends of the various ruling dynasties are important as they reflect the divine selection. The tales also relay the idiosyncrasies of these godlike men. An indulgence of Xuanzong was a stable of 40,000 dancing horses.

Zhou royal house, and the founding of their first capital in Tai, long before they conquered all of north China. It is a classic hero myth in which the protagonist has mysterious, possibly divine origins, an extraordinary birth, is abandoned, rescued, develops precociously, and performs great deeds. His great achievement, though, is characteristically Chinese—he invents farming, and establishes the agricultural way of life. This hymn shows how the Hou Ji myth became the basis of an annual spring sacrifice to sanctify the coming agricultural year. Much more typical in the *Classics* are stories about the founding Sage Kings of China, discovered in the *Book of History*. In the beginning, some 5,000 years ago, there were the Three Sovereigns named Fu Xi, Shen Nong, and Huang Di (the Yellow Emperor).

They were the inventors of, respectively: writing, agriculture, and the calendar—all fundamental features of Chinese civilization. There is no historical evidence for the existence of such individuals, but some time around the third millennium B.C., perhaps even earlier, all three basic inventions undoubtedly occurred. They were probably gradual developments rather than inventions by individuals, but they marked the beginning of civilization in the strict sense in China. So these figures are "culture heroes" by whom the main features of Chinese civilization were fathered. (There are no "mothers" as in many other national mythologies.)

The Three Sovereigns were followed by the Five Emperors, the last two of which, Yao and Shun, were the first two of the Three Sage Kings who began the Chinese empire. Yao chose Shun as his successor when he heard how he managed to live peacefully with his dreadful family who, among other things, tried to kill him by dropping a rock on his head when he was down repairing a well. Yao tested Shun with various administrative tasks, and gave Shun his two daughters in marriage, to see whether he could keep both of them happy. Shun passed these difficult tests and was chosen as king, rather than Yao's useless eldest son. And so began the custom of choosing the most virtuous man to rule the empire. Shun's successor was Yu, the founder of the first dynasty, the Xia. Yu's great achievement, it is said, was to implement measures for flood control. "If it wasn't for Yu we would all have been fishes," states an old Chinese saying.

The *Book of History* goes on to tell how the Xia kings became degenerate, and were replaced by the virtuous Shang kings chosen by the High God. In turn, the Shang lost the Mandate of Heaven, and were replaced by the founders of the Zhou Dynasty, ruling when the *Classics* were written. If this is mythology, rather than legend (or the elaboration of the stories about actual people), it is political not religious mythology. Given its emphasis on legitimacy and divine sanction for ruling China, its purpose is clearly ideological. It would not fit the Chinese definition of "myth," which is *shenhua*, (talking about spirits). However, it is not history, and clearly falls within the boundaries of what the West calls "mythology." For example, the story of the last king of the first dynasty, the Xia, is obviously mythological, as Jie Gui is depicted as a monster of vice. He

was strong enough to twist iron bars into rope, and he made war on everybody, wearing out his subjects with his tirades. To buy him off, one of the great chiefs presented one of his daughters to him for marriage. Jie Gui was so infatuated with his new wife, that he made her a bed of ivory and gems, and created a garden in which they could enjoy themselves during the summer months. He built a pool and filled it with wine, he hung meat in all the trees, and surrounded himself with exotic foods. Jie Gui became so debauched that his subjects, the Shang, now became tired of his self-indulgent behavior, and realized they had no choice but to overthrow him.

HOU JI, FATHER OF THE PEOPLE

Once there was a woman called Jiang Yuan, who became the mother of the people. Childless, she conceived her son, Hou Ji, by stepping in the toe-print of God. She suffered no pain in giving birth, but her husband disowned the child who was abandoned in the lane outside the house. The farm animals came and kept him safe. He was then thrown out into the forest, but the woodsmen found him and saved him. He was left in the ice and snow to die, but birds came and warmed him with their wings. He grew strong and tall, and began to grow his own food. He taught the ancient people how to grow beans and rice, wheat and melons, all the crops that feed the people today. So every year at harvest time, in honor of Hou Ji, grain is harvested to make wine and cakes, then a ram is sacrificed and eaten. Hou Ji is seen as the founder of the dynasty that taught people how to live the Chinese way.

Above **Flying apsara, a mythological nymph.** These flying beings come from Hindu mythology, but were adopted by the Chinese. Tang Dynasty (A.D. 581–755) emperors used these carvings as curtain raisers, to re-create a Buddhist paradise within their lavish palaces.

Right **Mythological sea monsters.** *Classic of the Mountains and Seas* is an anthology of stories collected in the first century B.C. It lists fantastic creatures that combine the physical attributes of a number of animals, such as whale with elephant tusks, or crocodiles with tiger tails.

CREATION MYTHOLOGY

Chinese creation mythology is not found in the very earliest sources, but has to be reconstructed from later writings such as the *Classic of the Mountains and Seas*, where Chinese myths are already influenced by Buddhism and Confucian historicizing. However, they can be checked against surviving oral traditions of tribal peoples like the Miao.

Records of creators, as opposed to an impersonal process of creation, were first found in the third century A.D.—significantly after the introduction of Indian ideas—in the form of a male creator, Pan Gu, and a female, Nu Gua. Pan Gu is similar in many respects to Mesopotamian and Indian creator figures. In one account, he separates heaven and earth; and in another the world develops out of his body.

Pan Gu

Pan Gu, fearing that the earth and sky might merge together, stood between them, his head keeping the sky aloft, and his feet treading down the earth. For 18,000 years, the distance between heaven and earth increased at a rate of 10 ft (3 m) a day. Pan Gu grew at the same rate to continue to hold heaven and earth apart. Eventually Pan Gu considered there was no risk of the sky and earth joining, so he fell asleep and eventually died. From his corpse came all the world's elements. His breath became the wind and clouds, his voice became thunder, his left eye became the sun, and his right eye became the moon. His four limbs and his trunk were transformed into the cardinal directions and the mountains, his blood became the rivers, and his veins became roads. His flesh became trees and soil, the hairs on his head became the stars, and the hairs on his body were transformed into grass and flowers. Finally, the fleas on his body became the ancestors of the different races of human beings.

Nu Gua

In another myth, Nu Gua is responsible for the creation of human beings, and is known from much earlier (pre-Buddhist) references to her as one who changes shape and transforms things. She may be, as with female beings in other societies, the original Chinese creator. Nu Gua wandered through the

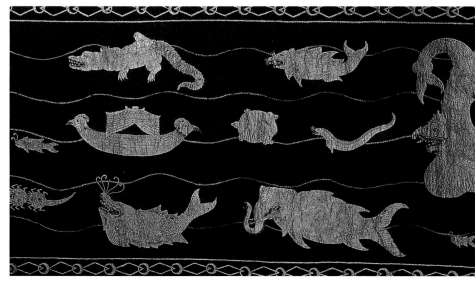

world longing for companionship. She sat down at the bank of a river, and began to model the river clay into a little figure. When Nu Gua stood the finished figure on the ground, it immediately came to life, dancing and laughing with happiness. Nu Gua was so happy she decided to fill the whole world with people, working until it grew dark. Nu Gua worked and worked, but realized that she could not possibly create enough people to populate the whole world. She called on her magic power, and taking a length of vine, she trailed it in the mud, and then whirled it about in the air. As soon as the drops of mud touched the ground, they were transformed into human beings.

In time, the Pan Gu and Nu Gua myths were combined, with the two represented as brother and sister. The problem of how to allow them to mate and produce human beings was solved by a special message from the Heavens authorizing this dramatic departure from propriety.

The mythic world of early China is best seen in a Han Dynasty work that purports to be a geography but is better described as a mythography. The *Classic of the Mountains and Seas,* in the manner of European travelers' tales, describes weird animals, monstrous human beings, gods and goddesses, and very strange far-off lands. The figures that are met in this tour of the world include a god of luck, a human figure covered in fur with a tiger's tail, the Ape God Howl, a snake god with nine human heads, and the nine-tailed fox. And the lands found included the land of the hairy folk, the land of the lop-eared people, and the land of the low people with fish tails for feet.

DAOIST MYTHOLOGY

The fourth century B.C. Daoist work attributed to Zhuang Zhou or Master Zhuang (Zhuangzi) opens with a myth of the world in constant transformation.

In the northern abyss there is a fish. Its name is Kun. It is gigantic, and no one knows how many thousands of *li* (a mythical measurement) it stretches. It is transformed and becomes a bird called Peng with a back so large that no one knows how many thousands of *li* it is wide. Peng springs into the air and flies, and its wings are like clouds floating in the sky. This bird floats above the waves toward the Pool of Heaven. This may be a product of Zhuang's extraordinary imagination, but it reads like a cosmological myth.

From the second century A.D. on, Daoism became an organized religion complete with priests, disciplinary and moral rules, rituals, and penitential practices. It quickly developed a pantheon of gods and goddesses. At the top was a trinity comprising the Celestial Venerable of the Original Beginning, the Jade Emperor, and Lord Lao up in Heaven, who was none other than Laozi, the alleged author of the *Book of the Way and its Virtue* deified. These figures, and a bewildering array of spirit beings, are described in a vast body of scriptures only explored in recent times.

One striking feature of the Daoist tradition is the emphasis on the female, something which goes back to Laozi who, in the *Book of the Way and its Virtue,* described the source of all as "the gateway of the mysterious female." This is reflected in the evolution of one cult with an extended mythology, that of the Queen Mother of the West, who lives on an enormously high mountain in the far West, and possesses the secret of immortality. The palace of the Queen Mother of the West has nine stories, and is believed to be built entirely of jade. Around the palace are magnificent gardens where the Peach Tree of Immortality is believed to grow. The Immortals are said to live here, in an endless series of amusements and banquets.

Daoism, too, developed the mythology and iconography of the Eight Immortals which have become an integral part of popular Chinese religion. Daoists believed that human beings can become Immortals (*xian*) through special practices, and many of these Immortals were revered. Finally, around the thirteenth century A.D., eight of these immortal humans were

Above **Wen Ch'ang, the god of literature.** This god was invoked for success in examinations. In a moment of despair, he threw himself into the sea, but a fish saved him. He is usually shown standing on a fish, with an inkwell and writing brush.

Left **A fantastic horned beast.** This animal plaque was inspired by an ancient geographical gazetteer that catalogued strange spirits and supernatural flora and fauna found in distant parts of the countryside.

THE CHINESE PANTHEON

The Chinese Pantheon is arranged in an imitation of earthly organization. It appears as a vast government administration complete with ministers and support staff. They keep registers, write reports for their superiors, and every year give an account of their administration to the sovereign god, the August Personage of Jade, Yu Ti. There is a definite hierarchy of rank and clearly delineated areas of power. The gods are promoted or lowered in rank, or even dismissed, depending on their performance. The gods are judged by the August Personage of Jade. This explains the large number of changing divinities which inhabit Chinese mythology. There are also many versions of the hierarchy, and differences over who is the High or Emperor God.

Opposite page **Guan Yin, Buddhist goddess of mercy and compassion.** This goddess is one of the best loved of all Chinese deities, particularly among women. She was sometimes portrayed as the Gentle Mother, carrying a child in her arms.

singled out, and their images and/or symbols are found in temples, while their stories are told and re-told in print, in operas, and more recently in films. The Eight Immortals of Daoism are the following.

Lu Tongbin

This Immortal is portrayed as a scholar with a fly-whisk and a sword. Probably one of the most popular of the Immortals, Lu is the subject of a great number of myths, such as his killing of the Yellow Dragon; his conversion of the courtesan, White Peony; and the Yellow Millet Dream, a dream that foresees a successful career, that ends in his murder.

Zhong Liquan

The Immortal of longevity who is said, in ancient times, to have discovered the Elixir of Life, he always holds a fan to revive the dead, and sometimes carries a peach from the Tree of Immortality.

Cao Guojiu

This figure is always illustrated in court dress. He is said to have been the brother of an empress. As the patron of actors, he carries a pair of castanets. He has the reputation of being a bad-tempered murderer.

Li Tieguai

Li is always depicted as a beggar with a crutch and a begging bowl. He was the first Immortal rescued from his poverty by none other than the Queen Mother of the West. He is also known as "Iron Crutch."

Zhang Guolao

This Immortal is usually riding backward on a white mule, carrying a cylindrical musical instrument made of bamboo. He was born old, persecuted throughout his life by his family, and after many adventures, was rewarded with immortality by the Jade Emperor. He folds up his mule like paper and puts it in his pocket, taking it out when he needs to fly away to perform deeds of mercy.

Han Xianzi

This patron of musicians holds peach blossoms and a jade flute. He received the gift of immortality after falling from his favorite peach tree.

Lan Caihe

A beggar and a street singer of dubious gender, Lan holds a basket of flowers. The stories about this curious figure show him (or her) singing songs that attack the pleasures of life.

He Xiangu

A female Immortal, she is often pictured holding a lotus or a kitchen ladle. After many years, she was released from servitude in the kitchen of her wicked stepmother. She gained immortality by eating a peach from the ancient Tree of Immortality.

BUDDHIST MYTHOLOGY

Chinese Buddhism continued the process of mythologizing the historical Siddhartha into the mythical Buddha, that had begun in India. Ancient Chinese texts emphasized the miraculous events of his life in India, to a far-off China that did not know of Buddhism until five or six centuries later. For example, at the moment of his birth, Chinese rivers are said to have overflowed their banks, mountains collapsed, and meteors appeared. Wise men were consulted by the emperor of the time, and they told him of a great sage who had been born in the West. The Daoists had another version, that the Buddha was really Laozi, who disappeared, on the back of an ox, into the West after completing his work, *Book of the Way and its Virtue*. (The West to the ancient Chinese was India, not Europe.)

Into the grotto of the Spring of the Peachblossom invite the Immortal One.

CHINESE DIVINATION PRAYER

The most interesting of the Chinese Buddhist myths relates to Guan Yin, a popular female deity. Historians have traced the evolution of Guan Yin from the male Indian bodhisattva Avalokitesvara, via the influence of Chinese fertility figures. Serious-minded Buddhists saved her Buddhist credentials by arguing that a bodhisattva can change shape or sex at will. One story says that if she finds she is not taken seriously by the men she appears to, because of her femininity, she changes into a male, and back again to show that sex differences are irrelevant to spiritual power. Chinese women, however, find her femininity sympathetic when seeking good marriages or male children.

Above **Buddha Sakyamuni.** This Buddha is often pictured accompanied by the bodhisattvas, Mahakasyapa and Ananda.

Below **Guan Yin on a lotus flower.** A popular goddess, she is credited with the ability to release prisoners and remove poison from snakes.

JAPANESE MYTHOLOGY

Right **Shinto goddess Nakatsu-Hime-Zo.** Originally a consort to Emperor Ojin, a deified form of the war god, Hachiman, this goddess became an incarnation of the compassionate bodhisattva (enlightened being), Kannon.

Below **Bodhisattva, from the Descent of the 25 Blessed.** These beings accompany Amida, a great Buddha of wisdom, when he descends from paradise to lead his followers back to "the Lotus Land of Bliss."

Ancient Japanese mythology is primarily enshrined in two great collections from the early eighth century A.D., the *Kojiki* (Record of Ancient Matters), and the *Nihongi* (Written Chronicles of Japan). This makes reconstruction of earlier mythology very difficult because these works have a very special status not only in Shinto religion, but also in state ideology. They are devoted to establishing the divine origin of the Japanese emperors, and the uniqueness of the Japanese islands and people.

However, we can read between the lines to find their origins. Modern ethnology has established the mixed (Polynesian and mainland east Asian) origin of the Japanese people which suggests a variety of influences on Japanese mythology. The beginning of the Japanese creation story has remarkable similarities to Polynesian creation myths, while the emphasis on the divine origins of the imperial line is closer to Chinese and Korean origin stories.

THE NOTION OF KAMI

As organized in these very earliest of Japanese writings and in "the way of the Kami" (Kami-no-michi, or Shinto), the focus is on the kami, or spirits. This term has a far wider meaning than "gods," but the concept of kami is very elusive. Motoori Norinaga (1730–1801), an important figure in the modern revival of Shinto, wrote that kami embraced not only gods, but human beings (especially emperors), natural objects, and "anything whatsoever which was outside the ordinary, which possessed superior power, or which was awe-inspiring." And he went on to say that powerful evil as well as exceptional good marked

a kami. The number of kami is indefinite, and the stories about them, the myths, are not necessarily religious, in our sense.

The Japanese deified the forces of nature because they felt these forces were more powerful than humans were, and venerated them under the name kami. Anything considered outside the ordinary, or a being that seemingly possessed superior power came under the name kami, including human beings, high mountains, tall trees, birds, beasts, plants, seas, and so on. The kami have bodies like those of human beings, and are endowed with all the human qualities and defects. When the kami die, their spirit lives on. At times, their souls can leave the body and manifest as an object. The kami can also do both good and evil. The successive generations of sacred emperors were also called kami.

SHINTO MYTHOLOGY

It might be questioned whether the ancient Japanese really believed that all men of the world were descended from the kami, or that this only applied to the Japanese people and the Japanese islands. In practice, of course, at the time that Shinto originated, there was probably no thought that any other land or any other people existed. In later times, during the national revival of the eighteenth and nineteenth centuries, the notion of the special and unique status of Japan was drawn from these myths by proponents of the *Kokugaku* (national revival).

The religion of the ordinary people, however, at the beginning of the Empire was a kind of shamanism, like that of most of northern Asia, and based on spirit mediums who contacted the spirits and were taken over by them to communicate messages from the spirit world to the physical world. Japanese mythology often refers to communications with spirits in dreams and ecstatic trances.

THE INTRODUCTION OF BUDDHISM

Shortly before kami mythology was organized and written down, Buddhism was introduced to Japan from China. Just as the original Indian Buddhism had been altered in China, in Japan Buddhism

underwent a further transformation into Japanese forms, which generated a new Buddhist mythology. This partially involved an identification of preexisting kami with buddhas and bodhisattvas, as well as the mythicizing of founders of Japanese Buddhist sects.

In the early literature, especially works such as the anthology of poetry, the *Manyoshu*, oral traditions of a mythological nature may be discovered which match more recently collected folk traditions, and probably precede both imperial ideology and attempts to match Buddhist stories. Rituals, festivals, folk customs, proverbs, and popular sayings also give clues to the myths now lost by the theologians of Shinto and Buddhism.

The invention of myths, however, still continues to the present day. The proliferation over the last

century of what the Japanese call "New Religions," is often accompanied by new myths about their origins, founders, and special powers. The Japanese people frequently adapt, in their eclectic fashion and for their own purposes, the religious mythology of other traditions.

Make the offering to Buddha of cherry blossoms.

SAIGYO, TRAVELER-POET AND
BUDDHIST MONK (A.D. 1118–1190)

A CREATION STORY

The kami, according to the Japanese, were responsible for the creation of the world as we know it. In the *Kojiki*, we are told that in the beginning there were the kami of the center of heaven, and then the kami of birth and growth appeared. The brother and sister kami, Izanagi, "the male who invites," and Izanami, "the female who invites," were the eighth pair of deities to appear after heaven and earth had been created out of chaos. Izanagi and Izanami were

Above **View of a Japanese landscape.** Ritual landscapes represent the harmony between people and the natural universe. Kami, or deities, are said to live in certain areas of the landscape.

Above **Amaterasu, the sun goddess.** Susano-o, the storm god, became so destructive that the sun goddess hid in a cave. The evil gods were delighted, because the world was thrown into darkness, which hid their wicked deeds. The good deities eventually persuaded Amaterasu to come out of hiding.

ordered to create the islands of Japan. They stood side by side on the "Floating Bridge of Heaven," lowered a heavenly jeweled spear into the ocean, and began to stir. When the water began to coagulate they lifted the spear out of the water, and the droplets fell from its tip and became an island, the first solid land. The two gods then descended onto this island, and built a heavenly pillar and a splendid palace. Izanagi and Izanami circled the pillar until they met. They examined each other's bodies, and realized that they fitted together. The first result of this union was a deformed creature called "Leech Child," who the couple abandoned at sea on a camphorwood boat. Izanagi and Izanami were told by the gods that the reason for this unfortunate birth was the result of Izanami speaking first during their courting ritual. Once again, the couple circled the pillar, and gave

birth to the Eight Great Islands of Japan, as well as the other great kami. Amaterasu, the sun goddess, was their favorite child, and was sent up on a ladder to her place in the heavens. The moon god Tsuki-yomi came next and was sent to heaven to complement and as a consort of the sun. Then came Susano-o, a cruel and badly behaved god given to destruction and to making loud noises, so he was expelled to become the storm god.

Death of Izanami and Izanagi's Descent into Hell

While giving birth to the god of fire, Izanami was so badly burnt that she died. Before her death, she managed to give birth to the water goddess, the earth goddess, and the gourd of heaven, who together could control the god of fire, and prevent the world

RUSTIC GODS

All aspects and phenomena of nature are considered manifestations of different divinities. In addition to generalized divinities, each species of tree has a special god. Large and beautiful trees are worshipped, and are often decorated with a rope of plaited straw, from which hang little pieces of paper letting people who pass by know of the divine quality of the tree. Offerings are also placed in front of the tree for those faithfully devoted to specific rustic gods.

from being destroyed. A desperately unhappy Izanagi came to the land of Yomi (the land of the dead) to see if he could reclaim Izanami, but he was refused. Izanami told Izanagi not to look at her, but against her wishes, he broke off a tooth of his wooden comb, lit it, and used it as a torch to see her. He was shocked at her horribly transformed appearance. In revenge, Izanami created eight female spirits, who pursued Izanagi to the end of the world. He bathed and purified himself from the contamination of his contact with death, and from his bathwater a number of other kami were produced.

Amaterasu and Susano-o

Amaterasu and Susano-o had a stormy relationship. Susano-o delighted in destroying his sister's creations. He broke down the earth walls of her rice fields in spring, and at harvest time made "the heavenly piebald colts" lie down in the fields. He filled irrigation ditches, and deposited excrement in the temples built for the Festival of the First Fruits. The storm god also destroyed all the crops. Despairing, Amaterasu hid in the rocky cave of heaven, blocking the entrance with a boulder, and as a result the world was plunged into darkness. This conflict of the siblings gives an explanation for the change of the seasons, from spring, to autumn, to winter.

Amaterasu was enticed out of hiding by a display of hanging jewels and a mirror in the tree outside her cave; a wild and obscene dance by the other kami also attracted her curiosity. She was persuaded to come out of the cave, and once more the world was lit up by the rays of the sun.

The last, but certainly not least, of the creations of the kami is the Japanese imperial line. Amaterasu sent her grandson, Ninigi, down from heaven to rule Japan. Ninigi's great-grandson, Jimmu, eventually became the first emperor of Japan, and all Japanese emperors since this time have been considered divine. Amaterasu's image and her emblems, now the insignia of the emperor, are enshrined in the great imperial shrine of Isé, which became the center of her cult and is considered the most sacred place in Japan.

BUDDHIST MYTHOLOGY

When Buddhism came to Japan, on the whole it did not oppose the kami, but sought to assimilate them into the beliefs of Buddhism. For example, a story arose that the Emperor Shomu had a dream, in 742 B.C., in which Amaterasu herself said: "This land is the country of the kami. The people should worship them, but the wheel of the sun is Dainichi Nyorai. The true nature is Vairocana (Illumination). If sentient beings understand this logic, they should convert to Buddhism." This passage introduces a distinctively Japanese Buddha, Dainichi (the Indian Vairocana), and identifies him with the sun, subsuming and subordinating Shinto to Buddhism. However, it does not seek to completely eliminate the kami.

Temmu, the emperor who first promoted Buddhism in Japan, was influenced by a Buddhist sutra (The Sutra of the Golden Light), which depicts the Buddha appointing four God Kings to protect any king or kingdom that accepts his teaching. These God Kings are also known as the Four Heavenly Kings, Guardians of the Four Directions, Protectors of Buddhist Law. They

Above *Izanami and Izanagi Creating the Japanese Islands* by Kobayashi Eitaku (1843–1890). These divinities also produced the major deities. The death of Izanami marked the in-trusion of death into the world. The grief felt by Izanagi introduced the notion of mourning.

Left *A Snowstorm at Kinroyzan Temple* by Kuniyoshi Utagawa (1796–1861). The conflict between Amaterasu and Susano-o set in motion the change of seasons. When the storm god became too boisterous, the sun goddess would hide her rays, and winter would begin.

Opposite page **One of the four God Kings of Buddhism.** These characters were the protectors of Buddhist law. Images of them are found within temples. Traditionally, these guardians hold a sword to conquer greed, anger, and ignorance. The other hand holds a rope to catch those who oppose Buddha.

Right **Amida seated on a lotus flower.** Amida, which means Infinite Life, is one of the great savior figures in Japanese Buddhism. Followers believe that, at the hour of death, Amida will take them to an idyllic place called the Pure Land.

Below *Calligraphy* by Matsuo Basho (1643–1694). The development of Zen Buddhism influenced many aspects of art and life. The Sixth Patriarch, Huineng, wrote two poems on a monastery wall. This form of poetry is now known as Haiku, and expresses the essence of nature.

are often realized standing at the corners of altars. Ferocious looking, sometimes portrayed with fiery halos, and often stepping on *tentoki* (tiny creatures), they are depicted as warriors protecting the Buddhist realm.

The most influential text in Japanese Buddhism is undoubtedly the Lotus Sutra, which is a powerful story of miraculous events and a vision of Buddha-worlds, revealed by the Sakyamuni on Vulture Peak before he enters Nirvana. It has something for everyone from sophisticated metaphysical notions to simple faith-based practices which will enable anyone to achieve enlightenment. However, it is the mythological elements, the stories within it that have left the greatest impression on the Japanese. It has been called the "gospel" of Japanese Buddhism. For example, devotees are introduced to an extraordinary vision of a giant stupa (a Buddhist tower-temple), made of the seven kinds of precious stones, soaring into the sky, but floating in the air, unsupported. It is filled with millions of grotto-rooms and is decorated with ten billion jeweled balls. Gentle music echoes within it, and from this vision comes a voice that proclaims the glory of the Buddha.

Amida

The mythology of Amida, the savior Buddha, is another major element in Japanese Buddhism. It presents the Pure Land, "the Lotus Land of Bliss," a kind

of heaven providing fulfillment, and filled with delights ranging from beholding the Buddha, to the satisfaction of all the senses. This land is presided over by Amida who, along with Kannon (the Japanese version of the Chinese bodhisattva, Guan Yin), is found represented in temples throughout Japan. Pure Land Buddhism also taught devotees about a graphically depicted hell especially reserved for murderers, butchers, and meat-eaters.

This idea was further developed in the Pure Land Sutra. Those who reach Amida's Pure Land have escaped, not only Hell but all suffering and rebirth. The Pure Land is full of fragrances, flowers and fruit, trees decked with jewels, and huge jeweled lotus flowers. This garden has no rocks or hills, but is crisscrossed with calm streams that have sweet-smelling water and floating flowers. The water feels hot or cold according to one's specific wishes, and once again, peaceful music is played throughout this glorious place.

Zen Buddhist Mythology

Zen Buddhism developed a considerable mythology and iconography around the figure of Daruma (Bodhidharma), the alleged founder of the Chinese Chan School of Buddhism, from which came Zen. Further back lay the founding story of Zen, how Mahakasyapa was the only disciple of the Buddha who smiled to show he understood when the Buddha held up a flower. Then came stories about the succession of Indian and Chinese Zen Patriarchs, and, finally, the Japanese teachers. Perhaps the most famous one of all is the story of the Sixth Patriarch, the Chinese monk Huineng, and the real founder of Zen. He was a poor man from South China who went north to find enlightenment from the famous teacher, the Fifth Patriarch, Hongren. He was set to work in the kitchen, but only Hongren recognized his qualities. The master, who was dying, announced that the monk who wrote the poem best expressing what Buddhism was about would be his successor. The favorite of the monks wrote a poem about polishing the mirror of the mind to reflect reality. In the middle of the night, Huineng awoke, and wrote two poems on the wall of the monastery. They argued that there was no mirror, that the Buddha-nature was in everybody, just waiting to be discovered, so no polishing was needed. This is the essence of Zen told in story form.

Another famous story is told of how the child monk, Toyo, solved the problem set by his Master

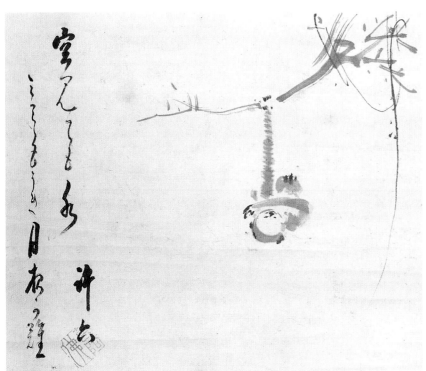

Mokurai, who asked, "What is the sound of one hand clapping?" First, he suggested it was the music floating up from the geisha quarters; then the sound of water dripping; then the whisper of the wind; then the hoot of the owl; and finally the chirping of the cicadas. The Master rejected them all. Finally, he achieved *satori* (enlightenment) when he realized that it was a "soundless sound," that all sound is illusory.

Dogen, founder of the Soto school of Zen, translated and commented on Chinese collections of sayings and stories of the Zen masters. Whether one calls such stories myths is a matter of definition. Some incidents may actually have occurred. They teach a lesson through the words and actions of a great and illustrious Master.

One favorite is the story of Nanquan killing the cat. One day the monks in Nanquan's monastery got into an argument about a cat. Nanquan called for the cat to be brought, and he held it up. "Can anyone tell me," he said, "why I should not kill it?" No one spoke up, so he cut the cat in two.

The point of such stories lay in the commentaries. Some say Nanquan didn't actually kill the cat, as the action of killing is shocking to Buddhists. Some say he did it to teach a lesson, but commentators differ greatly on what the lesson is: Don't argue? Life and death are relative? Worry about the things that

matter? Others still point to the action, a sudden violent act to induce enlightenment, which is akin to the Zen practice of the Prior striking meditating monks, sharply, with a stick.

FOLK MYTHOLOGY

There are many local cults in Japan which are not part of State Shinto, and which are not based on the ancient writings. Jean Herbert, an academic, has described the process of "kamification" by which people, who in life were thought to have displayed special powers, came to be worshipped in death. While many of these figures are clearly historical, others appear to be the product of myths. The stories about the Uji-gami, or ancestral kami of clans or families, and the particular patron kami of various professions often appear to have been borrowed from myths. For example, Nomi-no-sukune, the patron of Sumo wrestlers, is said to have been famous in his home village for his prodigious strength. He was brought to court where he was tested against the Grand Champion and killed him with one blow. He became a high official and was responsible for abolishing human sacrifice.

Rain Gods
Rain also had its special gods, such as the god Taka-Okami, who lives on mountains, and Kura-Okami, who dwells in valleys, and can cause snow as well as rain. In the description of Izumo province, it is stated that, to the west of Mount Kaminabi, the wife of the god Aji-Suki-Taka-Hikone gave birth to the god Tak-Tsu-Hiko, and advised him to build a temple, as a mark of respect to the rain gods.

Mountain Gods
The sacred Mount Fuji is worshipped as a kami by many Japanese sects, and has an enormous and complex mythology. It is said to be the axis of the world, and the source of heaven and earth. It is claimed to have arisen miraculously out of the earth in the third century B.C. A story tells of how an emperor was once enticed into the crater by the goddess of Fuji, and he was never seen again.

Sea and River Gods
Most Japanese rivers have their kami respected and feared because of their creation of floods. A fearsome dwarf god, Kappa, is blamed for drownings, but

Right **Mount Fuji, home of the mountain gods.** The extinct volcano is the sanctuary for mountain gods and goddesses. Chief god and lord of the mountains, O-Yama-Tsu-Mi was born from the dismembered parts of the fire god's body.

Below **The Feast of Inari.** The god of rice is called Inari. He is closely related to the food goddess, Uke-mochi. Inari is a symbol of prosperity, and many festivals are held to celebrate and encourage his benevolence.

called Namazu, which lay bound underground with wisteria vines under a stone until he escaped. His movements were said to have caused the all-to-frequent earthquakes.

Wind Gods

From the breath of Izanagi came the wind god, Shina-Tsu-Hiko, who blew away the mist which covered the land. There are actually many wind gods. Some are responsible for gentle breezes. Fishermen believed in Haya-ji, the typhoon god, who carried wind in a bag on his back.

Thunder Gods

There is a curious mythology relating to "thunder-trees," which are protected against lightning by Kami-nari, the thunder god. One story in the *Nihongi* is about the felling of a forest to build an imperial fleet. The official in charge, Kahabe-no-omi, refused to stop operations when told by the thunder god that they were attacking thunder-trees. He persisted, despite torrential rain, thunder, and lightning, and the official eventually burnt the thunder god, who had taken the form of a fish. There is another story that relates the punishment of the Empress Saimei for daring to cut some sacred trees to build her Palace of Logs.

Left *The Waterfall* by Kasushika Hokusai (1760–1849). Kappa, a river god, is responsible for waterfalls. The symbol of water also represents purification, which came into existence when Izanagi washed himself after being contaminated by death.

people can escape his wrath by bowing to him, which forces him to bow in return, causing the flood water to pour out of his skull. Many waterfalls have water goddesses, complete with stories and shrines. There are several sea gods who were created when Izanagi washed off the impurities of death, such as the god of the bottom of the sea, the god of the middle waters, and the god of the surface.

Earthquake Gods

Earthquakes are sometimes attributed to Nai-no-kami, the earthquake god, and sometimes to a giant fish,

In many places rocks are worshipped as kami because of their striking shapes. One is especially venerated as the stone which Empress Jingo (A.D. 170–269)

Below **Snakes and serpents**. One legend tells of an eight-headed snake who visited the province of Izumo once a year to devour a daughter from each family. The storm god eventually defeated this terrifying creature, by putting out eight cups of wine for each of its heads.

carried on her belly to delay the birth of her child until she had completed a military expedition against her foes, the Koreans.

Goddess of Food

There are several food gods—of rice, of fish, of vegetables—each with their accompanying stories. Uke-mochi is the general goddess of food. Amaterasu is said to have sent her brother/consort, Tsuki-yomi, to seek her secrets. Uke-mochi produced a meal from her mouth, which so disgusted him that he killed her and threatened to stop the the food supply. Amaterasu intervened, and ordered that a shrine be set up next to her own great shrine of Isé. From the corpse of Uke-mochi, seeds and crops, farm animals, and silkworms were produced.

DRAGONS AND SNAKES

In ancient Japan, the people believed in a snake god, Orochi, who lived on the very top of mountains. The Buddhist religion told of the dragon god, Ryujin, who ruled the clouds, the rain, and the water. There was the dragon, Yasha, one of the demon-gods who protected Buddhism. All of these deities have wide mouths, sharp fangs, pointed horns, and all-seeing eyes.

In Japanese folklore there are tales told of people who turned into snakes after death because of their evil ways and miserly habits. A male becomes a serpent because his desires are not satisfied. Women are often associated with snakes because of the tales told

Below **The accomplished and lucky tea kettle.** An abbot bought a tea kettle. When water was boiled in this kettle, it turned into a raccoon, and ran about the room. The savvy abbot decided to take it around the countryside as a performing show.

of them being fierce and possessive toward their lovers. Snakes are not always thought of as symbols of evil, but also of love with no bounds. Long ago in the Keicho era, there lived a beautiful girl in Senju, in the province of Musashi. A bachelor called Yaichiro fell in love with her, and sent her many letters of love, but she did not respond. Yaichiro died of sorrow, and the girl married someone else. On the morning after the wedding, the couple didn't emerge from their room. When the bride's mother entered, she found the bridegroom dead, and a snake crawling out of the bride's eyes. The villagers believed that the snake was the heartbroken Yaichiro.

Serpents and dragons are also associated with nature. Natural disasters, especially devastating floods, are linked to them. It is believed that after storms they are washed out of their dens and come into the open. There are four types of dragons in Japanese mythology: the heavenly dragons who guard the palace of the gods, the spiritual dragons who bring the blessed rain, the earth dragons who determine the course of rivers, and the dragons who are the guardians of all the earthly treasures.

HELL AND DEMONS

Hell, or Jigoku, is underground, and is divided into eight regions of fire and eight regions of ice. Emma-o is the ruler of Jigoku, and the judge of the dead. He is identified with the Chinese deity, Yanluo Wang, and his origins are from the Hindu god of death, Yama.

In Jigoku, Emma-o is surrounded by 18 generals and thousands of soldiers, as well as nasty demons and guards with horses' heads. According to one tradition, death begins as a journey across a vast, empty

Opposite page **Oni (demon) skewering the damned.** These demons work alongside Emma-o, the ruler of Jigoku. They are responsible for keeping the tortured souls of the underworld under tight control.

plain. In other versions of the tale, infernal beings guard the dead during their journey. At the entrance to Jigoku lies a steep mountain, which the deceased have to climb, and on the other side of the mountain is a river with three crossings. One of the crossings is a shallow ford, which those who have committed only minor sins may cross. Another is a bridge over which good people may pass. The third is a horrific torrent filled with monsters, through which evil sinners must struggle. On the other side of this third crossing waits a horrible old woman who strips her victims naked. They are then taken by the Jigoku guards to Emma-o, who judges only men; his sister decides the fate of women. The god sits between two severed heads, and a magic mirror reflects the sinner's past wrongdoings. Emma-o then judges the individual's sins, and allocates them to the appropriate part of Jigoku. The souls of the dead can, however, be saved with the help of a bosatsu, the Japanese form of the bodhisattva.

The Oni

The Oni are giant, horned demons. They are said to have come to Japan from China with the arrival of Buddhism, and Buddhist priests perform annual rites to expel them. The Oni can be a variety of colors, and they have three fingers, three toes, and sometimes

three eyes. They are usually cruel and lecherous, and they are said to sweep down from the sky in chariots, to steal the souls of people who are about to die. One story tells of how the diminutive hero Momotaro freed young girls whom the Oni had captured.

The Oni of Jigoku take sinners to Emma-o, and are said to be responsible for creating illness and disease.

Above **Woman reading a love letter in front of her servants, Edo period (1614–1868).** In one Japanese myth, a beautiful girl rejects the advances of a lovelorn boy, with fatal consequences.

TIBETAN MYTHOLOGY

Right **Padmasambhava and his wives.** Padmasambhava was called to Tibet by the Dharmaja (King of Law) in the eighth century. This Indian monk introduced Tantric Buddhism to Tibet, and is often represented seated on a lotus, holding a thunderbolt *(vajra)*, a skull, and a trident.

Folk history, with its broad range of exciting and instructive myths, is an important part of Tibetan culture. These traditional accounts explain the stuff of existence— the origins of the world and of their people, the development of agriculture and technology, the might and splendor of their kings and their realm, and their conversion to Buddhism. These stories are not fixed, but part of a living, evolving, oral culture, open to embellishment and elaboration. Traveling bards spread the stories far and wide, although different regions in the vast Tibetan cultural arena have their own particular traditions. Some of these myths have been written down, and are often further embroidered through episodes rediscovered in the various visions of the historiographers.

The gradual taming of the environment and its forces is an important theme in the mythological history of Tibet. Padmasambhava, or Guru Rinpoche, the eighth-century tantric master revered for bringing Buddhism from India to Tibet, epitomizes this process. Similarly, the exploits of the warrior hero of Tibet, King Gesar of Ling, are far too numerous and extensive to be included here.

The core of the epic of Ling, which might well be compared to the *Iliad* and the *Odyssey*, or the Hindu tale, the *Mahabharata*, tells of the stories of Gesar's birth, childhood, and marriage; how he became ruler; and his wars against the demon king of the

north and the Turkic peoples. Typically, King Gesar and his army defeat the foe, often through trickery and cunning, as much as might, returning home with a booty of medicinal herbs, cattle, magic jewels, and other treasures. Gesar allows the defeated tribes to maintain their autonomy, causing them to become allies. This process can be seen to mirror the political process of "Tibetanization" through adopting Tibetan Buddhism. There may be kernels of factual history embedded in these myths, however, the Tibetan idea of historiography is more about instilling desirable values, glorifying the people and their complex society through the triumph of good over evil, and bringing the past to life. For the Tibetan people, this folk history is real, no matter if there are variations on names, places, and motives in different sources. This extensive genre consists of a rich tapestry of verse and prose that are performed in dramatic dances, in

Right **Map of the world, according to Tibetan cosmology.** Mount Sumeru, the axis of the universe, is in the inner circle. It is surrounded by four continents with their four islands within the cosmic ocean. The guardian of the north sits on a white lion on Mount Sumeru.

THE MONKEY DESCENDANTS AND EVOLUTION

We can speculate about this myth of the origin of Tibetan people, and look at what we understand from scientific evidence about the processes of physical and cultural evolution. Does this origin story contain some kernel of prehistoric truth?

Old and Middle Stone Age tools and the evidence of habitation have been discovered at archaeological sites on the Tibetan plateau. Genetic mapping suggests that modern humans may have originated about 40,000 years ago, west of Tibet and north of India. Clear evidence for early modern human inhabitation on the northern edge of the Tibetan plateau in the Tsaidam Basin dates from 33,000 years ago.

song, and also in simple story-telling. The following origin myths are well known throughout Tibet, and were recorded by Tibetan historiographers in the first section of the *Mani Kabum*, a twelfth-century ancient text that has been "rediscovered" and is currently being studied.

THE ORIGINS OF THE TIBETAN PEOPLE

There was once a magical monkey, living very high up in a very fine cave on Mount Kong-pori, a sacred peak in the Yarlung Valley in central Tibet. Because this monkey had visited the high realm of the Buddhas and made contact with Chenrezig, a great compassionate Buddha-to-be, he spent all of his time in meditation, patiently developing his skills in compassion, peace, and loving-kindness.

One day his sublime practice was interrupted by a passionate rock srinmo-demoness, who was overcome with lust when she saw the radiant monkey. The monkey, however, had vowed to meditate until he reached enlightenment, and was not attracted to this rock srinmo-demoness. She threatened that she would marry a violent rock demon, and produce many destructive offspring who would destroy many living beings, if the monkey did not succumb to her wishes, and take her as his wife.

The monkey was stuck. He knew he could prevent this great destruction, though it would cost him his vow. Because of his com-passion he united with the rock srinmo-demoness, and she bore him six wild red-faced monkey-children. Their father took them to a bountiful forest full of many fruit-bearing trees so they could eat well, and grow up happily. But before long there was no more food left to eat, and the youngsters became hungry.

Filled with great compassion for their plight, the monkey sought assistance from Chenrezig, who intervened by producing grains including barley, rice,

and buckwheat. As the monkey-children satiated their hunger, their hair and tails grew shorter, they learned to speak, and became human. The six original tribes of the Tibetan people are descended from these children. This is why Tibetans are both spiritual and compassionate, traits inherited from their monkey ancestor, an emanation of Chenrezig; and strong and courageous like the srinmo-demoness, an emanation of Tara, the Buddhist protectress of Tibet.

Above **Green Tara.** This goddess symbolizes compassion, and is the Buddhist protectress of Tibet. Ancient legend has it that Green Tara was a Nepalese princess, reincarnated because of her study of and devotion to Buddhism.

CONVERSION OF TIBET TO BUDDHISM THROUGH PINNING THE DEMONESS

Right Skull decoration from Jokhang Monastery. King Song-tsen Gampo built the Jokhang Monastery. The symbol of the skull serves as a reminder of life's impermanence, and the use of skulls as cups played an important part in Tibetan rituals.

Below Buddha's first sermon. This seventeenth-century fresco shows five high-caste followers gathering around Buddha in a deer park. This represents the beginning of his public life. Buddha is seated on a lotus flower, and the scene below him illustrates the ever-widening circle of Buddhist devotees.

The Tibetan Empire had become great, and the ruler King Song-tsen Gampo, who reigned between A.D. 627–649, commanded respect from all the neighboring countries. Despite his already happy marriage with the Nepalese Princess Khri-tsun, he desired a second refined and beautiful younger wife. So, a marriage was arranged with Princess Kong-jo from the nearby country of China.

With negotiations finalized, and wedding plans in place, the young princess and her entourage embarked on the long journey to Lhasa in central Tibet, protected by two strong Tibetan bodyguards, Laga and Luga. The princess carried a beautiful statue of the Buddha Sakyamuni, her most precious offering to the Tibetan court. She encountered many difficulties on this journey, and the special chariot that carried this statue seemed to be particularly prone to mishap. On reaching the plains of Lhasa, the chariot became completely bogged, and nothing Laga and Luga did could free it. Despairing, Princess Kong-jo consulted her feng shui charts to determine the cause of the problem. To her dismay she discovered that the very energy of the earth of Tibet was trying to repel this statue of the Buddha Sakyamuni and, with it, all the teachings of Buddhism.

Reflecting very deeply, Kong-jo realized that the very earth of Tibet, Land of Snows, was actually a huge and powerful reclining srinmo-demoness. To add to the Princess's troubles, there were also treacherous otherworldly beings inhabiting the land and supporting this demoness. Despite these considerable obstacles, other aspects of the landscape were proven to be quite favorable. Kong-jo's feng shui calculations determined that a series of Buddhist temples and stupa-reliquaries could pin down the negative earth forces and otherworldly beings, and curtail their destructive activity. She could then get started on building the temple to house the precious Buddha Sakyamuni statue.

Princess Kong-jo was received with much celebration by the Tibetan court. It was only Queen Khri-tsun who was not so pleased with the arrival of this second wife. On hearing of Kong-jo's plans to build a temple in Lhasa for the precious Buddha-statue, Khri-tsun claimed the right, as senior consort, to build her temples first. Kong-jo suggested that Khri-tsun build a great temple in the middle of the lake near Lhasa, which, along with other protective measures, should, firstly, be filled with earth. This angered the jealous Queen Khri-tsun, who then asked the King for permission to build 108 Buddhist temples wherever she wanted.

Foundations were dug, and stones were laid, but no matter how much was built by day, the malignant beings in the earth destroyed the work by night. In desperation, Khri-tsun consulted Kong-jo, knowing that her feng shui skills would resolve the impasse. Kong-jo again explained the remedies, including the filling of the lake with earth, which would enable the great temple of Lhasa to be built. Khri-tsun didn't fully understand the instructions, and when she tried to fill in the lake it became a muddy mess. This confirmed the Queen's sneaking suspicions that Kong-jo was deceiving her out of spite.

Queen Khri-tsun explained her difficulties to the King, who comforted her. Through his own divination he realized that a temple should, indeed, be built near the lake. So, the King and Queen rode to the lake, and taking a ring from his finger, the King told Khri-tsun to build a temple wherever his ring fell. The ring flew high into the air, bounced from

the Queen's saddle, and fell into the lake. Khri-tsun was dismayed, but the King promised to help her. Together they did their best, but whatever was built by day, was again, crumbled by night.

With all building attempts thwarted, the frustrated King reconsidered Kong-jo's scheme. With reflection he gained a full understanding of the supine srinmo-demoness. As the demoness flailed her limbs about, the newly built temples were destroyed. The King decided to build 12 Buddhist temples, successfully pinning the srinmo-demoness by the hands, feet, knees, elbows, shoulders, and hips. These Buddhist temples were built throughout the entire Tibetan domain and finally, both queens were able to build their temples. The precious statue of the Buddha Sakyamuni, also known as Jowo

KING GESAR OF LING

King Gesar is also known as Gesar of Khrom. Some historians suggest that this name was adapted from Caesar of Rome, speculating that the tales of the King of Ling were overlaid with exploits told by Arabs in west central Asia, during the time of the great Tibetan Empire (seventh to ninth centuries A.D.). The might of Tibetan military power spread to Mongolia, through Turkestan, and even further west to the Arab conquerors of the old Persian dominions; south through the whole Himalayan region into Nepal and the plains of India; and in the east into Gansu, Qinghai, Sichuan, and Yunnan Provinces in China.

Rinpoche, found its final place in the great temple of Lhasa, called the Jokhang Monastery. Finally, the compassion of the Buddha's teachings radiated through the Land of Snows.

Above **Life of Buddha Sakyamuni.** After his birth from his mother's right side, the Buddha takes seven steps on seven lotus flowers. Two god figures receive him with a sacred cloth. When the Buddha Sakyamuni statue was enshrined, compassion filled the country of Tibet.

RECOMMENDED READING

European Mythology

Berresford-Ellis, Peter. *A Dictionary of Celtic Mythology*. Oxford University Press: Oxford, 1992.

Berresford-Ellis, Peter. *A Dictionary of Irish Mythology*. Oxford University Press: Oxford, 1987.

Burgess, Glyn S. (translator). *The Lais of Marie de France*. Penguin USA: New York, 1986.

Crossley-Holland, Kevin (ed.). *Norse Myths*. Random House: London, 1981.

Cunliffe, Barry. *The Ancient Celts*. Penguin: London, 1999.

Davidson, H.R. Ellis. *Gods and Myths of Northern Europe*. Viking Press: New York, 1990.

Davies, John. *The Celts*. Cassell: London, 2000.

Gantz, Jeffrey (ed.). *The Mabinogion*. Penguin: Harmondsworth, 1976.

Green, Miranda J. *Celtic Myths*. British Museum Press: London, 1993.

Jones, Gwyn and Thomas Jones (eds.). *The Mabinogion*. Everyman Library: London, 1949.

Larrington, Carolyne (translator). *The Poetic Edda*. Oxford University Press: Oxford, 1997.

Lönnrot, Elias. *The Kalevala (World's Classics*, edited by Keith Bosley). Oxford University Press: Oxford, 1989.

MacCana, Proinsias. *Celtic Mythology*. Hamlyn: London, 1970.

Malory, Sir Thomas. *Le Morte d'Arthur* (edited by R.M. Lumiansky). Collier Books: New York, 1986.

Matthews, Caitlín. *Mabon and the Mysteries of Britain*. Arkana: London, 1987.

Spirin, Genaddy. *The Tale of the Firebird* (translated by Tatiana Popova). Philomel Books: New York, 2002.

Sturluson, Snorri. *Edda* (translated by Anthony Faulkes). Everyman Library: London, 1995.

Tennyson, Alfred. *Idylls of the King (Penguin Classics*, edited by J.M. Gray). Penguin USA: New York, 1989.

Tolkien, J.R.R. and E.V. Gordon (eds.). *Sir Gawain and the Green Knight*. Oxford University Press: Oxford, 1967.

de Troyes, Chrétien. *Arthurian Romances (Penguin Classics*, translated by Carleton W. Carroll). Penguin USA: New York, 1991.

Virtanen, Leea and Thomas Dubois. *Finnish Folklore*. University of Washington Press: Seattle, 2001.

Egyptian and African Mythology

Bartels, L. *Oromo Religions: Myths and Rites of the Western Oromo of Ethiopia—an Attempt to Understand*. Reiner: Berlin, 1983.

Courlander, Harold. *A Treasury of African Folklore*. Marlowe & Company: New York, 1996.

Hart, G. *Egyptian Myths*. British Museum Press: London, 1990.

Idowu, E.B. *Olodumare—God in Yoruba Belief*. Longmans: London, 1962.

Itayemi, P. and P. Gurrey. *Folk Tales and Fables (Africa* series). Penguin: Harmondsworth, 1953.

Kenyatta, Jomo. *Facing Mount Kenya: The Tribal Life of the Gikuyu*. Martin, Secker, & Warburg: London, 1938.

Knappert, Jan. *An Encyclopedia of Myth and Legend: African Mythology*. Diamond Books: London, 1995.

Lurker, M. *The Gods and Symbols of Ancient Egypt*. Thames & Hudson: London, 1980.

Mahfouz, Naguib. *Voices from the Other World: Ancient Egyptian Tales* (translated by Raymond Stock). American University: Cairo, 2003.

Omer-Cooper, John. *History of Southern Africa (Second Edition)*. James Currey: London, 1994.

Parrinder, E.G. *African Mythology*. Paul Hamlyn: Feltham, 1968.

Parrinder, E.G. *West African Religions*. Epworth Press: London, 1949.

Pelton, R. *The Trickster in West Africa*. University of California Press: Berkeley, 1980.

Shaw, Ian (ed.). *The Oxford History of Ancient Egypt*. Oxford University Press: Oxford, 2002.

Spence, Lewis. *Ancient Egyptian Myths and Legends*. Dover Publications: New York, 1991.

Storm, Rachel. *Egyptian Mythology: Myths and Legends of Egypt, Persia, Asia Minor, Sumer and Babylon*. Lorenz Books: London, 2000.

Middle East and Asian Mythology

Aston, W.G. (translator). *Nihongi: Chronicles of Japan from the Earliest Times to A.D. 697*. Tuttle: Rutland and Tokyo, 1972.

Birrell, Anne. *Chinese Mythology: An Introduction*. John Hopkins University Press: Baltimore, 1993.

Black, Jeremy and Anthony Green. *Gods, Demons and Symbols of Ancient Mesopotamia: An Illustrated Dictionary*. University of Texas Press: Austin, 1992.

Blacker, Carmen. *The Catalpa Bow: A Study of Shamanistic Practices in Japan*. Allen & Unwin: London, 1975.

Ching, Julia. *Mysticism and Sacred Kingship in China: The Heart of Chinese Wisdom*, Cambridge University Press: Cambridge, 1997.

Christie, Anthony. *Chinese Mythology*. Paul Hamlyn: London, 1968.

Crawford, Harriet E.W. *Sumer and the Sumerians*. Cambridge University Press: Cambridge, 1991.

Curtis, Vesta Sarkhosh. *Persian Myths*. British Museum Press: London, 1993.

Dalley, Stephanie (translator). *Myths from Mesopotamia: Creation, the Flood, Gilgamesh, and Others*. Oxford University Press: Oxford, 1991.

Danielou, A. *Hindu Polytheism*. Routledge and K. Paul: London, 1964.

Dawood, N.J. (translator). *Aladdin and Other Tales from The Thousand and One Nights*. Penguin Books: Harmondsworth, 1957.

Dimmitt, C. and J.A.B. van Buitenen. *Classical Hindu Mythology: A Reader in the Sanskrit Puranas*. Temple University Press: Philadelphia, 1978.

George, Andrew (translator). *The Epic of Gilgamesh: The Babylonian Epic Poem and Other Texts in Akkadian and Sumerian*. Penguin USA: New York, 2000.

Girardot, N.J. *Myth and Meaning in Early Taoism*. University of California Press: Berkeley, 1983.

Kitagawa, J.M. *Religion in Japanese History*. Columbia University Press: New York, 1966.

Knappert, Jan. *Islamic Legends: Histories of the Heroes, Saints, and Prophets of Islam*. E.J. Brill: Leiden, 1985.

Norbu, Namkhai. *Drung, Deu and Bön: Narrations, Symbolic Languages and the Bön Tradition in Ancient Tibet*. Library of Tibetan Works and Archives: Dharamsala, 1995.

O'Flaherty, W. *Hindu Myths*. Penguin: Harmondsworth, 1975.

Rappoport, Angelo Solomon. *Myth and Legend of Ancient Israel*. Ktav: New York, 1966.

Samuel, Geoffrey, Hamish Gregor and Elisabeth Stutchbury (eds.). *Tantra and Popular Religion in Tibet*. International Academy of Indian Culture: New Delhi, 1994.

Thomsen, H. *The New Religions of Japan*. Tuttle: Rutland, 1963.

INDEX

Italic numbers refer to illustrations and maps, while **bold** numbers refer to break-out boxes and family trees.

PICTURE CREDITS

The Publisher would like to thank the following picture libraries and other copyright owners for permission to reproduce their images. Every attempt has been made to obtain permission for use of all images from the copyright owners, however, if any errors or omissions have occurred Global Book Publishing would be pleased to hear from copyright owners.

Key: (t) top of page; (b) bottom of page; (l) left side of page; (r) right side of page; (c) center of page.

The Art Archive, London:
30(t), 71, 74(t), 131(b); Antenna Gallery Dakar Senegal/ Dagli Orti: 110(b), 111; Archaeological Museum Aleppo Syria/Dagli Orti: 125(t), 126; Archaeological Museum Baghdad/Dagli Orti: 122(b), 124(b); Archaeological Museum Istanbul/Dagli Orti: 8–9; Archaeological Museum Naples: 42(b); Ateneum Helsinki/Dagli Orti: 51; Biblioteca Estense Modena/Dagli Orti: 64(t), 64(r), 99(b); Biblioteca Nazionale Marciana Venice/Dagli Orti: 65(b), 70(b); Biblioteca Nazionale Turin/Dagli Orti: 73(t), 80(b); Bibliothèque des Arts Décoratifs Paris/Dagli Orti: 87(t); Bodleian Library Oxford: 18, 68(t), 70(t), 137(b) [Ouseley Add 24 folio 127v]; Bodleian Library Oxford/The Bodleian Library: 130(b) [Ouseley Add 176 folio 311v], 133 [Bodley Or 133 folio 33v], 138 [Pers b1 folio 15a], 149(t) [Douce OR.a1 folio 44r]; British Library: 10–11, 30(b), 65(t), 73(b), 80(t), 140(t), 141, 144, 145(t), 148; British Museum: 151, 156, 157(t); British Museum/Dagli Orti: 120(t), 127(b); British Museum/ Eileen Tweedy: 28; British Museum/Jacqueline Hyde: 95; Cabinet des Estampes Strasbourg/Dagli Orti: 81; Cathedral of Santiago de Compostela/Dagli Orti: 66(l); Cathedral Treasury Aachen/Dagli Orti: 66(b); Christie's/Eileen Tweedy: 124(t); Collection Antonovich/Dagli Orti: 85(b), 94(b); Conseil Général Saint Brieuc/Dagli Orti: 12(b); Dagli Orti: 5, 21, 39(t), 45(t), 82–83, 84(b), 88, 91(t), 92(l), 96, 97(t), 122(t), 127(t); Dagli Orti (A): front cover (b), 100; Egyptian Museum Cairo/Dagli Orti: 91(b); Eileen Tweedy: 34(b); Freer Gallery of Art: 152(b); Gustavium Garden Uppsala/Dagli Orti: 37(b); Hermitage Museum Saint Petersburg/Dagli Orti: 56(t); Historiska Muséet Stockholm/ Dagli Orti: 37(t), 41(t), 45(b); JFB: 66(t); Lucien Biton Collection Paris/Dagli Orti: 158(b), 167(b); Musée Alésia Alise Sainte Reine France/Dagli Orti: 14, 16(b), 29(t); Musée des Arts Africains et Océaniens/Dagli Orti: 108(r); Musée des Arts Africains et Océaniens/Dagli Orti (A): 1, 102; Musée des Beaux Arts Tours/Dagli Orti: 78(t); Musée Condé Chantilly/Dagli Orti: 15(t), 15(b), 67(b), 72, 76(t), 131(t); Musée Guimet Paris: 171; Musée Guimet Paris/Dagli Orti: 168(t); Musée du Louvre Paris/Dagli Orti: 7, 86(b), 87(b), 89(t), 90, 93(t), 97(b), 120(b), 123(t), 125(b), 128, 132(t); Museo Civico Treviso/Dagli Orti: 69; Museo del Duomo Friuli/Dagli Orti: 40; Museo Nazionale d'Arte Orientale Rome/Dagli Orti: 170(b); Museum of Anatolian Civilisations Ankara/Dagli Orti: 132(b); National Army Museum London: 115(t); National Bank of Mexico/Dagli Orti (A): 134; National Gallery Budapest/Dagli Orti (A): 12(t); National Museum Bucharest/Dagli Orti: 58(b), 62(b); National Museum of Prague/Dagli Orti: 19(b), 58(t); National Palace Museum Taiwan: 153; Nationalmuseet Copenhagen Denmark/Dagli Orti: 16(t); Neuschwanstein Castle Germany/ Dagli Orti: 79; Oriental Art Museum Genoa/Dagli Orti (A): 159, 162(t), 166(t); Prehistoric Museum Møesgard Hojbjerg Denmark/Dagli Orti: 42(t); Private Collection/Dagli Orti: 85(t), 92(r), 137(t); Private Collection/Dagli Orti (A): 98(b); Private Collection Paris/Dagli Orti: 50(l), 147(t), 167(t), 169; Richard Wagner Museum Bayreuth/Dagli Orti: 32; San Clemente Basilica Rome/Dagli Orti: 57; San Zeno Maggiore Verona, Italy/Dagli Orti (A): 135(b); Sibelius Museum Turku Finland/Dagli Orti (A): 53(b); Tate Gallery London/Eileen Tweedy: 76(b); Topkapi Museum Istanbul/Dagli Orti (A): 135(t); Turkish and Islamic Art Museum Istanbul/Dagli Orti (A): 136; Turkish and Islamic Art Museum Istanbul/Harper Collins Publishers: 139; Victoria & Albert Museum London/Eileen Tweedy: 2, 68(b), 118–119, 142; Victoria & Albert Museum London/Sally Chappell: 41(b), 143.

Art Resource, New York:
Victoria & Albert Museum, London: 44(b).

Bridgeman Art Library, London: 53(t), 74(b); Arni Magnusson Institute, Reykjavik, Iceland: 49(t); Kunsthistorisches Museum, Vienna, Austria: 63(t); Musée des Arts Décoratifs, Paris, France/Peter Willi: 61(t); Museum of Fine Arts, Boston (Kobayashi Eitaku, Japanese, 1843–1890, Izanami and Izanagi Creating the Japanese Islands, Japanese, Meiji era, about 1885, Object Place: Japan, Hanging scroll; ink and color on silk, 126 x 54.6 cm [image] 226 x 78.9cm [overall], Museum of Fine Arts, Boston William Sturgis Bigelow Collection 11.7972 © 2003 Museum of Fine Arts, Boston. All rights reserved): 161(t); Private Collection: 62(t); Private Collection/Charmet: 60; Private Collection/Lauros/Giraudon: 52, 54; Private Collection/The Stapleton Collection: 34(t); Royal Library, Copenhagen, Denmark: 38, 46; Victoria & Albert Museum, London, UK: 161(b).

Corbis: Brian A. Vikander: 170(t).

iStockphoto: Steve Estvanik: front and back cover (t).

Mary Evans Picture Library, London: 13, 19(t), 20(t), 20(b), 23, 24(t), 24(b), 25, 26, 27(t), 27(b), 29(b), 31(l), 33, 35, 36(b), 43, 48, 49(b), 50(r), 55, 56(b), 59, 61(b), 63(b), 75, 77, 78, 89(b), 94(t), 121, 123(b), 129(t), 129(b).

Werner Forman Archive, London: 22(b), 101, 104(b), 112(b), 146, 158(t); Anspach Collection, New York: 115(b); Basho Kenshokai, Ueno: 162(b); British Library, London: 150(b); British Museum, London: 104(t), 106, 110(t), 116(t); Courtesy Christie's: 112(t); Dallas Museum of Art (formerly Schindler Collection): 103(tl), 103(tr), 103(b); De Young Museum, San Francisco: 145(b); Dorset Nat. Hist. & Arch. Soc.: 17(b); Courtesy Entwistle Gallery, London: 107(r), 108(l); Kasmin Collection: 107(l); Mr & Mrs Myron S. Falk, Jr., New York: 155(c); Musée Royal de l'Afrique Centrale, Tervuren, Belgium: 105(t), 109(l); Musées de Rennes: 22(t); Museum für Völkerkunde, Berlin: 105(b), 116(b); National Commission for Museums and Monuments, Lagos: 99(t), 113; National Gallery, Prague: 165; National Museum of Ireland: 31(r); P. Goldman Collection, London: 157(b), 164(t), 114; Prince of Wales Museum of Western India, Mumbai: 140(b); Private Collection: 147(b), 150(t), 155(t), 160; Private Collection, London: 149(b); Private Collection, New York: 109(r), 117(t); Private Collection, Prague: 154(b); Shaanxi Provincial Museum, Xian: 152(t); Spink & Son, London: 168(b); Statens Historiska Museum, Stockholm: 36(t), 39(b), 47; Tishman Collection, New York: 117(b); Victoria & Albert Museum, London: 154(t); Yamato Bunkaken, Nara, Japan: 163.

Old World
MYTHOLOGY

Produced by Global Book Publishing
Level 8, 15 Orion Road, Lane Cove,
NSW 2066, Australia
Ph: (612) 9425 5800   Fax: (612) 9425 5804
Email: rightsmanager@globalpub.com.au